Social Networking

The Fairleigh Dickinson University Press Series in Communication Studies

General Editor: Gary Radford, Department of Communication Studies, Fairleigh Dickinson University, Madison, New Jersey

The Fairleigh Dickinson University Press Series in Communication Studies publishes scholarly works in communication theory, practice, history, and culture.

Publications in Communication Studies

Anastacia Kurylo and Tatyana Dumova (eds.), *Social Networking: Redefining Communication in the Digital Age* (2016)

Phil Rose, *Roger Waters and Pink Floyd: The Concept Albums* (2015)

Ronald C. Arnett and Pat Arneson (eds.), *Philosophy of Communication Ethics: Alterity and the Other* (2014)

Pat Arneson, *Communicative Engagement and Social Liberation: Justice Will Be Made* (2014)

Erik A. Garrett, *Why Do We Go to the Zoo?: Communication, Animals, and the Cultural-Historical Experience of Zoos* (2013)

Philip Dalton and Eric Kramer, *Coarseness in U.S. Public Communication* (2012)

Catherine Creede, Beth Fisher-Yoshida, and Placida Gallegos (eds.), *The Reflective, Facilitative, and Interpretive Practices of the Coordinated Management of Meaning* (2012)

Jolanta Aritz and Robyn C. Walker, *Discourse Perspectives on Organizational Communication* (2011)

S. Alyssa Groom and J. M. H. Fritz, *Communication Ethics and Crisis: Negotiating Differences in Public and Private Spheres* (2011)

R. C. MacDougall, *Digination: Identity, Organization, and Public Life* (2011)

Deborah Eicher-Catt and Isaac E. Catt (eds.), *Communicology: The New Science of Embodied Discourse* (2010)

Dan Cassino and Yasemin Besen-Cassino, *Consuming Politics: Jon Stewart, Branding, and the Youth Vote in America* (2009)

Michael Warren Tumolo, *Just Remembering: Rhetorics of Genocide Remembrance and Sociopolitical Judgment* (2015)

Brent C. Sleasman, *Creating Albert Camus: Foundations and Explorations of His Philosophy of Communication* (2015)

On the Web at http://www.fdu.edu/fdupress

Social Networking

Redefining Communication in the Digital Age

Edited by Anastacia Kurylo
and Tatyana Dumova

FAIRLEIGH DICKINSON UNIVERSITY PRESS
Madison • Teaneck

Published by Fairleigh Dickinson University Press
Copublished by The Rowman & Littlefield Publishing Group, Inc.
4501 Forbes Boulevard, Suite 200, Lanham, Maryland 20706
www.rowman.com

Unit A, Whitacre Mews, 26-34 Stannary Street, London SE11 4AB

British Library Cataloguing in Publication Information Available

Library of Congress Cataloging-in-Publication Data Available

Names: Kurylo, Anastacia, editor. | Dumova, Tatyana, 1962- editor.
Title: Social networking : redefining communication in the digital age / edited by Anastacia Kurylo
and Tatyana Dumova.
Description: Lanham : Fairleigh Dickinson University Press, 2016. | ?2015 | Series: Fairleigh dickin-
son university press series | Includes bibliographical references and index.
Identifiers: LCCN 2015047556 (print) | LCCN 2016006594 (ebook) | ISBN 9781611477382 (cloth :
alk. paper) | ISBN 9781611477399 (Electronic)
Subjects: LCSH: Online social networks. | Social media. | Social movements--Technological innova-
tions. | Social networks--Research--Methodology.
Classification: LCC HM742 .S6297 2016 (print) | LCC HM742 (ebook) | DDC 302.30285--dc23
LC record available at http://lccn.loc.gov/2015047556

∞™ The paper used in this publication meets the minimum requirements of American
National Standard for Information Sciences Permanence of Paper for Printed Library
Materials, ANSI/NISO Z39.48-1992.

Printed in the United States of America

Contents

List of Figures and Tables

TABLES

FIGURES

Acknowledgments

Any book is a collective endeavor including authors, editors, and publishers. The editors of this book are grateful to all contributing authors for their commitment and dedication to the project. Also, the editors wish to acknowledge the following Fairleigh Dickinson University Press and Rowman & Littlefield Publishing Group representatives for their professionalism, patience, and diligence:

Harry Keyishian, Director, Fairleigh Dickinson University Press
Gary P. Radford, Editor, Fairleigh Dickinson University Press
Julie E. Kirsch, Vice President, Publishing, Rowman & Littlefield
Brooke Bures, Associate Editor, Rowman & Littlefield
Zachary Nycum, Assistant Editor, Rowman & Littlefield

The editors are indebted to all who have helped this book to come to completion.

Anastacia Kurylo
Tatyana Dumova

Foreword

As I write this foreword to *Social Networking: Redefining Communication in the Digital Age*, I am reminded of the omnipresence and power of social media in the contemporary world. This book is a collection of ten thoughtful and comprehensive essays that map the historical, political, cultural, economic, and communicative impacts of social networking technologies in a modern era. An important feature of the book is its examination of social networking sites (SNS) in a multicultural and multinational world, a perspective often ignored in competing texts. In the words of the authors, *Social Networking* aims to "transcend an American or European approach and embrace non-Western perspectives." This is a laudable goal and especially important as scholars and students of new media attempt to understand similarities and differences in social uses of SNS in an interconnected and yet culturally diverse universe.

Reminiscent of my own research on intercultural new media studies (Shuter, 2012), several essays in this book explore the cultural nuances of SNS for advocacy, including Occupy Wall Street, Arab Spring in the Middle East, and networked activism in China. Social networking in times of crisis, a particularly interesting chapter in the book, also has unique cultural implications. Consider, for example, how social media was used in China by consumers to bring attention to faulty construction of department store escalators after Xiang Liujuan, a thirty-one-year-old mother, fell to her death when a panel at the top of an escalator gave way (Hernandez, 2015). Concerned that government-controlled mass media would not bring attention to the incident, relatives of the victim posted pleas for help on Weibo, a Chinese version of Twitter. Their posts ignited a crescendo of social media attention including WeChat, a very popular Chinese messaging system, which eventually caught the attention of commentators on Chinese mass media. In countries where the government owns and controls mass media, citizens are more apt to rely on social media to bring attention to crises because they have access to these platforms, and governments tend to exert less control over digital media than mass media.

Culture is at play even when students use social networking sites in the university classroom for educational purposes, a chapter of considerable interest in *Social Media*. Research strongly suggests that not only do university students from different cultures vary in how frequently they use digital media and SNS in the classroom, but they also differ significantly in the ways they prefer instructors to manage classroom digital behavior (Shuter, Cheong, & Chen, 2015). Like face-to-face communication, digital behavior, even in the university classroom, appears to be influenced by cultural values. Moreover, interpersonal concepts such as self-disclosure, which are also examined in this book, seem to be rooted in culture and, when enacted on social media, reveal their cultural origins.

Social Networking is an interdisciplinary text designed for students of social media, including upper level undergraduate and graduate students as well as researchers and practitioners. It is a must-read in a digital era.

Robert Shuter
Research Professor, Arizona State University, Hugh Downs School of Human Communication; Professor Emeritus, Marquette University; and Director, Center for Intercultural New Media Research

REFERENCES

Hernandez, J. (2015, July 29). A death on an escalator shows the power of social media in China. *New York Times*, p. A9.

Shuter, R. (2012). Intercultural new media studies: The next frontier in intercultural communication. *Journal of Intercultural Communication Research* 41 (3): 219–223.

Shuter, R., P. Cheong, & Y. Chen. (2015, November). *The influence of cultural values on US and Danish students' digital behavior in university classes.* Paper to be presented at the conference of the National Communication Association, Las Vegas.

Introduction

Social Networking Without Walls

Anastacia Kurylo and Tatyana Dumova

Internet-based social networking technologies have great potential to meet people's social needs, build communities, and connect cultures in today's global society. While assessing the dazzling growth of social media networks in recent years, media pundit Marshall McLuhan's pronouncement comes to mind: "For the 'message' of any medium or technology is the change of scale or pace or pattern that it introduces into human affairs" (1964, p. 8). Indeed, social networking sites (SNS) and applications have experienced truly remarkable growth and have become an integral and essential part of everyday life. Breaking previously established patterns of technology adoption, social networking platforms and tools almost simultaneously reach hundreds of millions of users around the globe, both in developed and developing countries, bridging demographic, social, and cultural divides.

According to the Pew Research Center's Internet and American Life Project, 26 percent of American adults used at least one social networking site in 2008; by 2011 this number grew to 47 percent and in 2014, to 74 percent (Pew Research Center, 2011, 2014). As of 2015, Facebook, Twitter, Instagram, Pinterest, and LinkedIn were among the most popular social networking platforms among adults in the United States (Duggan et al., 2015). Facebook, which originated as a networking tool for American college youth, was embraced by the older population, and currently, more than half (56 percent) of American online users over the age of 65 are on the network (Duggan et al., 2015); it is also the second most visited website in the world (Alexa, 2015). The number of Facebook's active global users grew from 1 million in 2004 to 1 billion in 2012, and to 1.35 billion in 2015 (Sedghi, 2014), literally turning Facebook into a "global social utility." Capitalizing on this growth,

Facebook's initial public offering (IPO) in 2012 created a business venture with an estimated $227 billion of economic impact affecting 4.5 million jobs globally in 2014 (Deloitte, 2015).

Along with Facebook, Twitter—a short-messaging service considered an oddity at the time of its founding—quickly became a major source of news for Americans (Barthel, Shearer, Gottfried, & Mitchell, 2015). At present, Twitter has near to 1 billion registered users, and 500 million messages are sent per day from 302 million active accounts across the globe (Smith, 2015). Notably, only one-third (34 percent) of all tweets are composed in English, and Jakarta is the "twitting capital" of the world, leaving great Western metropolises behind (Lipman, 2012). Instagram, a mobile multimedia sharing and social networking service, and Pinterest, a photo and image sharing platform, have close to a 300-million- and 70-million-member base respectively (Beese, 2015; Semiocast, 2013); both have developed global communities of users. While 70 percent of Instagram subscribers are from outside the United States (Instagram, 2015), most of Pinterest's members hail from America (Semiocast, 2013). LinkedIn, a professional and business-bound networking service, expanded from 4,500 members in 2003 to 364 million members in 200 countries in 2015. Its interface is available in twenty-four different languages and 75 percent of users come from countries other than the United States (LinkedIn, 2015). It should be noted that in the burgeoning social networking universe, these are only some of the most popular social networking sites.

While the practice of Internet-based social networking permeates the barriers of space and time, the worldwide trajectory of online social network penetration depends on many technological, economic, and demographic factors. It also results in centripetal tendencies of regionalism and localism that add to the peculiarities of adoption patterns, an assortment of revenue models, marketing practices, target audiences, and the vast variety of trendsetters such as Facebook, Twitter, LinkedIn, YouTube, Flickr, Fotki, Tumblr, QZone, Tencent Weibo, Sina Weibo, Renren, Douban, Google+, VKontakte, Odnoklassniki, LiveJournal, Snapchat, Vine, Nexopia, Delicious, Goodreads, hi5, Draugiem.lv, StudiVZ, Tuenti, Nasza-klasa.pl, Academia.edu, Decayenne, Tagged, XING, Skyrock.com, Mixi.jp, Cyworld, DeviantArt, aSmallWorld, Qube, GovLoop, Athlinks, Teazel, and many others. Similar to other social media, the overall dynamics of online social networks can be tied to the centrifugal forces of globalization that are gradually bridging cultural divides in today's world. Being part of the globalization trend, the use of online social networking continues to vary due to social, cultural, and political reasons:

> In the West, places like the UK and the USA, they are used for hanging out and having fun. In China and Hong Kong it's about learning. In Eastern

Europe it's about community and connecting with others, explaining why some of the largest and most engaged social communities in the world reside here. For example, using local sites such as Vkontakte, social networking has reached 77.1% penetration in Russia, one of the highest in our study. When we look at the Middle East, we see that many use social networks for earning respect from others, but also importantly, changing other's opinions. This explains why, during the Arab Spring, users naturally turned to social media to spread information. (Universal McCann, 2012)

Along with these developments comes the increasing amount of time people allocate for social networking compared to other social media applications. Building upon the user-centered nature of social media, social networks currently serve as the locomotives of the participatory Internet, exemplifying Tim Berners-Lee's ideas about the social nature of the Web (Berners-Lee, 1999). Central to understanding the underlying trends and developments in the field of social networking is the convergence of various social media formats, which blurs the existing boundaries between social media platforms and expands their overall functionality (Dumova, 2012).

Social Networking provides a cross-discipline examination of the implications of social networking to expose the inherent, yet often subtle, differences in social media adoption and usage. The book offers a critical analysis of social networking as a technological phenomenon and sheds light on its role in interpersonal communication, self-expression, cultural adaptation, and social change. The chapters in this volume examine the diffusion of social networking as a communication innovation, in a variety of contexts, and uncover patterns of adoption in different geographical regions and cultures, transcending an American or Eurocentric approach and embracing non-Western perspectives.

The book explores the phenomenon of online social networking in the contexts and settings of a global multicultural society caught in the turmoil of the information and communication revolution. Ultimately, the authors delve into the social, economic, political, cultural, and professional dimensions of social networking and explore how social networking technologies are used by individuals, small groups, organizations, and society at large. Thus, the volume addresses subject matter that is of keen interest to academics and practitioners alike, and fulfills a pressing demand by bringing together international experts from a variety of fields including communication, marketing and advertising, public relations, journalism, business, and education. *Social Networking* provides a much-needed forum for sharing innovative research practices and exchanging new ideas among academics and industry professionals. Additionally, it offers an interdisciplinary perspective on social networking by bringing together experts from a range of academic and professional fields. In doing so, this book is a definitive volume not only providing up-to-date coverage of online social networks, but also capturing their evolution in the twenty-first century.

CHAPTER OVERVIEWS

The history, theory, and practice of social networking technologies are introduced in the first two chapters. These topics are explored with respect to established and novel theoretical approaches. Additionally, discussion is offered in light of recent technological and theoretical advancements.

In chapter 1 titled, *Together and Apart: Social and Technical Networks*, Guy Merchant provides an overview of online social networking and traces its history to its similarities with, as well as points of divergence from, a lineage of pre-digital social networks. Towards this end, the metaphor of a network is discussed. Terms such as networked individualism and the distinction between social and technical networks are explicated. The definition of social networking sites and its implications are also explored. Overall, in this chapter, Merchant presents an introduction to the importance, relevance, and conceptualization of social networking sites. This broad-based understanding serves as a launching pad from which one can progress to the rest of the book.

Although online social networking is relatively new, scholars have already established and adapted theories that help to understand this phenomenon. Chapter 2, *The Application of Traditional Social Network Theory to Socially Interactive Technologies*, by Corey Jay Liberman explores how existing theories and models related to nonmediated environments explain rationales for membership in online communities and networks. The author discusses network-related terminology such as centrality and how various conceptualizations including the theories of homophily, mutual interest, and self-interest provide frameworks through which to understand the ways socially interactive technologies mediate members' online interactions. Liberman compares these relevant theoretical frameworks in ways that highlight their unique contributions to understanding social media networking.

In chapter 3, *Social Networking Sites, Self-Disclosure, and Personal Engagement*, Pamela J. Kalbfleisch explores how people personally engage with social networking sites. Willingness to self-disclose on social networking platforms is considered as well as reciprocity of self-disclosure and other relevant topics. Personal benefits and disadvantages of interpersonal communication using social networking sites are presented as well as the role of relational initiation and maintenance, declining relationships, and dissatisfaction in relational quality as displayed on social networking sites. In this chapter, Kalbfleisch discusses the personal benefits gained through engagement in online social networking in order to explain what drives people to construct and manage online identities, make their personal information public, and spend considerable time on making connections online.

In the following three chapters, an overview of social networking technologies is provided and contexts for applications of social networking are discussed. Each chapter explores a specific type of social media technology, framing the discussion within the larger societal context and expanding on how its use offers unique benefits and equally unique challenges to users. A discussion of the unique integration of social networking technologies within a variety of cultural settings as well as across disciplines and areas is presented.

Chapter 4, *Mobile Social Networking,* by Giuseppe Lugano explores social networking practices that are enabled, supported, or mediated by mobile communication technologies including (but not limited to) old-generation feature mobile phones, new-generation smartphones, laptops, tablet computers, or other devices using mobile broadband connection. Advancements in the last decade have allowed mobile social networking to broaden the scope of mobile telephony from interpersonal communication towards a wider range of online social networking activities. With an understanding of mobile social networking as an inherently interdisciplinary research area, Lugano is able to draw from research on technological, economic, and social aspects to explore the role and significance of mobile social networking.

In chapter 5, *Students, the Ivory Tower, and Educational Uses of Social Networking Sites,* Anastacia Kurylo and Yifeng Hu look at the uses of social networking for teaching and learning. The chapter applies the lens of the *Ivory Tower* stereotype of academia to examine the gap between students' personal and professional uses of social media technologies. Exemplars of educational institutions where SNSs are incorporated to bridge this technology divide are discussed. In this way, Kurylo and Hu identify the roles educators can play in narrowing this technological gap.

In chapter 6, Pamela E. Walck and Hans K. Meyer highlight the existing research in the area of social bookmarking in their chapter titled, *The Illusion of Control: A Historiographical Examination of Social Media, Bookmarking, and Perceived Control in the Digital Sphere.* To do so, they offer an interdisciplinary analysis incorporating multiple disciplines, including psychology, marketing, and information processing. They note the relevance of gender in the functionality of tagging and folksonomies on social media platforms, such as Pinterest. Walck and Meyer examine bookmarking as a technology that has adapted to accommodate more educated audiences. The chapter provides a historical context and elucidates the gatekeeping role of bookmarking as well.

The next three chapters of the volume discuss topics related to the use of social networking for civic activism, advocacy, and social movements. Given the many challenges facing humanity, from the political to income inequality to climate change, the importance of volunteering and social activism cannot be understated. From Occupy Wall Street to Arab Spring in the Middle East, social networking has clearly proven itself as more than an avenue for personal and even professional engagement.

In chapter 7, Hayley Watson, Kush Wadhwa, Lemi Baruh, and Salvatore Scifo explore *Social Networking in Times of Crisis*. They identify the challenges of using Web 2.0 technologies in crisis situations and discuss the various functions and benefits enabled by social networking tools for crisis response and management. The authors address the ethical issues inherent in the use of social networks during crisis, provide vivid examples, and offer suggestions for optimizing the use of online social networks in crisis management.

Chapter 8 titled, *Social Networking Technologies and Social Movements*, by Zeynep Günel and Lemi Baruh elaborates on the effects of SNSs on social movements. The chapter presents numerous examples from an array of cultures to demonstrate the importance and breadth of impact social networking sites have and may continue to have on social movements around the world. Their analysis of the role social networking sites played in movements like Occupy Wall Street, 15-M in Spain, Gezi Park in Turkey, Ukrainian Maidan, and Arab Spring demonstrate that online social networks serve to connect activists to activists and activists to publics, at both the local and global level. Günel and Baruh address the challenges of as well as the potential for social networking in social movements.

Chapter 9, authored by Zixue Tai, titled *Networked Activism in China*, provides an overview of networked activism in China. The chapter uses the lenses of mass collaboration, grassroots surveillance, and networks of protest to expose a view of how social networking is used in China for activist purposes. The discussion exposes the intersection of netizens, digital activism, and collective action in China. Tai demonstrates the inherent value of social networking resulting in quick mobilization. Insights discussed in the chapter demonstrate the unique way in which disgruntled Chinese netizens are able to use socially networked online public space to disseminate information and coordinate collective action despite heavily-controlled by the Chinese party-state mainstream media.

In the final chapter, *Social Network Research Methods: Approaches and Key Issues*, Tatyana Dumova considers the implications of a social network perspective for the study of social media networks and discusses issues pertaining to research of online social networks. The discussion in this chapter zeroes in on social network methodology as a multidisciplinary technique for analyzing social network data and the challenges it presents for accomplished network researchers and students of online social networks. Emphasis is placed on levels of analysis, sampling strategies, data archiving and reduction, data mining, and related ethical issues. Challenges of automated data collection from massive social networking sites like Facebook or Twitter are addressed.

CONCLUSION

The international scope as well as the interdisciplinary and multicultural composition of the book welcomes all students of social media including upper-level undergraduate and graduate students, academics, researchers, and practitioners to enter into a discussion of social media and social networking sites. *Social Networking* invites its readers to explore cutting-edge ideas and pursue new scholarship in this burgeoning and integral area of research.

REFERENCES

Alexa. (2015). *The top 500 sites on the web.* Retrieved from http://www.alexa.com/topsites.

Barthel, M., E. Shearer, J. Gottfried, & A. Mitchell. (2015, July 14). *The evolving role of news on Twitter and Facebook.* [Pew Research Center's report]. Retrieved from http://www.journalism.org/2015/07/14/the-evolving-role-of-news-on-twitter-and-facebook/.

Beese, J. (2015, January 22). *5 Insightful Instagram statistics that you should know.* Retrieved from http://sproutsocial.com/insights/5–instagram-stats/.

Berners-Lee, T. (1999). *Weaving the Web: The original design and ultimate destiny of the World Wide Web by its inventor.* San Francisco, CA: Harper Collins.

Deloitte. (2015). *Facebook's global economic impact.* [Report.] London: Deloitte. Retrieved from http://www2.deloitte.com/content/dam/Deloitte/uk/Documents/technology-media-tele-communications/deloitte-uk-global-economic-impact-of-facebook.pdf.

Duggan, M., N. B. Ellison, C. Lampe, A. Lenhart, & M. Madden. (2015, January 9). *Social media update 2014.* [Pew Research Center Report]. Retrieved from http://www.pewinternet.org/2015/01/09/social-media-update-2014/.

———. (2015, January 9). *Demographics of key social networking platforms.* [Pew Research Center Report]. Retrieved from http://www.pewinternet.org/2015/01/09/demographics-of-key-social-networking-platforms-2/.

Dumova, T. (2012). Social interaction technologies and the future of blogging. In T. Dumova & R. Fiordo (Eds.), *Blogging in the global society: Cultural, political and geographical aspects* (pp. 249–274). Hershey, PA: Information Science Reference.

Instagram. (2015). *Our story.* Retrieved from https://instagram.com/press/.

LinkedIn. (2015). *About LinkedIn.* Retrieved from https://press.linkedin.com/about-linkedin.

Lipman, V. (2012). The world's most active Twitter city? You won't guess it. *Forbes.com.* Retrieved from http://www.forbes.com/sites/victorlipman/2012/12/30/the-worlds-most-active-twitter-city-you-wont-guess-it/.

McLuhan, M. (1964/1994). *Understanding media: The extensions of man.* Cambridge, MA: The MIT Press.

Pew Research Center. (2011). *Social networking sites and our lives.* Retrieved from http://www.pewinternet.org/2011/06/16/social-networking-sites-and-our-lives/.

———. (2014). *Social networking fact sheet.* Retrieved from http://www.pewinternet.org/fact-sheets/social-networking-fact-sheet/.

Sedghi, A. (2014, February 4). Facebook: 10 years of social networking, in numbers. *The Guardian.* Retrieved from http://www.theguardian.com/news/datablog/2014/feb/04/facebook-in-numbers-statistics.

Semiocast. (2013). *Pinterest has 70 million users: More than 70% are in the U.S.* Retrieved from http://semiocast.com/en/publications/2013_07_10_Pinterest_has_70_million_users.

Smith, C. (2015, June 5). By the numbers: 150+ amazing Twitter statistics. *Digital Marketing Stats*. Retrieved from http://expandedramblings.com/index.php/march-2013-by-the-numbers-a-few-amazing-twitter-stats/10/.

Universal McCann. (2012). *Wave 6: The business of social* (Social media tracker 2012). Retrieved from http://www.umww.com/global/knowledge/view?Id=226.

Chapter One

Together and Apart

Social and Technical Networks

Guy Merchant

Since its inception the Internet has been a channel for communication and social connection, but it is only with the spread of social networking that such communication has become a significant part of everyday life. Social networking sites are situated at the confluence of these new forms of social interaction and a cultural imaginary that now extends beyond the limits of nation-states and jurisdictions. Although the growth of social networking can be attributed to the adoption and reach of digital technologies themselves, it is also the product of a desire for new or enhanced practices of communication and connection. This kind of connectivity encourages us to be always present in the lives of others, to be continually producing our identity through the ongoing activity of consumption and self-publishing. Newer mobile applications serve to magnify such activity with real-time alerts and updates on portable devices available at almost any time or place, leading to what has been described as "hyperconnectivity" (Wellman, 2001).

It could be argued that to be fully part of the twenty-first century one needs to perform a sustained and continuously refreshed social presence, making visible one's experiences through multiple connections with others. There are many examples of spaces in which this is observable—the photo-sharing app Instagram is a case in point. Here the image-trail that we leave is addressed to the other, validated by family and friends, through views, likes, and comments, all wittingly enacted on a canvas that is patently larger than the individual connections themselves, always located in a wider network of connections. Instagram is dominated by pictures of *me and my friends* (note here the ubiquitous selfie); *where we are*; and *what we are doing*. In this sense those who participate are repeatedly improvising and embellishing the

9

@ reference point that they inhabit, in relation to other @s, and from time to time in relation to #things, #places, and #events. [1]

This may be the brave new world that we have created, but it remains undertheorized and only partially researched. We do not yet have a full enough picture of contemporary social networks, partly because they are inherently promiscuous but also because they are based on new or emerging practices. I suggest that these practices are best seen as part of an assemblage, an ongoing flow of lived experience, attitude, and belief, marked only by the trace of textual threads that meander across multiple spaces and sites both on- and offline. Moreover they have become imbricated with new kinds of identity performance as individuals continually rehearse and revise their private and public selves in this expanded social world.

In a previous era, and one within living memory, connectivity was achieved in very different ways. One of the dominant technologies of communication was the phone, and most phone communication was one-to-one. Those who have recently become @s were then listed by real name in alphabetical order, with a verifying address and number, having a uniformly brief entry in that compendium of subscribers, the telephone directory. Its encyclopaedic volumes of wafer-thin paper simply indicated the possibility of contact rather than themselves being a living testimony to acts of connection. In landline culture, social networks were implicit, the promise of connection existed in potential and intermittent exchanges.

On Facebook, Twitter, LinkedIn, and the like, connections have an organic feel, as lines of communication traverse social space, crossing, tying and forming temporary knots and entanglements. Here we are reminded of the image of the rhizome, the subterranean network of roots (think mushrooms, potatoes, or couch grass) in which "any point [. . .] can be connected to anything other, and must be" (Deleuze & Guattari, 2004, p. 7). Included in these rhizomic connections are the communities and neighborhoods, the family ties, the friendships, as well as the wider social groups with which we affiliate.

As others have observed, network*ing* suggests an active, ongoing activity, and one in which contact is both initiated and reciprocated (boyd & Ellison, 2008, p. 211). This certainly fits well with the organic, rhizomic pattern of communication and interaction described above—but although this verb *networking* has become rapidly absorbed into popular discourse what it means in different contexts and to different populations is still unclear. In this chapter, I explore what is at stake by elaborating on some key aspects and characteristics of online social networking, addressing our current understanding of the field, and the social and cultural practices that we see evolving.

By placing this within a wider context that includes what we know about networks and more specifically about *social* networks, I point to the ways in which new technologies expand and change how we communicate and, as a result, how we organize, entertain, and learn. Rather than suggesting a uniformity or inevitability to all this, I emphasize the heterogeneity of social networks, how social networking sites have evolved, how they have been taken up in different localities, how they alternately challenge and reinforce traditional social divisions, and, importantly, how they are woven into the texture of everyday life as part of a mesh of complex multidimensional connections—a larger network. To begin I offer a brief history of social networking sites before focusing in on the underpinning idea of the network and what it now means to us.

A BRIEF HISTORY OF ONLINE SOCIAL NETWORKING

It is generally agreed that online social networking has its origins in the Usenet groups and bulletin boards that were established to promote community and information sharing between interest groups in the early spread of Internet-based communication. These groups were predominantly comprised of computer programmers and enthusiasts, and their communication tended to focus on issues related to technology and computer science. A common feature of these sites was an online chat function through which subscribers could write and receive responses in real time.

These technologies formed the basis for early social networking sites (SNSs), and they were subsequently enhanced by adding in a facility for making individual users' online networks visible to others. Some of the first services to perform this function were Classmates, a forerunner of Friends Reunited (established in 1995), which attempted to reconnect people who had attended school together, and Six Degrees of Separation (launched in 1997), which allowed people to list their friends for others to view. Another early networking site that used the idea of a friends list was LiveJournal. Set up in 1999, LiveJournal popularized the blog format (see Davies & Merchant, 2010) as a way of regularly updating those on one's friendlist or blogroll.

According to boyd and Ellison (2008) the period between 1997 and 2001 was marked by the development of various niche community tools, such as AsianAvenue (now AsianAve), BlackPlanet, and MiGente, as well as by the rapid spread of social networking to other parts of the English- and non-English-speaking world. By 2003, the list of services included such popular sites as Friendster, LinkedIn, and MySpace, and there was substantial growth in the number of subscribers. With the demise of Friendster, MySpace became one of the most popular SNSs, its success often being attributed to widespread adoption by teenagers. However, in May 2005, MySpace was purchased by News Corporation and then became a focus of media attention and controversy. This coincided with the growing popularity of Facebook.

Although evidence suggests that the world of SNSs is now dominated by Facebook, with a reported 1.23 billion active accounts at the time of writing (Consenza, 2014), the market is volatile and characterized by the ongoing development of apps with particular characteristics and functions. Examples of these sorts of apps are Twitter (with its 140 character format and high profile for real-time news and information) and Snapchat (with its time-limited image exchange service).

Unfortunately most of the information currently available concerns SNSs that are popular amongst English language speakers, but it is certainly the case that region- and language-specific sites have an important role to play. In addition, some of the multilingual practices that exist within the larger online social networks are often overlooked (but see for example, the study of multilingualism in Flickr by Lee & Barton, 2011). Table 1.1 shows some of the higher profile SNSs that are currently available. This is included to illustrate how online social networking is not simply a phenomenon in the English-speaking world, and that, despite the wide appeal of Facebook, it is certainly not the only online space for social networking.

Arguably, more important than following the rising fortunes of SNSs is a focus on how social groups and communities take up the affordances of new technology and make them work to fulfill their diverse needs and purposes, whether this takes the form of new expressions of activism (McCaughey & Ayers, 2013), social enterprise (Donner, 2006), or financial transaction (Morawczynski, 2009). The same is true for the everyday interactions of partners and friends, parents and siblings, families and interest groups which are

SNS	Country of origin	Registered users*	Made publically available
Cyworld	South Korea	24,000,000	1999
Facebook	USA	1,280,000,000	2004
Hyves	Netherlands	10,097,000	2004
Mixi	Japan	242,323,160	2000
Orkut	Brazil	100,000,000	2004
QZone	China	480,000,000	2005
Skyrock	France	22,000,000	2007
Tuenti	Spain	12,000,000	2007
VKontakte	Russia	249,409,900	2006

Table 1.1. *Source*: Wikipedia (2014).

often, to a greater or lesser extent, transacted through a range of digital media such as Facebook, Instagram, Skype, and instant messaging—as well as in co-present interactions in shared spaces—and entwined in everyday events and activity. In other words, it is becoming increasingly apparent that SNSs sit in a web of connections and interactions which include the social and the technical, the actual and the virtual, as well as what is present and absent.

NETWORK AS METAPHOR

When academics first started to write about social networks, the sort of online connections I refer to above would have been hard to imagine, but as the Social Web entered public consciousness, new possibilities presented themselves. With this the whole idea of creating a "narrative of the self" (Giddens, 1991) became instantly available, and the tools for engaging in the practices of self-publication were often free of charge and popular. Staking out one's place on the social graph (Merchant, 2011) made typing in updates, uploading images and videos, liking, and commenting popular pastimes for many. In fact a whole new language was invented to describe these practices from "friending" (making an online connection) to "following" (looking at someone's updates), to "tagging" (or labelling) and "tagging in" (including someone in an update or post).[2]

The adoption of these practices cut across traditional divisions in society. Of course, that is not to say that such divisions were erased, or that online communication ushered in a new egalitarian era, but merely to point to the spread of participation and the rise and availability of what came to be known as online social networking. As a result, networking is now such a commonplace term that it might seem that there is little to be gained by defining or redefining it, but an exploration here will help to give some purchase on how networking has evolved, and how it can be used to describe current practices.

As a way of thinking about social interaction, the metaphor of a network is appealing in a number of ways—after all, it suggests a patterning, a connection between points, a way of imagining how tapping away at a keyboard in Nottingham, England might connect us to someone doing more or less the same thing in New York. Yet imagining a network invites a certain kind of abstraction of the social, one which is perhaps best captured in the diagrams that are a common characteristic of network analysis. Here the material, the physical, and the affective—the embodied self in context—is elided, as the individual, and the singularity of activity in situ, is reduced to a dot (or node). Similarly, little is revealed about the content of the communicative connection or, for that matter, its fluidity. It is frozen in time, with social proximity simply represented in terms of frequency or duration of contact.

But network is, of course, a distinctively modern metaphor, and one that was first used in a technical sense to describe the complex interconnected travel systems that grew up in the nineteenth century. It was only later that it was applied to media, such as early broadcast radio and television. Nowadays, the word network readily associates with the world of digital connection and to the Internet itself.

It is no accident that this metaphor was first taken up in the social sciences at the same time as early computer networks were being developed (Emirbayer & Goodwin, 1994) and from that point it was just a matter of time before the lines between social and technical networks would become blurred. Writing in 1978 to launch the first issue of the academic journal *Social Networks*, Freeman, Mitchell, and Ziegler (1978) underlined the need to bring together different strands of social network research, research which was beginning to attract the attention of academics working in a number of disciplines including sociology, anthropology, human geography, economics, biology, social psychology, communication, and political science. From then onward, the hope that studying social networks might emphasize the interdependence of individuals and the idea that social network analysis had the potential to bridge micro- and macrosociological concerns by illustrating how the "flow of material and nonmaterial resources" is patterned (Schuller, Baron, & Field, 2000, p. 19) have animated a substantial body of research.

Literature in this field illustrates how social networks support the routine life of people and their capacity to cope with adversity, emotional upheaval, economic hardship, and the everyday challenges of life—including everything from child care to house maintenance (Wellman & Wortley, 1990). The theoretical strength of the network metaphor has enabled researchers to map the extent of social ties, to examine both individual and collective dimensions, and to begin to retheorize the concept of community. In these accounts, communication is foregrounded as attention is placed on the "flow of information (and other resources)" within and between groups (Garton, Haythornthwaite, & Wellman 1997, p. 1). In other words, how social beings are linked, how they participate by creating allegiances and friendships in both formal and informal contexts are important considerations. Social network analysis helps us to map the relationship between the individual and the larger social systems in which he or she participates, and as a result the relationships themselves often become the unit of analysis.

In his searching critique of this work, Latour (2005) is dismissive of the ways in which the idea of the network has been deployed by social scientists. As Latour asserts:

> Network is a concept, not a thing out there. It is a tool to help describe something, not what is being described. It has the same relationship with the topic at hand as a perspective grid to a traditional single point perspective

painting: drawn first the lines might allow one to project a three-dimensional object onto a flat piece of linen; but they are not *what* is to be painted, only what has allowed the painter to give the impression of depth before they are erased. (p. 131)

Latour (2005) distinguishes between technical networks (electricity, trains, the Internet) and social networks (formal and informal connections between people). In order to develop a more robust concept of networks Latour lists their defining features. These are:

1. Traceability: "A point-to-point connection which is 'physically traceable' and can be 'recorded empirically.'"
2. Space: All networks leave empty "what is not connected."
3. Cost: Connection isn't freely available, it requires maintenance and repair.
4. Immateriality: There is no "durable substance" in a network, it has to be continually enacted.

Central to Latour's thinking is the ambition to describe more complex, multidimensional networks in which human and nonhuman actors (such as technologies) are entangled in multiple kinds of relations. These concepts will be useful to bear in mind in the ensuing discussion of social networking.

SOCIO-TECHNICAL NETWORKS

Although Latour (2005) marks a clear distinction between social and technical networks, the study of online social networking shows how they interweave, creating what appears to be a seamless web of communication. In the work of Barry Wellman we see how these social and technical arrangements are evolving. Wellman has documented the ways in which social networks have changed with the rise of rapid global communication and increased population mobility (see, for example, Hampton & Wellman, 2003; Wellman, 2002; Wellman & Wortley, 1990). Wellman and his colleagues, based on their in-depth studies of a community in metropolitan Toronto, provide empirical data and theoretical models that extend our knowledge of networks. In this body of work, computer-supported networks sometimes receive a lot of attention, even to the extent of generating what seems like quite a narrow definition. For example: "When a computer network connects people or organisations, it is a social network" (Garton et al., 1997, p. 1). But for the most part, the work is helpful in illuminating the relationship between technical networks and social relationships, and illustrates the significance of traceability, and point-to-point connection (Latour, 2005).

Wellman's theory of how the patterning of relationships may evolve from "close-knit" groups to "glocalised communities" and on to "networked individualism" (Wellman, 2002, p. 12) has received a lot of attention from those interested in new technology, not only because of the way it fits with the rise of mobile computing but also because of the way in which it suggests high levels of agency. In Wellman's work, community is defined socially rather than spatially. Social connection, and ultimately one's sense of belonging, may now begin to depend on "place-to-place connectivity, and not door-to-door" (Wellman, 2002, p. 14). This is certainly the case for the diasporic youth who are the focus of a recent study by Rowsell and Burgess (2014) in which research participants worked across communicative platforms to link with those who were both geographically close and distant, connecting to deeply-felt identifications with collectivities such as national, religious, and ethnic heritage.

Networked individualism is a term used by Wellman (2002) to describe this shift from place-to-place communication to person-to-person communication ushered in with high-speed connectivity through mobile devices. As he suggests:

> Where high speed place-to-place communication supports the dispersal and fragmentation of organizations and community, high speed person-to-person communication supports the dispersal and role-fragmentation of workgroups and households. The shift to a personalized, wireless world affords *networked individualism*, with each person switching between ties and networks. People remain connected, but as individuals rather than being rooted in the home bases of work unit and household. Individuals switch rapidly between their social networks. Each person separately operates his networks to obtain information, collaboration, orders, support, sociability, and a sense of belonging. (p. 15–16)

Building on this agentive view, Benkler (2006) argues with some optimism that networked individuals are able to "reorganise their social relations in ways that fit them better" and to "loosen bonds that are too hierarchical and stifling" or fill in the gaps where "their real-world relations seem lacking" (Benkler, p. 367).

In sum, the idea of networked individualism is certainly a powerful evocation of the social world we see in everyday urban life in which we might imagine an invisible web of networks. However, when we consider online social networking, our account must extend beyond person-to-person communication to include "the crowd" those who are reached through the affordances of one-to-many and many-to-many social media. In his analysis, Gergen (2003) uses the image of the Japanese "floating world to conjure up the following vision:

We may imagine here that dwelling about us at all times are small communities that are unseen and unidentifiable. However, as we stroll the thoroughfare or sip coffee in a café their presence is made constantly known to us. Each mobile phone [. . .] is a sign of a significant nucleus, stretching in all directions, amorphous and protean. (p. 105)

This view places the mobile device at the very center, and helps us to imagine the connectivity of the networked individual. Although the view might sound a little technocentric, we are reminded that activity is embedded in, and continuous with, everyday social space. And as it turns out, most mobile social networking practices are more concerned with thickening existing social ties than forging new ones (Carpenter, Green, & LaFlam, 2011; Ellison, Steinfield, & Lampe, 2007), helping to establish a sort of absent presence with others (Licoppe, 2004). Mobile devices then, as Sheller (2004) observes, enable their users to hold multiple connections and identities in play at any one time. As a result, as I have argued elsewhere (Merchant, 2011), the boundaries between online and offline social networking are become increasingly porous, as mediated communication is absorbed into co-present interaction.

This is illustrated by a study of young people's use of mobile technology, in which Davies (2014) carefully tracks the ways in which her participants use both image and written text in person-to-person interaction, through instant-messaging and Facebook as part of their everyday social activity as they move around the urban environment. Here the distinctions between meanings made on- and offline, between those present and those who are absent begin to dissolve. These young people are simultaneously together and apart in their interactions. In this way, we see that the texture of social interaction is complex, and mediated through a variety of channels. What we think of as sites for social networking do, however, still play a significant part in this web of communication, and they are the focus of the following section.

SOCIAL NETWORKING SITES

Even though the boundaries between online and offline communication are beginning to blur, directing our attention to the characteristics of social networking sites will help to focus on the social nature of the changing landscape of communication. In what follows, I begin by mapping the terrain of online social network.

As I mentioned at the start of this chapter, the Internet has always worked as a channel for communication and social connection. In countering some of the more extravagant claims of Web 2.0 enthusiasts, who suggest that the growth of the Social Web constitutes a paradigm shift, Tim Berners-Lee

(2000) argued since 1999 that the Web "is more a social creation than a technical one" (p. 123). Yet it is also true that the most noteworthy development of recent years is the scale of adoption of technologies and the popular spread of the "read/write web" (Richardson, 2006). The online textual universe is now extremely large and varied, and encompasses well-established participative practices such as email groups, listservs, and bulletin boards, as well as more recent developments such as music-, photo-, and video-sharing sites, MMOGs and 3D virtual worlds (Davies & Merchant, 2009). These platforms and the communicative practices that they support could be seen as the basis of online social networking as a popular and broad-based activity.

An important aspect of online social networking is the development of environments that are specifically designed to support and develop friendship and social interaction and whose overt purpose is to provide a context and appropriate tools for doing so. I prefer to use the term *social networking sites* (SNSs) to describe these environments and to distinguish them from other forms of technologically supported interaction. Facebook, Instagram, and Twitter are the most popular SNSs at the time of writing (Consenza, 2014), but the category also includes VKontakte (which caters to Russian speakers), and QZone (which uses Mandarin), and a host of other smaller applications (see table 1.1). The rapidly changing world of online communication and the development and spread of mobile apps has contributed to the changing fortunes of a number of providers. Friendster, Bebo, and MySpace are notable examples of SNSs that have declined in popularity over the last five years. Consenza (2014) gives an impression of the global spread of popular SNSs and shows how region and language pattern social networking.

In their commentary on SNSs, boyd and Ellison (2008) make a distinction between "networking," which they argue implies active relationship *initiation*, and "network," which for them suggests relationship *maintenance* (p. 211). The distinction is helpful as a way of categorizing different kinds of online social activity but glosses over the fact that relationship maintenance and development can be just as active and arguably equally as significant as relationship initiation. boyd and Ellison (2008) tie their definition of SNSs to three core characteristics. These are:

- Individual users or members construct a public or semi-public profile on the site
- Users/members create and list connections with others (friends, followers, or buddies)
- Users/members traverse the site through their own and others' friendlists

Although it could be argued that these characteristics are shared with other environments that may not focus explicitly on friendship (Blogger, YouTube and similar applications come to mind), the emphasis on presence, connection, and community are certainly germane to an understanding of social media. There is clearly a fuzzy boundary between the characteristics of wider online social networking and the smaller area of specific SNSs as defined above. This is most evident in Web-based services that have supported the growth of a community, or communities of interest—or what Gee (2004) refers to as an affinity space. Examples of these are the Flickr photo-sharing community, music recommending sites like Blip.fm, and those other online spaces that benefit from having their own "in house" communication tools. It is useful, then, to distinguish between those environments specifically de-signed to promote social interaction and friendship and those that support social networking around a specific activity or "social object" (Ito et al., 2008; Merchant, 2010).

One of the unifying features of social networking sites is the way that they support public displays of friendship and connection. In blogs this is often shown as a blogroll, in other sites it is a friendlist, whereas in the microblogging site Twitter this function is fulfilled by the lists of who "follows" you as well as who you "follow." In this way, according to Greenhow and Robelia (2009), users "make visible their social networks" or to be more precise, they give an online performance of those connections that they *think are significant* to their imagined audience. The concepts of performance and audience (which have their origins in the work of Goffman, 1959) suggest that where individuals use multiple SNSs we might expect to see differences in their friendlists—differences that would reflect their engagement in differ-ent communities and different activities. Indeed, there is some evidence to suggest this (Rowsell & Burgess, 2014; Subrahmanyam, Reich, Waechter, & Espinoza, 2008).

In order to complete the picture of online social networking, SNSs must now be viewed in what I referred to above as the "wider textual universe" of online communication in which all the email exchanges, i-m chats, bulletin boards, and so on feature. This is important, firstly in order to be more specific about the difference between SNS activity and social networking online, and secondly to open to a more expansive view of social networks in which activity and interaction across a range of platforms can be conceptual-ized.

CONCLUSION

In this overview of social and technical networks, emphasis has been placed on the ways in which new media are used to elaborate upon and enhance everyday social interactions. One of my central concerns has been to illus-trate how emerging social and technological arrangements can be conceived of as rhizomic networks. Although the features of SNSs like friendlists, blogrolls, and inventories of followers make visible and public some of the ways in which we are connected, what Latour (2005) refers to as traceability remains latent, in the sense that only some of the data is accessible, more is locked into specific applications, sites, kinds of activities, and so on. However, the emergence of the phenomenon of networked individualism does suggest that the sort of point-to-point connection described by Latour operates with increased fluidity and frequency. As a result, the recognition that networks are made up of people *and* technologies is now gaining currency, as Contractor, Monge, and Leonardi (2011) argue:

> Ubiquitous computing, both inside and outside formal organizations, is making it increasingly difficult to separate people's interactions with other people from people's interactions with technologies. Consequently, it may make more sense to begin treating technologies as endogenous to social networks, rather than exogenous to them. (p. 684)

Networks, then, are more complex than social connections, and are perhaps better conceived of as heterogeneous assemblages of diverse objects acting and reacting to one another. From this perspective it may be helpful to see them as collections of activity involved in creating meanings that are both material and semiotic, through connections that are transient, coming into existence through a constant making and remaking. This suggests that multiple kinds of relations must be repeatedly performed in order to sustain a network.

The sort of dialogic exchanges that have been observed in Twitter (Gillen & Merchant, 2013), the flow of news and current affairs (Vis, 2013), and the enactment of micro-celebrity (Page, 2012) can then be seen as traces of networks that link embodied individuals, with objects, events, images, ideas, and the technologies that mediate them. In a similar vein the kinds of online conversations documented by Vásquez (2014) in her study of consumer reviews shows how subscribers provide advice, warning, and public endorsement based upon everyday actions and interactions that flow back and forth, online and offline. Despite some of the concerns expressed about online social networking (see for example, Cassell & Cramer, 2008), it is more helpful to see them as part of a larger tapestry in which human and nonhuman actors are sometimes together and sometimes apart.

The densely connected relationships enacted on SNSs are more often than not anchored to relationships and social activities in the real world (see Dowdall, 2009). This not only raises new and complex issues of privacy and self-expression (Livingstone, 2008), but also involves specific strategies for making connections and relationships visible—in short for enacting identity in the social world. As Spencer-Oatey (2007) suggests:

Identity helps people "locate" themselves in social worlds. By helping to define where they belong and where they do not belong in relation to others, it helps to anchor them in their social worlds, giving them a sense of place. (p. 642)

This sense of location, however, is unlikely to be fixed as members of SNSs continually negotiate and renegotiate a sense of who they are within the landscape of discursive practices and subjectivities. In this regard we can apply the notion of "performativity" (following Butler, 1990) to describe the ways in which identity is repeatedly enacted through linguistic and nonlinguistic representations on SNSs.

As counter to arguments for the leveling effect of digital culture, it appears then that the weight of a historical and social past is pervasive, and that performances of gender, race, and class are still very much in evidence as prevailing discursive practices (see for example, Gómez, 2010; Kehily & Nayak, 2008; Koutsogiannis & Adampa, 2012). They invite performances of identity to which one is strongly anchored. At the same time, however, they co-exist and intersect with a kaleidoscope of identifications (often related to media consumption and popular culture)—transient identities that may be relatively easy to make or remake (Merchant, 2006).

Online performances, just like the offline practices they are connected to, seem to be oriented toward an audience—a known or imagined other, to whom one is giving an account of oneself. As Butler (2005) argues:

An account of oneself is always given to another, whether conjured or existing. . . . The very terms by which we give an account, by which we make ourselves intelligible to ourselves are not of our making. They are social in character, and they establish social norms, a domain of unfreedom and substitutability within which our "singular" stories are told. (p. 21)

And yet, in continually producing these accounts the very fluidity of online social networking, its capacity to work across boundaries, to experiment, to bring in new voices, and to draw in different media offers the possibility for reworking what appears to be given. Bringing together what has been kept apart by the limitations of technical networks and the separation of social networks creates opportunity—and that in itself is a source of hope.

REFERENCES

Barton, D., & C. Lee. (2013). *Language online: Investigating digital texts and practices.* Abingdon: Routledge.

Benkler, Y. (2006). *The wealth of networks: How social production transforms markets and freedom.* London: Yale University Press.

Berners-Lee, T. (2000). *Weaving the Web: The original design and ultimate destiny of the World Wide Web by its inventor.* New York: HarperCollins.

boyd, d., & N. B. Ellison. (2008). Social network sites: Definition, history and scholarship. *Journal of Computer-Mediated Communication* 13:210–320.

Butler, J. (1990). *Gender trouble: Feminism and the subversion of identity.* Abingdon: Routledge.

Butler, J. (2005). *Giving an account of oneself.* New York: Fordham University Press.

Carpenter, J., M. Green, & J. LaFlam. (2011). People or profiles: Individual differences in online social networking use. *Personality and Individual Differences* 50 (5): 538–541.

Cassell, J., & M. Cramer. (2008). High tech or high risk: Moral panics about girls online. In T. McPherson (Ed.), *Digital youth, innovation, and the unexpected* (pp. 53–76). MacArthur Foundation, Cambridge, MA: MIT Press.

Consenza, V. (2014). World Map of Social Networks. Retrieved from http://www.vincos.it/world-map-of-social-networks.

Contractor, N., P. Monge, & P. Leonardi. (2011). Multidimensional networks and the dynamics of sociomateriality: Bringing technology inside the network. *International Journal of Communication* 5:682–720.

Davies, J. (2014). (Im)material girls living in im(material) worlds: Identity curation through time and space. In C. Burnett, J. Davies, G. Merchant, & J. Rowsell (Eds.), *New literacies around the globe: Policy and pedagogy* (pp. 72–88). London: Routledge.

Davies, J., & G. Merchant. (2009). *Web 2.0 for schools: Learning and social participation.* New York: Peter Lang.

Davies, J., & G. Merchant. (2010). Negotiating the blogosphere: Narratives of the self on-screen. In V. Carrington & M. Robinson (Eds.), *Contentious literacies: Digital literacies, social learning, and classroom practices* (pp. 81–94). London: Sage.

Deleuze, G., & F. Guattari. (2004). *A thousand plateaus: Capitalism and schizophrenia.* London, Continuum.

Donner, J. (2006). The use of mobile phones by microentrepreneurs in Kigali, Rwanda: Changes to social and business networks. *Information Technologies and International Development* 3 (2): 3–19.

Dowdall, C. (2009). Masters and critics: Children as producers of online digital texts. In V. Carrington & M. Robinson (Eds.), *Digital literacies: Social learning and classroom practice* (pp. 43–61). London: Sage.

Ellison, N., C. Steinfield, & C. Lampe. (2007). The benefits of Facebook 'Friends': Social capital and college students' use of online social network sites. *Journal of Computer-Mediated Communication* 12:1143–1168.

Emirbayer, M., & J. Goodwin. (1994). Network analysis, culture, and the problem of agency. *American Journal of Sociology* 99 (6): 1411–1454.

Freeman, L., J. Mitchell, & R. Ziegler. (1978). Editorial. *Social Networks* 1:1–3.

Garton, L., C. Haythornthwaite, & B. Wellman. (1997). Studying online social networks. *Journal of Computer-Mediated Communication* 3:1–22.

Gee, J. P. (2004) *Situated language and learning: A critique of traditional schooling.* London: Routledge.

Gergen, K. (2003). Self and community in the new floating worlds. In K. Nyiri (Ed.), *Mobile democracy: Essays on society, self and politics* (pp. 103–114). Vienna: Passagen.

Giddens, A. (1991). *Modernity and self-identity: Self and society in the late modern age.* Oxford, UK: Polity.

Gillen, J., & G. Merchant. (2013). Contact calls: Twitter as a dialogic social and linguistic practice. *Language Sciences* 35:47–58.

Goffman, E. (1959). *The presentation of self in everyday life.* London: Penguin.

Gómez, A. G. (2010). Disembodiment and cyberspace: Gendered discourses in female teenagers' personal information disclosure. *Discourse & Society* 21 (2): 135–160.

Greenhow, C., & B. Robelia. (2009). Informal learning and identity formation in online social networks. *Learning, Media and Technology* 34 (2): 119–140.

Hampton, K., & B. Wellman. (2003). Neighboring in Netville: How the Internet supports community and social capital in a wired suburb. *City and Community* 2 (4): 277–311.

Ito, M., H. Horst, M. Bittanti, d. boyd, B. Herr-Stephenson, P. Lange, C. Pascoe, & L. Robinson (with S. Baumer, R. Cody, D. Mahendran, K. Martinez, D. Perkel, C. Sims, & L. Tripp). (2008). *Living and learning with new media: Summary of findings from the Digital Youth Project.* Retrieved from http://digitalyouth.ischool.berkeley.edu/report.

Kehily, M., & A. Nayak. (2008). Global femininities: Consumption, culture and the significance of place. *Discourse: Studies in the Cultural Politics of Education* 29 (3): 325–342.

Koutsogiannis, D., & V. Adampa. (2012). Girls, identities and agency in adolescents' digital literacy practices. *Journal of Writing Research* 3 (3): 217–247.

Latour, B. (2005). *Reassembling the social: An introduction to Actor-Network Theory.* Oxford: Oxford University Press.

Lee, C., & D. Barton. (2011). Constructing glocal identities through multilingual writing practices on Flickr.com. *International Multilingual Research Journal* 5:1–21.

Licoppe, C. (2004). "Connected" presence: The emergence of a new repertoire for managing social relationships in a changing communication technoscape. *Environment and Planning D: Society and Space* 22 (1): 135–156.

Livingstone, S. (2008). Taking risky opportunities in youthful content creation: Teenagers' use of social networking sites for intimacy, privacy and self-expression. *New Media & Society* 10 (3): 393–411.

McCaughey, M., & M. Ayers. (2013). *Cyberactivism: Online activism in theory and practice.* London: Routledge.

Merchant, G. (2006). Identity, social networks and online communication. *E-Learning* 3 (2): 235–244.

Merchant, G. (2010). View my profile(s). In D. Alvermann (Ed.), *Adolescents' online literacies* (pp. 51–70). New York: Peter Lang.

———. (2011). Unravelling the social network: Theory and research. *Learning, Media and Technology* 37 (1): 4–19.

Morawczynski, O. (2009). Exploring the usage and impact of "transformational" mobile financial services: The case of M-PESA in Kenya. *Journal of Eastern African Studies* 3 (3): 509–525.

Page, R. (2012). The linguistics of self-branding and micro-celebrity in Twitter: The role of hashtags. *Discourse and Communication* 6 (2): 181–201.

Richardson, W. (2006). *Blogs, wikis, podcasts and other powerful Web tools for classrooms.* London: Sage.

Rowsell, J., & J. Burgess. (2014). A tale of multiple selves: Im/materializing identities on Facebook. In C. Burnett, J. Davies, G. Merchant, & J. Rowsell (Eds.), *New literacies around the globe: Policy and pedagogy* (pp.103–120). Abingdon: Routledge.

Schuller, T., S. Baron, & J. Field. (2000). Social capital: A review and critique. In S. Baron, J. Field, & T. Schuller (Eds.), *Social capital* (pp. 1–38). Oxford: Oxford University Press.

Sheller, M. (2004). Mobile publics: Beyond the network perspective. *Environment & Planning D: Society & Space* 22 (1): 39–52.

Spencer-Oatey, H. (2007). Theories of identity and the analysis of face. *Journal of Pragmatics* 39 (4): 639–656.

Subrahmanyam, K., S. Reich, N. Waechter, & G. Espinoza. (2008). Online and offline social networks: Use of social networking sites by emerging adults. *Journal of Applied Developmental Psychology* 29:420–433.

Vásquez, C. (2014). *The discourse of online consumer reviews.* London: Bloomsbury.

Vis, F. (2013). Twitter as a reporting tool for breaking news: Journalists tweeting the 2011 UK riots. *Digital Journalism* 1 (1): 27–47.

Wellman, B. (2001). Physical place and cyber place: The rise of networked individualism. *International Journal of Urban and Regional Research* 25 (2): 227–52.

———. (2002). Little boxes, glocalization, and networked individualism. In M. Tanabe, P. Besselaar, & T. Ishida (Eds.), *Digital cities II: Computational and sociological approaches* (pp. 10–25). Berlin: Springer.

Wellman, B., & S. Wortley. (1990). Different strokes from different folks: Community ties and social support. *American Journal of Sociology* 96 (3): 558–588.

Wikipedia. (2014). List of social networking sites. Retrieved from http://en.wikipedia.org/wiki/
    List_of_social_networking_websites.

NOTES

1. The @ suffix is used to designate individual subscribers, and # to signal a "tag" or label.
2. See Barton & Lee (2013) for a fuller discussion of online language.

Chapter Two

The Application of Traditional Social Network Theory to Socially Interactive Technologies

A Reconceptualization of Communication Principles

Corey Jay Liberman

In today's media-saturated world, a simple search engine request by a user on the Internet for "online social networking sites" can yield over 300,000 unique results. Some of these sites are well-known, such as Facebook, Tumblr, Instagram, LinkedIn, and Flickr. Others are more inconspicuous, such as weRead, Travellerspoint, Influenster, Cucumbertown, and Tylted. Regardless of their popularity, based on the total number of registered users, all online social networking sites do share one thing in common: they are all mediated environments that provide the ability for individuals to create relationships with others in non–face-to-face environments. Of course, such mediated environments have forced scholars, practitioners, and users of social media to ask numerous questions about the nature of communication and relationships. For example, has the mere definition of relationship changed with the introduction and utilization of online social networking platforms (Manago, Taylor, & Greenfield, 2012)? What does it mean when someone says online friend (Chan & Cheng, 2004)? How do such variables as trust, honesty, love, and passion change when technology enters into the process of networking (Ramirez & Zhang, 2007)? Does the strength of an online relationship pale in comparison to that of a nonmediated one (Bryant, Sanders-Jackson, & Smallwood, 2006)? Perhaps one of the most important questions, however, is the following: what is the necessary prerequisite for network membership in cyberspace? Based on existing research dealing with nonmediated social networks, two valid answers to this query can be provided.

First, and very similar to McPherson, Smith-Lovin, and Cook's (2001) argument that individuals are more likely to form relationships with those who possess attitudinal (what we think), behavioral (what we do), and demographic (who we are) similarities as compared to those who possess dissimilarities, which is emblematic of the sociological/anthropological homophily principle (birds of a feather flock together), the same is true of network affiliation in mediated environments: similarity facilitates communication which fosters connections. As an example, Cucumbertown, mentioned earlier, is an online social network for those involved and interested in the culinary world and members communicate with one another about recipes located throughout the world. Network connections, here, are predicated on similarity; a disinterest in cooking is going to bar one from network inclusion.

Second, and made poignantly clear by Monge and Contractor (2003), another prerequisite for network membership in a mediated environment is that the individual in question must accrue some form of gain, whether it be at the individual level or at the collective level (or both). Again using Cucumbertown as an example, the benefit of an individual posting her recipe for *clafoutis*, a very popular French dessert made of fruit, is that she will have access to others' recipes as well, including, perhaps, *zerde* (a Turkish pudding dessert), *mantecado* (a Spanish crumble cake), and/or *pavlova* (an Australian cake). This, according to Monge and Contractor (2003), is an example of one's decision to become part of a communication network based on collective (or mutual) interest: the idea that one's gain is accompanied by another's gain. However, one might also gain without necessarily providing a gain for another. As an example, one who joins the online social network known as Travellerspoint, an online community where individuals share their travel experiences with others, might very well become a member merely to gain information about destinations such as Thailand, Bolivia, Cuba, the Netherlands, or Hungary, rather than to provide useful information for others. This, according to Monge and Contractor (2003), is an example of one's decision to become part of a communication network based on individual self-interest.

This chapter will shed light on how existing theory and research dealing with social networks in nonmediated environments can be used to explain rationales for, processes associated with, and effects of individuals' membership in online communities. Beginning with a brief discussion of centrality, a term that has permeated the social network literature for the past three decades, and then using the theory of homophily, theory of mutual interest, and theory of self-interest as guiding frameworks, it will become clear that although the mediated landscape has changed the ways in which communication networks are formed, the existing literature is extremely relevant for understanding the social activities that occur in the online world.

BASIC NETWORK TERMINOLOGY AND CENTRALITY

It is important to mention, at the outset, that social networks are not a recent novelty. Scholars within the fields of sociology and communication have long noted that creating and maintaining social ties with others is important in defining one's sense of identity, in shaping one's attitudes and behaviors, in garnering social support, and as a reflection of one's self. In fact, these four important variables associated with social networks have not changed since individuals have taken much of their everyday activities online. However, although social networks are not new, the media through which individuals interact with others are. As Kane, Alavi, Labianca, and Borgatti (2014) make clear, it is common for individuals to conflate the terms "network" and "social media," where the former connotes the culmination of actors who are part of one's socially constructed community, whereas the latter are "information technologies . . . which support interpersonal communication and collaboration using Internet-based platforms" (p. 275). In fact, Bryant, Sanders-Jackson, and Smallwood (2006) went so far as to adopt a new phrase, socially interactive technologies, which refer to the media that enable networking to occur in online, computer-mediated environments. As such, for the remainder of this chapter, the phrase social network will be used to describe the individuals communicatively connected to each other based on certain similarities, whereas the phrase socially interactive technology, or SIT, will be used when referencing the mediated devices enabling such connections to occur in cyberspace.

In its simplest form, a social network can be defined as a collection of individuals whose relationships with one another come to build a social structure (Burt, 2000). At the macro level, then, there is the entire structure, which is the combination of all individuals within a particular network and the relationships that each has with others. At the micro level, however, there are both individuals and the relationships that they create with each other. According to basic terminology from those who study social networks and conduct what is known as social network analysis research (see Scott & Carrington, 2011), the individuals within a network are referred to as nodes and the relationships between and among nodes are called ties (Hanneman & Riddle, 2011). As such, a social network can be conceived of as the emergent structure based on the ties between and among once isolated nodes. The great majority of socially interactive technologies allow users to visualize the tie-node-structure that comes to construct the social network in question (Ellison, Steinfield, & Lampe, 2007). This is the first way in which existing social network theory, dating back at least six decades (see, for example, Bavelas, 1948), can be used to explain online networking practices among users to-day. As an example, aNobii is an online social network that enables those who share a common interest in books to learn more about them from others who are well-versed in this same pastime. Once an individual becomes a registered user of this social network, she becomes an individual node within it. Assuming that the registered user wishes to learn a bit more about the book *Blink*, written by Malcolm Gladwell, she will merely put this information into a registered-node-only search engine, one that requires a username and password to access, after which all of the users who recently posted information (in the form of a review) about this book will appear and the user in question can then add the reviewers to her list of network friends. Now, not only is the individual user a node within an already-existing network (the aNobii network), but, by becoming online friends with others, predicated on an interest in Malcolm Gladwell's text, the creation of ties begins to occur and the aNobii structure becomes augmented. This, in essence, is no different than meeting a new person at a coffeehouse, exchanging contact information, and becoming part of her network of friends: it is merely happening in a mediated environment.

Many scholars who study social network structures are interested in the extent to which one's network position is potentially more significant, salient, or powerful as compared to another. The term centrality, popularized by Freeman (1979), connotes one's importance based on positional location within a given network. That is, within a given structure, certain nodes are likely to be more noteworthy than others. One of the four centrality measures, degree centrality, has received much attention in the scholarly literature and has come to increase our understanding of individual, node-level influence on one hand, and collective, structural-level implications on the other (see Bonacich, 1987, for an in-depth review). In short, degree centrality is defined as having more ties as compared to other nodes within one's network (Marsden, 2002). Assume that in a network of 100 nodes, Individual Y has a total of 54 ties and Individual Z has a total of 38 ties. In this case, Individual Y has, compared to Individual Z, higher degree centrality. What are the implications of having more social connections, comparatively speaking, within a network structure? Research has found, for example, that individuals who are better connected have (a) increased power (Krackhardt, 1990), (b) increased access to information (Tsai, 2001), (c) increased influence among other nodes (Faust, 1997), (d) fostered more trust in others (Buskens, 1998), and (e) increased the likelihood of effective leadership (Friedkin & Slater, 1994). All of these five effects of being well-connected within a network, if used for good intentions, are beneficial. However, is there a way of gauging degree centrality in online social networks, and if so, what are the likely effects of this?

In many online social networks, there is certainly a way of gauging one's degree centrality. As a first example, on Facebook, two fundamental and quantitatively-possible ways of determining and measuring one's importance in his or her network, as compared to all other nodes, is to count the number of friends that one has and the number of groups to which one belongs (Brandtzaeg, Luders, & Skjetne, 2010; Park, Kee, & Valenzuela, 2009). This, in essence, is analogous with degree centrality's claim that the most important node in the network is the individual with access to the most others, comparatively speaking. Statistical probability argues that those with more Facebook friends and those who belong to more groups (which, thus, increase connection possibilities), have access to more individuals. On Facebook, it is likely that those with more friends are going to have access to more information (e.g., gossip, news, social events), access to more people (individual nodes will actually become one's social bridge to another network of social actors), and an increased likelihood of social support. In fact, results from Ellison, Steinfield, and Lampe's (2007) study indicated that among the benefits of having many Facebook friends is the accruement of what the authors call social capital: the positive, psychological effects associated with creating, cultivating, and maintaining relationships with others (Coleman, 1988). Among the most important variables correlated with social capital in Ellison, Steinfield, and Lampe's (2007) study was higher self-esteem, and, although they "can definitively state that there is a positive relationship between certain kinds of Facebook use and creation of social capital," they "cannot say which precedes the other" (p. 1161). In other words, as a result of their study, an interesting query emerges: Is self-esteem a prerequisite for, or an effect of, having many Facebook friends, which translates into high degree centrality producing increased social capital? For purposes of this chapter, the answer to this query is somewhat insignificant. What is important, rather, is that centrality in a mediated environment can be measured, quantitatively, and comes to have some significant meaning within the communication context.

As a second example of degree centrality in an online network, Recipefy, a mediated community of individuals who share culinary recipes for foods from across the world, provides three interesting ways of determining one's level of measurable, quantitatively-based importance within the overall network structure. First, once a registered user posts a recipe for one of six culinary categories (appetizers, starters, main courses, side dishes, desserts, and drinks), other users, who either read the posted recipe, use the posted recipe, or a combination of both, then have the option to like the said recipe. In the online, mediated world, to like something means exactly what it does in colloquial English: to approve of it. If, for example, a registered user posted his recipe for a tiramisu mousse cheesecake and then received seven likes, this is emblematic of this individual's centrality in the network. In fact, there is a search option whereby one can search tiramisu mousse cheesecake and see all of the posted recipes, thus enabling the quantitative comparison among posters. As such, a user who receives seven likes as compared to a user who receives five likes is, comparatively speaking, more important: in this case based on the taste of his/her culinary creation. This symbol of importance, based on the testimonial evidence of one's cooking abilities, becomes a degree-centrality marker.

A second way of gauging degree centrality is by determining one's popularity within the Recipefy network. If we take a moment to think about the vernacular surrounding the definition of degree centrality forwarded earlier, that one is more important in his or her network based on having more social connections as compared to others, this is a common way of operationalizing the term popular within the field of sociology. For example, Cillessen and Rose (2005) define popularity as "[being] well-liked by others . . . generally display[ing] high levels of prosocial and cooperative behavior . . . [being] well-known, socially central, and [oftentimes] emulated" (p. 102). Based on this definition, those with such traits have an increased likelihood of developing more social connections as compared to those who do not. From within the Recipefy network, a registered user increases her popularity when she gains additional likes and when individuals leave specific comments about the user, the posted recipe, or both. In this case, admiration, reverence, and emulation have everything to do with one's recipe and one's ethos and, hence, talent equates to popularity which equates to degree centrality. In the end, users are ranked in terms of their popularity within each of the six culinary categories and being popular within the Recipefy network increases the likelihood that others will use her recipe(s): an indirect measure of success and talent and a direct measure of degree centrality.

Finally, within the Recipefy network, there is an option for registered users to view the most followed posters within the SIT. These individuals either have posted the most recipes, the best recipes (based on the sheer number of likes), have the most positive comments about their posted recipes, or a combination thereof. As a registered user, one can begin following the most followed posters. Each and every time the user posts a new recipe, the follower will immediately (and automatically) be updated. What is amazing about the most-followed option in the Recipefy SIT, and which makes it, conceptually, theoretically, and pragmatically similar to nonmediated social networks, is that a user can follow those who follow those who are most viewed. This last sentence may have seemed both syntactically and semantically flawed, but it was neither. At the start of this chapter, the idea of homophily was presented, which, in sum, argues that birds of a feather flock together. Another way of representing this, in verbal form, is that a friend of a friend is a friend (if Individual A is friends with Individual B and Individual B is friends with Individual C, it is quite likely that Individual A and

Individual C will also be friends with each other) (Louch, 2000). This idea emanates from the field of psychology and has its main roots in Fritz Heider's (1958) well-known Balance Theory, which helps to explain the human desire for psychological, cognitive, and relational consistency. The previous sentence, that a user can follow those who follow those who are most viewed, can most aptly be explained as follows: that a social network structure emerges in the Recipefy community when a registered user not only begins to follow a most viewed poster, but also when she begins to follow others who wish to follow most viewed posters. This, in the end, is how the Recipefy network becomes socially, communicatively constructed and how one can determine not only how the combination of nodes connected by ties creates a community, but also why certain individuals are more central to the community as compared to others.

In sum, this section has argued that both mediated and nonmediated social networks have structures that emerge when individuals (nodes) form relationships (ties) with others creating a sense of shared community. Although the communicative processes through which nodes become part of a network are strikingly different in the mediated landscape, certain social actors are more important based on their position within the larger network structure, as evidenced by one's friends and group memberships on Facebook and one's popularity (determined by likes, comments, and most followed status) on Recipefy. In the end, therefore, the ideas, principles, and theories related to nonmediated social networks that have emerged, and which have been supported, over the past half-century are certainly not for naught when discussing mediated communities. Rather, they have proven extremely useful for understanding the emergence of social structures via the online media provided in the age of technology.

BIRDS OF A FEATHER NETWORK TOGETHER: THE THEORY OF HOMOPHILY

One question that has caused scholars to ponder is whether homophily, or similarity, precedes network affiliation or whether it is a cause of it. That is, is Bradley a fan of the Dave Matthews Band because all of his friends are fans or did Bradley become friends with them in the first place because they enjoy the same genre of music? The obvious question to ask is why scholars have not studied this. The answer is that they have. At least they have tried to study it. The problem, however, is that studying social networks is not an easy task to accomplish. The one issue that makes determining whether homophily is an antecedent to, or effect of, network membership is that few studies are longitudinal (Morgan, Neal, & Carder, 1996). In other words, few empirical analyses look at the initial creation of a network and then study the nodes that later become a part of it. Rather, the great majority of empirically-based examinations are cross-sectional: they look at one particular network at one particular (usually random) moment in time (Burt & Ronchi, 1994). Among the methodological flaws associated with a cross-sectional design is retrospective accountability. Individuals, for example, are supposed to re-member, with great accuracy, why they joined the network in question. Un-fortunately, as Killworth and Bernard (1976), and later Bernard, Killworth, and Sailer (1982), found, network members are highly inaccurate when it comes to remembering why and with whom they form social connections. That said, although longitudinal studies will provide more information about whether similarity is the cause for or the effect of network membership, it is clear that attitudinal and behavioral commonalities are inherent among net-work nodes.

In their oft-cited piece, McPherson, Smith-Lovin, and Cook (2001) argue that homophilous variables, such as gender, age, religion, education, occupa-tion, and social class, come to be overrepresented within social networks and underrepresented between social networks. Using a purely hypothetical ex-ample, if there are a total of one thousand Catholics and a total of ten social networks to which all can belong, it is much more likely that they will all belong to the same two or three, rather than one hundred individual Catholics belonging to each of the ten individual networks. The conclusion, in the end, is both expected and remarkable at once: that similar nodes are likely to congregate in the same social communities. It is expected because, from the time that we are young until the time when we enter adulthood, we enter into homophilous groups (Kiesner, Poulin, & Nicotra, 2003). Some examples of this follow: children's playgroups are often determined by gender and age; a travelling soccer team for fifth grade boys is predicated on athletic talent; the mathematics class that a high school sophomore joins is based on her aca-demic ability; the college that one enters is based on such things as academic standing, SAT score, and personal essay; the sorority that one joins is based on, among other things, her interest in the organization's philanthropic dedi-cation; the way one dresses is a function of his new job; and how a family landscapes its garden is often a reflection of the neighborhood. Although this list could be endless, it does point to one extremely important claim about social networks: the people within them, whether they be friends, teammates, classmates, sorority sisters, colleagues, or neighbors, are quite similar.

On the other hand, however, it is remarkable that such similarity exists within network structures. As much as people might yearn for difference and exposure to something new, they also strive for comfort and predictability (Rogers & Bhowmik, 1970). Assume, for a moment, that you just did some-thing awful that will absolutely have a very grave effect on the relationship you share with your best friend. Assume, further, that you seek advice about how to remedy the situation. In all likelihood, you know exactly the person from whom you will solicit advice. What about this person is so appropriate given the nature of the situation? If you actually take a moment to think about this hypothetical situation and take a moment to think about why you would reach out to this particular individual for advice as opposed to another, I am confident that the answer to this query is as follows: because the advice that they would offer is the same advice that you would offer yourself. That is, this is the person who thinks most like you. In fact, there is a strong chance that this individual would not think that you did anything wrong in the first place. This, in the end, is the benefit of having similar nodes in one's network. As McPherson, Smith-Lovin, and Cook (2001) claim, "by interacting with others who are like ourselves, anything that we experience as a result of our position gets reinforced . . . it comes to typify 'people like us'" (pp. 415–416). That said, however, having such an abundance of similarity within networks also damages individuals by not exposing them to heterophilous (dissimilar) others, from which would stem different perspectives, different interests, different jokes, different favorite foods, different music genres, and different ways of life.

Since the major emphasis of this chapter is highlighting the link between traditional theories associated with nonmediated social networks and the networks formed as a result of online technologies, examples of homophilous ties, creating communities of individuals who are strikingly similar, abound. One prime example of the homophily principle in action via SITs, where individuals are collectively bound together for a particular reason, is Cafe-Mom, an online network of women whose marketing tagline is "the meeting place for moms." In essence, mothers can communicate with other mothers about such topics as children's health, forthcoming or current pregnancy, toddlers, babies, teens, behaviorally-troubled children, learning disabilities, and how to financially budget with a new child. All of the women who are part of this network have at least two variables in common: they are either current or soon-to-be mothers and they are seeking advice from others who have been in the same (or a similar) situation. It is not to say that non-mothers cannot join the network, nor is it to say that mothers without concerns, who are not in need of advice, cannot, and do not, join. It is to say, however, that mothers in need of advice and mothers who wish to offer the advice that they have accumulated through experience are more likely to join. After all, this is the key argument embedded in the theory of homophily. Not that only those who are similar are going to network together. Rather, those who are similar to one another are more likely to network together as compared to those who share dissimilarities.

A second example of similarity breeding network connections and creating an online, social community is a social networking service known as Ravelry, which allows users to share ideas and information about the fiber arts, including, though not limited to, spinning, crocheting, knitting, weaving, and needlepoint. Registered users, for example, communicate with one another about such topics as color choice, patterns, stitch design, fabrics, different textiles, and even how to fix mistakes while knitting and weaving. Merely by searching through the groups, blogs, and forums created and used by registered nodes, it becomes clear that interest in the fiber arts becomes a prerequisite for membership in this online network. Similar to joining a local community group, becoming a member of the Ravelry online network enables both attitudinal and behavioral congruity, whereby individuals' thought and behavioral patterns become aligned, to produce relational outcomes. In this case, Ravelry allows fiber artists, both experienced and inexperienced, to share information with one another and, based on even a cursory review of the user comments on the blog, it is quite clear that individual network members are benefitting from the advice offered from others.

Homophily theory has long helped explain membership in offline networks and continues to receive much attention in the scholarly literature, both in terms of rationale(s) for joining networked communities, as well as the effects of said membership. Recently, for example, data have revealed that (a) individuals part of the GLB community are more likely to network with each other as compared to their straight counterparts for purposes of social support and comfort (Ueno, Wright, Gayman, & McCabe, 2012); (b) homophily is a statistically significant predictor of intra-network altruism among associated members (Curry & Dunbar, 2013); (c) individuals part of a homophilous, as opposed to a heterophilous, network of friends are more likely to smoke and more likely to be physically inactive (Flatt, Agimi, & Albert, 2012); and (d) being part of a homophilous network, wherein individuals might reinforce potentially dangerous behaviors, increases one's tendency to engage in pathological gambling practices (Meisel et al., 2013). In addition, results from research that has looked at the relationship between homophily and online behavior using SIT has begun to surface, including the following: (a) that age as a homophily variable might be the most important predictor of one's communicative decisions in the virtual world afforded by the Internet (Huang, Shen, & Contractor, 2013); (b) that, on Twitter, not only do those with similar political views follow one another's posts, but also that their messages become extremely well-aligned with one another (Park, 2013); (c) that individuals communicating with others about consumer products via electronic word-of-mouth are more persuasive agents when homophilous variables exist (Canhoto & Clark, 2013); and (d) that individuals who were socially connected to homophilous others via Facebook felt more social comfort and emotional support as compared to those who were networked with more heterophilous nodes (Wright, 2012). Although scholars have clearly started to address the link between SITs and homophily, more time must be devoted to this area of inquiry, as evidenced by the sheer quantity of interaction that transpires via computer-mediated technologies.

NETWORKING FOR COLLECTIVE GAIN:
THE THEORY OF MUTUAL INTEREST

One of the most-cited, emergent theories dealing with social, communication networks and the rationale for their existence and maintenance is the theory of mutual interest (Monge & Contractor, 2003). In short, this theory argues that an individual joins a particular social network not only because he or she will benefit from becoming part of the community in question, but also that the community will benefit from the individual's membership. A prime example of this theory as it relates to network membership is one's decision to join the United States Army. Although from a social network perspective, this community can become extremely complicated (it is one of three military departments, along with the Navy and the Air Force, and comprises both active and reserve constituencies), the Army mission statement by which all associated members identify is as follows:

> To fight and win our Nation's wars by providing prompt, sustained land dominance across the full range of military operations and spectrum of conflict in support of combatant commanders. We do this by:
>
> • Executing Title 10 and Title 32 United States Code directives, to include organizing, equipping, and training forces for the conduct of prompt and sustained combat operations on land.
> • Accomplishing missions assigned by the President, Secretary of Defense and combatant commanders, and Transforming [*sic*] for the future.

(Organization, n.d.)

On the one hand, this mirrors the principle of homophily mentioned earlier, arguing that accepting this mission statement as one's own becomes a prerequisite for network membership and, in this case, for joining the United States Army. However, it also mirrors mutual interest, inasmuch as an individual's decision to join the army network will be beneficial both at the individual level (patriotism, comradery, bravery, education, training, leadership) and the collective level (increased recruitment, increased veterans). In fact, Monge and Contractor (2003) speak about the relationship between the notion of mutual interest and collective action (the sociological principle upon which the armed forces is predicated), wherein network membership benefits ego on one hand and the already-existing community on the other. Although definitional variations exist, collective action can be defined as the advantages that accrue when working with others as opposed to working independently (Oliver, Marwell, & Teixeira, 1985). From a network paradigm, the power-in-numbers perspective argues that there is a positive correlation between the quantity of actors in a given network and the likelihood of effective action on their behalf.

It becomes clear, after a review of many of the platforms available for media users today, that the theory of mutual interest does, in fact, drive the decisions of individual members. Based on the foregoing discussion, the prerequisite for the emergence of this theory as a guiding framework for network membership is that the new actor, as well as the actors already embedded within the community, both have to benefit from the individual's connection to, and participation in, the social system. One might even argue that all social actors within a network benefit when all other nodes contribute to the structure's existence and purpose. A first example of an online social network, whose membership can be explained using Monge and Contractor's (2003) theory of mutual interest, is DailyStrength, a community of individuals (both professional experts and laypersons) who provide social support to one another in such areas as terminal illness, loneliness, eating disorders, post-death bereavement, overall health, relationships, chronic disease, jealously, divorce, and depression. It is quite difficult to conceive of a physical, mental, or emotional issue that might plague an individual user and not find an available support group on this online network. DailyStrength's marketing tagline, "become a member now and join the largest, most comprehensive network of people sharing their knowledge, experiences, and support," illustrates that by becoming a registered user, an actor becomes both a beneficiary of others and a benefit to others in the process as well. If one were to read the active discussion boards of any of the current topics, including food allergies, alcoholism, miscarriage, and bisexualism, she would clearly realize that the entire community benefits with each and every joining actor. That is, with new actors come new stories, with new stories comes new advice, with new advice come new questions, with new questions come new discussion topics, with new discussion topics come new insights, with new insights come new perspectives, and with new perspectives come new solutions. It is possible to pictorially represent this chain of events and such representation would be emblematic of a circular motion of actions, each of which comes to influence the next. However, this circle does not stop once the shape is completed. Rather, once the shape is completed, the conversations merely become enriched. Once a conversation ends, all invested actors (not only the individual who began the conversation and the individuals who participated in it, but also those who viewed the public conversation) are better off as a result of the information and advice provided. This, in the end, is the thesis behind the theory of mutual interest: All invested parties benefit by collective action within the network.

A second example of this theory in action is ClusterFlunk, which is an online social networking site, exclusively for college students, where registered users can use collaborative learning techniques to perform schoolwork.

Assume, for example, that a student is enrolled in an introductory psychology course and is having trouble writing a paper on Albert Bandura's (1977) social learning theory. This student can post a message, beginning a discussion, which can ultimately prompt an idea for his thesis and might even lead to another node within the ClusterFlunk network to share some of his coursework related to Bandura's theory (notes, original publications, papers). It should become clear, even based on this brief explanation, how and why the original poster would benefit when another registered user responds. The question, at this point, is how the individuals who share the information with the requester benefit from this social interaction. That is, how is this representative of mutual interest? The ClusterFlunk network is founded upon the norm of reciprocity, where the "share with others when they have shared with you" doctrine is unofficially enforced (see, for example, Gouldner, 1960). The sharing principle is the bedrock of this community and if requests are one-way, and nonreciprocal, the entire network will fail. This, however, is not the case. This online, mediated community has existed for over two years and, according to the *Des Moines Register*, a newspaper in Iowa, A. J. Nelson and Joe Dallago, the two cofounders of ClusterFlunk, raised one million dollars earlier this year. As a result, the entire ClusterFlunk community is benefiting when each new collegiate user registers: the user is afforded access to information about a variety of topics including art, science, philosophy, history, and business, and the already-existing nodes are provided access to the new members' information and expertise. Hopefully the new information and expertise are in nonredundant, non-overlapping areas.

Research that links the theory of mutual interest to online communities has yet to accumulate empirical evidence. However, given how much social activity occurs via computer-mediated formats, and the importance of understanding how all nodes within a given structure can benefit when new ties are created, it is due time to examine the extent to which Monge and Contractor's (2003) theory of mutual interest can help explain both the motives for, and effects of, membership in networks via socially interactive technologies.

NETWORKING FOR INDIVIDUAL GAIN: THE THEORY OF SELF-INTEREST

The final theory that will be examined, and which drives a large amount of social network research, is the theory of self-interest (Monge & Contractor, 2003), arguing that membership in communities of actors can be purely ego-driven. That is, regardless of whether and to what extent other individuals already part of a given network benefit, nodes will join if they, themselves, can profit from inclusion. As an example, Lambda Pi Eta, the honor society of the National Communication Association, annually inducts undergraduate students who have (a) completed a total of at least 60 credits, (b) maintained a major Grade Point Average of at least a 3.25, and (c) maintained a cumulative Grade Point Average of at least a 3.0. Scholars who endorse the theory of mutual interest would argue that, when a student is invited into the honor society and ultimately joins, both constituencies become beneficiaries: the student is provided with the resources that accompany membership (i.e., prestige, increased access to contacts within the field, opportunity to become a member of the chapter's executive board) and the society, both at the national and individual chapter levels, gains something as well (i.e., increased membership, dues). However, an alternative theoretical perspective from which one can emanate when attempting to better understand a student's decision to become a member of Lambda Pi Eta, joining a network of fellow accomplished classmates, is the theory of self-interest. From this theoretical framework, the student in question joined for personal, narcissistic reasons: because of the prestige of being in an honor society, to have increased contacts, to have an opportunity to become an executive board member, and to be afforded the opportunity to put this accomplishment on a resume.

One example of a website, which can be viewed as a SIT, used for social networking purposes and whose user memberships can be linked to the theory of self-interest, is Instagram. In short, Instagram, whose marketing tagline is "capture and share the world's moments," provides registered users with the ability to post photos and videos, of themselves and/or others, which are subsequently viewed by network nodes (photos and videos are available to all registered Instagram users unless the node chooses to make her profile private). These users can then comment on the photos and videos and even like them, which, as mentioned earlier in the chapter, is analogous with the social approval that would emerge in a nonmediated, communicative environment. From a cursory perspective, it can be argued, potentially, that two nodes (one who posts and one who follows the posts of the other) both have something to gain, thus adding validity to the theory of mutual interest and collective action. However, a more in-depth look reveals a much more narcissistic rationale for becoming a member of the Instagram community. As a poster of photos and videos, the node is able to showcase her social life. It is difficult to navigate the visual messages within this online network without seeing the progression of users' lives posted: friends, family members, pets, selfies, and the list goes on. Instagram has provided a postmodern form of visual storytelling that has replaced the now-antiquated practice of scrapbooking. The question that remains, however, is what purpose does the story told through visual images serve? According to the theory of self-interest, the goal of such storytelling through visual communication is to gain followers (other members that routinely view one's uploaded photos and videos), to increase the quantity of likes (endorsement that the visual images are worthy of praise), and to highlight the activities of one's life. Likewise, the goal of Instagram followers is to visualize the lives of others (perhaps creating social comparison) and engaging in social experiences vicariously through a form of mediated technology. As such, the theory of self-interest can certainly explain one's rationale for becoming a node within the Instagram network: there is something to individually gain as a result of community membership.

A second example of an online social network whose membership is predicated on the theory of self-interest is Lafango: a social network of musicians, artists, photographers, and dancers who are able to upload their own, unique press kits in an effort to showcase their skills and work to talent seekers, in the hope that such recognition will transform into employment opportunities. Although there is a way of interacting with others within the Lafango network (through a blogging interface), and, like several of the examples provided throughout this chapter, there are ways of following other users and liking the press kits uploaded by them, the great majority of communicative activity is predicated on reasons that are ego-driven. In fact, according to the marketing strategy used by this website, "*lafango* is your true representation on the web," potential users should join because of the opportunities available to market themselves: a vivid, transparent example of network membership based on a self-serving interest. In addition, there are routine competitions among users so that nodes can stand out among the other actors within the Lafango network which, through the eyes of talent seekers, can become extremely important: especially within the fine and performing arts industries. Each day, in fact, there is one featured press kit, earned by the node's creator receiving more likes as compared to all others within the entire Lafango community. This individual's profile picture is featured on the site's homepage, with a link to the node's entire electronic press kit: yet another benefit linked to the individual, herself, rather than the community at large. It is important to mention, again, that this example, too, can, tangentially, be viewed from the theory of mutual interest perspective. That is, the entire Lafango network benefits, to an extent, when each new member joins: The collective talent of registered users increases (based on probability and statistics) when new members join, the prestige of winning a competition increases with more nodes in the network, and more talent seekers are going to search the website for musicians, photographers, artists, and dancers when more users join. However, the main rationales for joining, as mentioned earlier, are self-satisfying.

Similar to the theory of self-interest, there have yet to be studies that specifically link the independent variable of self-interest to one's desire to become a member of an online community. That said, however, and based on the foregoing discussion, it becomes clear that the relationship between the two exists: it is empirical data that are needed to support this claim. An interesting conclusion regarding online social networks is that the theory of mutual interest and the theory of self-interest, as explanatory frameworks for understanding the impetus for an individual to join a community, might not be mutually exclusive. In other words, perhaps both can shed light on rationales for joining certain online communities. As such, both might explain variability in one's decision to join (or not join) a particular computer-mediated network. In the end, it might just be that one theoretical perspective is more valid given the nodes, ties, structures, and SIT in question.

CONCLUSION

Online social networks have become mundane for social actors as we are navigating the second decade of the twenty-first century. While certain scholars and practitioners have attempted to study and delineate the negative ramifications of relational construction in mediated environments, others have spent their careers proposing the relational benefits to be gained from online networking. This chapter focused on neither. Rather, the argument forwarded was that, from a communicative, social network perspective, the processes and practices that occur through socially interactive technologies mirror those that occur in their nonmediated, face-to-face counterparts. Some of the most heavily-researched areas in the world of social networks, including degree centrality, the theory of homophily, the theory of mutual interest, and the theory of self-interest, all manifest themselves in online communities, producing the conclusion that individual nodes, and ties that they construct with others, are, to a large extent, predicated on rational decision-making premises. As such, it becomes clear that both the theories and data-gathering procedures that have guided network research for the past fifty years are conducive to analyzing and assessing the communities in which actors become a part in cyberspace.

It is important to note, however, that since these theories were developed, tested, and validated well before the introduction of socially interactive technologies, their applicability can be questioned. For example, the theory of homophily argues that similarity breeds similarity. However, with the agency afforded by the Internet for individual nodes to, in a sense, socially construct identities of their choosing (not necessarily aligned with their true selves), perhaps such mediated similarity is but a fabrication and a figment of the imagination. The theory of mutual interest argues that all nodes within a given social network must somehow benefit when each new member joins. However, given the sheer size of mediated communities, is it possible that individuals will still join SITs, and that these SITs will continue to survive, structurally, even if not all associated nodes somehow amass rewards? The theory of self-interest argues that nodes within a network have an interest in joining the said entity if they, individually, have an opportunity at narcissistic gain. However, could it be that, regardless of membership impetus, at least a percentage of one's decision emanates from this selfish motive?

While this chapter has raised some important questions about the link between existing social network theory and socially interactive technologies, it has also pointed to several more. That said, however, the field of communication is moving closer to understanding the antecedents, processes, and effects associated with network structures within mediated platforms. In the end therefore, although Kane et al.'s (2014) claim that there exist "novel and distinctive theoretical issues raised by social media [regarding] . . . social media networks" (p. 275), it is equally prudent to argue that it is more the media that are novel: the theoretical issues raised are an extension of network research conducted in nonmediated, non-online communities.

REFERENCES

Bandura, A. (1977). *Social learning theory*. New York: General Learning Press.

Bavelas, A. (1948). A mathematical model for group structure. *Applied Anthropology* 7:16–39.

Bernard, H. R., P. D. Killworth, & L. Sailer. (1982). Informant accuracy in social network data V: An experimental attempt to predict actual communication from recall data. *Social Science Research* 11:30–66.

Bonacich, P. (1987). Power and centrality: A family of measures. *American Journal of Sociology* 92:1170–1182.

Brandtzaeg, P. B., M. Luders, & J. H. Skjetne. (2010). Too many Facebook friends? Content sharing and sociability versus the need for privacy in social network sites. *International Journal of Human-Computer Interaction* 26:1006–1030. doi10.1080/10447318.2010.516719.

Bryant, J. A., A. Sanders-Jackson, & A. M. Smallwood. (2006). IMing, text messaging, and adolescent social networks. *Journal of Computer-Mediated Communication* 11:577–592. doi: 10.1111/j.1083-6101.2006.00028.x.

Burt, R. S. (2000). The network structure of social capital. In B. M. Staw & R. I. Sutton (Eds.), *Research in organizational behavior* (pp. 345–423). Greenwich, CT: JAI Press.

Burt, R. S., & D. Ronchi. (1994). Measuring a large network quickly. *Social Networks* 16:91–135.

Buskens, V. (1998). The social structure of trust. *Social Networks* 20:265–289.

Canhoto, A. I., & M. Clark. (2013). Customer service 140 characters at a time: The users' perspective. *Journal of Marketing Management* 29:522–544. doi: 10.1080/0267257X.2013.777355.

Chan, D. K., & G. H. Cheng. (2004). A comparison of offline and online friendship qualities at different stages of relationship development. *Journal of Social and Personal Relationships* 21:305–320. doi: 10.1177/0265407504042834.

Cillessen, A. H., & A. J. Rose. (2005). Understanding popularity in the peer system. *Current Directions in Psychological Science* 14:102–105.

Coleman, J. S. (1988). Social capital in the creation of human capital. *The American Journal of Sociology* 94:S95–S120.

Curry, O. S., & R. I. M. Dunbar. (2013). Sharing a joke: The effects of a similar sense of humor on affiliation and altruism. *Evolution and Human Behavior* 34:125–129.

Ellison, N. B., C. Steinfield, & C. Lampe. (2007). The benefit of Facebook "friends": Social capital and college students' use of online social network sites. *Journal of Computer-Mediated Communication* 12:1143–1168. doi: 10.1111/j.1083-6101.2007.00367.x.

Faust, K. (1997). Centrality in affiliation networks. *Social Networks* 19:157–191.

Flatt, J. D., Y. Agimi, & S. M. Albert. (2012). Homophily and health behavior in social networks of older adults. *Family and Community Health* 35:312–321. doi: 10.1097/FCH.0b013e3182666650.

Freeman, L. C. (1979). Centrality in social networks: Conceptual clarification. *Social Networks* 1:215–239.

Friedkin, N. E., & M. R. Slater. (1994). School leadership and performance: A social network approach. *Sociology of Education* 67:139–157.

Gouldner, A. W. (1960). The norm of reciprocity: A preliminary statement. *American Sociological Review* 25:161–178.

Hanneman, R. A., & M. Riddle. (2011). Concepts and measures for basic network analysis. In J. Scott & P. J. Harrington (Eds.), *The SAGE handbook of social network analysis* (pp. 340–369). Thousand Oaks, CA: Sage.

Heider, F. (1958). *The psychology of interpersonal relations*. New York: Wiley and Sons.

Huang, Y., C. Shen, & N. S. Contractor. (2013). Distance matters: Exploring proximity and homophily in virtual world networks. *Decision Support Systems* 55:969–977.

Kane, G. C., M. Alavi, G. Labianca, & S. P. Borgatti. (2014). What's different about social media networks? A framework and research agenda. *MIS Quarterly* 38:275–304.

Kiesner, J., F. Poulin, & E. Nicotra. (2003). Peer relations across contexts: Individual-network homophily and network inclusion in and after school. *Child Development* 74:1328–1343.

Killworth, P. D., & H. R. Bernard. (1976). Informant accuracy in social network data. *Human Organization* 35:269–286.

Krackhardt, D. (1990). Assessing the political landscape: Structure, cognition, and power in organizations. *Administrative Science Quarterly* 35:342–369.

Louch, H. (2000). Personal network integration: Transitivity and homophily in strong tie relations. *Social Networks* 22:45–64.

Manago, A. M., T. Taylor, & P. M. Greenfield. (2012). Me and my 400 friends: The anatomy of college students' Facebook networks, their communication patterns, and well-being. *Developmental Psychology* 48:369–380. doi: 10.1037/a0026338.

Marsden, P. V. (2002). Egocentric and sociocentric measures of network centrality. *Social Networks* 24:407–422.

McPherson, M., L. Smith-Lovin, & J. M. Cook. (2001). Birds of a feather: Homophily in social networks. *Annual Review of Sociology* 27:415–444.

Meisel, M. K., A. D. Clifton, J. Mackillop, J. D. Miller, W. K. Campbell, & A. S. Goodie. (2013). Egocentric social network analysis of pathological gambling. *Addiction* 108:584–591. doi: 10.1111/add.12014.

Monge, P. R., & N. Contractor. (2003). *Theories of communication networks*. New York: Oxford University Press.

Morgan, D. L., M. B. Neal, & P. Carder. (1996). The stability of core and peripheral networks over time. *Social Networks* 19:9–25.

Oliver, P., G. Marwell, G., & R. Teixeira. (1985). A theory of the critical mass: Interdependence, group heterogeneity, and the production of collective action. *American Journal of Sociology* 91:522–556.

Organization (n.d.). Retrieved from http://www.army.mil/info/organization/.

Park, C. S. (2013). Does Twitter motivate involvement in politics? Tweeting, opinion leadership, and political engagement. *Computers in Human Behavior* 29:1641–1648.

Park, N., K. F. Kee, & S. Valenzuela, S. (2009). Is there social capital in a social network site? Facebook use and college students' life satisfaction, trust, and participation. *Journal of Computer-Mediated Communication* 14:875–901. doi: 10.1111/j.1083-6101.2009.01474.x.

Ramirez, A., & S. Zhang. (2007). When online meets offline: The effect of modality switching on relational communication. *Communication Monographs* 74:287–310. doi: 10.1080/03637750701543493.

Rogers, E. M., & D. Bhowmik. (1970). Homophily-heterophily: Relational concepts for communication research. *Public Opinion Quarterly* 34:523–538.

Scott, J., & P. J. Carrington. (2011). *The SAGE handbook of social network analysis*. Thousand Oaks, CA: Sage.

Tsai, W. (2001). Knowledge transfer in intra-organizational networks: Effects of network position and absorptive capacity on business unit innovation and performance. *The Academy of Management Journal* 44:996–1004.

Ueno, K., E. R. Wright, M. Gayman, & J. McCabe. (2012). Segregation in gay, lesbian, and bisexual youth's personal networks: Testing structural constraint, choice homophily, and compartmentalization hypotheses. *Social Forces* 90:971–991. doi: 10.1093/sf/sor022.

Wright, K. B. (2012). Emotional support and perceived stress among college students using Facebook.com: An exploration of the relationship between source perceptions and emotional support. *Communication Research Reports* 29:175–184. doi: 10.1080/08824096.2012.695957.

Chapter Three

Social Networking Sites, Self-Disclosure, and Personal Engagement

Pamela J. Kalbfleisch

"TODAY, IF YOU OWN A SMARTPHONE, you're carrying a 24–7 singles bar in your pocket" (Ansari, 2015, p. 42).

"The prominent secret-sharing site Form-spring closed in 2013, but a new wave of websites and apps, such as Secret, Whisper and Yik Yak have more than filled the void." (Dickey, 2014, p. 42).

Navigating personal relationships has become more complicated as hundreds of social networking sites are available to meet others, to begin relationships, to maintain relationships, to dissolve relationships, to discuss relationships, and to discuss others. Personal engagement is high as people attempt to accomplish all aspects of relational management and personal navigation through a world where information is just a click or swipe away.

This chapter explores how people personally engage with social networking sites. The variety of social networking sites is considered as well as the research on issues of personal engagement with these sites. Willingness to self-disclose on social networking sites is considered as well as reciprocity of self-disclosure. Personal benefits and disadvantages in social networking sites are considered as well as how credible and attractive those engaged with social media sites are considered. Relational initiation, maintaining relationships, and dealing with declining relationships and dissatisfaction with relational quality is considered as displayed on social networking sites. Stalking behavior and jealously are considered as well as ending relationships. This chapter points to the rich nature of future research on personal engagement and social networking sites as researchers more fully examine this area of study and consideration.

BACKGROUND: ROMANTIC ENCOUNTERS
AND RELATIONSHIPS

Online dating services provide users with potential romantic partners through online profiles providing information about potential dates; communication with these potential partners, the mechanisms of which differ across social networking sites; and matching by using algorithms to assist the user with identifying potential matches (Finkel, Eastwich, Karney, Reis, & Sprecher, 2012). These sites include general self-selection sites, such as Match, Plen-tyOfFish, OKCupid; more targeted groups in niche self-selection sites, such as JDate, Gay, Sugardaddie; family/friend participation sites, where family and friends can use the site for matchmaking for someone else, such as Kizmeet, Heartbroker; video-dating sites, where users employ webcams for conversation, such as SpeedDate, Video dating, WooMe; sites that allow virtual dating where users create avatars for virtual dates online including OmniDate, Weopia, VirtualDateSpace; self-report matching sites where matches are made based on self-reported data, such as eHarmony, Chemistry, and PerfectMatch; matching sites that do not use self-report data to form matches such as GenePartner, ScientificMatch; and smartphone applications (apps) that use global positioning systems (GPS) to inform users of partners in the area such as Zoosk, Badoo, and Grindr (Finkel et al., 2012). These are but a subset of the myriad of online dating sites that are available to those looking for romantic or sexual connections.

Walther (1996) theorized that online environments provide users with increased opportunities to control and manage information compared with face-to-face communication. Users do this by being able to edit their self-presentation, selecting asynchronous conversations, and reallocating their cognitive resources to focus totally on self-presentation. These options are not as readily available in face-to-face interactions. Strategic communication can take the form of manipulation of information and visual input, such as photographs. Toma and Hancock (2011) found that this was the case and that this was particularly true of female photographs versus male photographs. Strategy can also come into play with the selective use of deceptive discourse (Toma & Hancock, 2011).

Social networking sites can be locations where people can gain information about people with whom they have romantic interest without necessarily being set up as dating sites (boyd, 2007). Facebook and MySpace are examples of social networking sites that are more general in nature but that could be used to glean information of this nature. People looking exclusively for casual sex might use sites such as OnlineBootyCall, AdultFriendFinder, and GetItOn; and those looking for partners for extra relationship affairs might use Ashley Madison, Illicit Encounters, and Waiting Room (Finkel et al., 2012). Sexual encounters can occur through mediated means or through meeting face-to-face (Chambers, 2013). In the case of massively multiplayer online games, partners can meet as avatars or characters in a complex online environment such as Second Life, The Sims, and World of Warcraft (Finkel et al., 2012).

These are but some of the social networking sites available. Other sites are focused on group dates or group meetings such as Ignighter, Meetcha, Grubwithus (Finkel et al., 2012) as well as other "meet-up" sites. List of Social Networking Websites (n.d.) on Wikipedia notes over two hundred social networking websites. Clearly this list is limited due to the difficulty of finding every site available. Some sites are specifically not easily found and rely on being difficult to find and search as well to guard the secrecy and anonymity of users. Users in the fictional *Mr. Mercedes* (King, 2014) met in a secretive social networking site, Under Debbie's Blue Umbrella, where they exchanged messages with a mass murderer who was trying to get the users communicating with him to kill themselves. Real-time users can currently log into this site using login information from the book. The Easter eggs found on this site by readers could be considered a further way to market the book or a manifestation of reader engagement with the fictional story.

SELF-DISCLOSURE

An issue of interest is why users would self-disclose on social networking sites where they may not know who could be reading their disclosures? This is especially the case when one considers the dangers inherent in providing personal information to others in a manner that could become very public. The short interactive horror film written by Nickel and Zada (2011), *Take This Lollipop*, is a Facebook app that uses information and photos taken from a person's Facebook presence to personalize a scenario where a bad man is coming to get the person who willingly provided her or his Facebook information and clicked on a lollipop with an embedded razor blade. While this film acts as entertainment, it does depict what happens when providing access to a Facebook account where personal information is available.

Self-disclosure is revealing personal information that is not already known to another person about oneself (Jourard, 1971). In an examination of why people self-disclose on social networking sites, Krasnova, Spiekermann, Koroleva, and Hildebrand (2010) found that people self-disclose in these environments because of the convenience of developing and maintaining relationships in social networking sites and because of the users' enjoyment of the social networking sites. Privacy concerns of self-disclosures were mitigated by their trust in the social networking sites and the availability of information dissemination controls. On the contrary, Taddei and Contena (2013) discovered that the perception of privacy risks did not directly influence the amount of self-disclosure in social networking sites. Rather, as Joinson, Reips, Buchanan, and Paine Schofield (2010) found, the degree of perceived information control makes users self-confident about their ability to control information dissemination. The users perceive less risk because of heightened trust in social networking sites' information dissemination controls.

This lower perception of risk may be particularly heightened with younger social networking site users who may have greater trust in information controls and who may see greater need to receive social support from social network site members. When looking at college students using social networking sites, Manago, Taylor, and Greenfield (2012) found that larger social networks were associated with social media users' higher levels of life satisfaction and perceived social support. This group used status updates to disclose emotional intimacy. Interestingly, Oh, Ozkaya, and Larose (2014) found that the frequency of social network site use, the numbers of social network site friends, and supportive interactions were positively associated with the users' perceived social support, affect, sense of community, and life satisfaction. This may encourage users to continue to add contacts as friends to build their social network and social support.

DIFFICULTIES FACED IN ONLINE SELF-DISCLOSURE

However, building connections may not lead others to perceive the person with a large number of contacts as desirable. Tom Tong, Van Der Heide, Langwell, & Walther (2008) identified those with extensive friend connections on Facebook as being perceived as less popular and desirable than those with a more moderate number of Facebook friends. Also, in her examination of perceptions of self-disclosure on Facebook, Bazarova (2012) found that users perceived greater message and relational intimacy from private disclosures (targeted one-on-one) than from those made publicly (wall postings). While self-disclosures shared privately were judged as appropriate, self-disclosures made publicly reduced perceiver likability for the person making the self-disclosures.

Reciprocity in self-disclosures is normatively expected in social relationships (cf. Altman & Taylor, 1973; Jourard, 1971), and taking turns self-disclosing is associated with increased liking in initial interactions (Sprecher et al., 2013). However, when comparing online to face-to-face interactions,

Lipinski-Harten and Tafarodi (2012) found that online chats appeared to produce less sequential connectivity, greater self-focus, and less other-focus than did face-to-face interaction.

Self-disclosure is used as a technique to develop relationships and obtain information about the other communicator or communicators. It can also be used in maintaining and repairing relationships. Social network users can provide private information about family issues, school issues, social issues, risk behaviors, sexual behavior, and personal vulnerability (Williams & Merten, 2008). However, the individuals reading these disclosures do not necessarily have as much ability to determine if they are truthful self-disclosures. Information that may be readily available face-to-face may be more obscure and difficult to find on social networks (Kim & Dindia, 2011). Social network users do use information provided by others on the websites, such as on a user's wall, to make evaluations of the user's credibility and attractiveness (Walther, Van Der Heide, Kim, Westerman, & Tong, 2008). Walther, Van Der Heide, Hamel, and Schulman (2009) found that when there is a discrepancy between a social network user's self-claims and those made by others, observers will place more weight on the claims made by others. This may present unique challenges to those attempting to develop and maintain relationships in social networking sites.

Dissolution of relationships can present its own set of challenges in social networking sites. Users can be unfriended and blocked from another person's account who no longer wishes to be in a relationship. LeFebvre, Blackburn, and Brody (2015) found that even face-to-face relationships that are dissolving can also play out on social networking sites. Users can communicatively dissolve relations publicly by updating relational status, untagging or deleting wall postings and pictures; by defriending, deleting, or blocking a former relational partner from their social networking site; and by defriending, blocking, and blocking family and friends of former relational partners. Users who are in dissolving relationships can manage positive impressions of themselves by their self-presentation online including new posts and pictures presenting a positive view of the activities the user is participating in without the former relational partner. Some users will attempt to invoke jealousy by making it clear they are ready for new relationships.

The public dissolution of relationships on social networking sites can make a difficult process even more unsettling as a person is ruled out of another's life on social networking sites. Some users cope with this by avoiding social media. Others may stalk a former relational partner or perceived relational partner through social media sites and other online information. Tokunaga (2015) found that patterns of negative relational maintenance behaviors are predictive of surveillance over social networking sites. Those with low-quality relationships and relational dissatisfaction were more likely to use surveillance tactics on their relational partner's social networking sites; Surveillance on social networking sites is related to users spending large amounts of time on their partner's profile pages.

CONCLUSION

Personal engagement with social networking sites has been measured with visits to sites, time on sites, number of friends, clicks through social media pages. Engagement has also been measured with content analysis of site information and with self-report and experimental studies. It is clear that for personal engagement, social media sites are a salient issue for those interested in studying how we navigate through life, not only face-to-face but also in social networking sites. Relationships are born, develop, maintain, decline, dissolve, and die or are reborn online and also in the face-to-face world. The immediacy of social media networks, the input of others to social media networks, and the potential public nature of social media networks are all reasons why we should turn to further study of personal engagement in these venues.

Research studies are conducted to answer some questions but others develop through this process as well. For example, how do people navigate between social networking sites and their face-to-face relationships? How do social networking sites assist in relational development or are they just another venue for this development? Are social media sites part of the decline of relationships? Could they be used to repair and heal? Of the variety of social networking sites, which ones draw the most personal engagement from people? Other points for future research include consideration of new research methods for examining communication and engagement in social media sites. How can we as scholar educators gain access and information on what, in some cases, is a secretive world and, in other cases, boldly public?

In conclusion, when considering personal engagement with social networking sites we are left wondering how social networking sites will develop and how we as human beings will adapt and engage personally. The plurality and changing nature of these sites warrant extensive examination and reconsideration of their role in self-disclosure and relationship maintenance. It is clear that the future is bright for those interested in studying personal engagement with social networking sites.

REFERENCES

Altman, I., & D. A. Taylor. (1973). Reciprocity of interpersonal exchange. *Journal for the Theory of Social Behavior* 3:249–261.
Ansari, A. (2015, June). Love in the age of like: Human beings have never had as many romantic options as they do now. Will that doom love or save it? *Newsweek* 185 (22): 40–46.

Bazarova, N. (2012). Public Intimacy: Disclosure interpretation and social judgments on Facebook, *Journal of Communication* 62:815–832. doi: 10.1111/j.1460–2466.2012.01664.x.

boyd, d. (2007). Why youth (heart) social network sites: The role of networked publics in teenage social life. In D. Buckingham (Ed.), *Youth, Identity, and Digital Media* (pp. 119–142). Cambridge, MA: The MIT Press.

Chambers, D. (2013). *Social media and personal relationships: Online intimacies and networked friendship.* Houndmills, UK: Palgrave Macmillan.

Dickey, J. (2014, July). The antisocial network: Inside the dangerous online world kids can't quit. *Newsweek* 184 (1): 40–45.

Finkel, E. J., P. W. Eastwich, B. R. Karney, H. T. Reis, & S. Sprecher. (2012). Online dating: A critical analysis from the perspective of psychological science. *Psychological Science in the Public Interest* 13 (1): 3–66. doi: 10.1177/1529100612436522.

Joinson, A. N., U.-D. Reips, T. Buchanan, & C. B. Paine Schofield. (2010). Privacy, trust, and self-disclosure online. *Human-Computer Interaction* 25:1–224. doi: 10.1080/07370020903586662.

Jourard, S. M. (1971). *The transparent self* (rev. ed.). New York: Van Nostrand Reinhold.

Kim, J., & K. Dindia. (2011). Online self-disclosure: A review of research. In K. B. Wright & L. M. Webb (Eds.), *Computer-mediated communication in personal relationships* (pp. 156–180). New York: Peter Lang.

King, S. (2014). *Mr. Mercedes.* New York: Gallery Books.

Krasnova, H., S. Spiekermann, K. Koroleva, & T. Hildebrand. (2010). Online social networks: Why we disclose. *Journal of Information Technology* 25:109–125. doi: 0268-3962/10.

LeFebvre, L., K. Blackburn, & N. Brody. (2015). Navigating romantic relationships on Facebook: Extending the relational dissolution model to account for social networking environments. *Journal of Social and Personal Relationships* 32:78–98. doi: 10.1177/0265407514524848.

Lipinski-Harten, M., & R. W. Tafarodi. (2012). A comparison of conversational quality in online and face-to-face first encounters. *Journal of Language and Social Psychology* 31:331–341. doi: 10.1177/0261927X12446601.

List of social networking websites. (n.d.). Retrieved from http://en.wikipedia.org/wiki/list_of_social_networking_websites.

Manago, A. M., T. Taylor, & P. M. Greenfield. (2012). Me and my 400 friends: The anatomy of college students' Facebook networks, their communication patterns, and well-being. *Developmental Psychology* 48 (2): 369–380. doi: 10.1037/a0026338.

Nickel, J., & J. Zada. (2011, June 13). *Take this Lollipop.* Retrieved From www.takethislollipop.com.

Oh, H. J., E. Ozkaya, & R. Larose. (2014). How does online social networking enhance life satisfaction? The relationships among online supportive interaction, affect, perceived social support, sense of community, and life satisfaction. *Computers in Human Behavior* 30:69–78. doi: 10.1016/j.chb.2013.07.053.

Sprecher, S., S. Treger, J. D. Wondra, N. Hilaire, & K. Wallpe. (2013). Taking turns: Reciprocal self-disclosure promotes liking in initial interactions. *Journal of Experimental Social Psychology* 49:860–866. doi: 10.1016.jesp.2013.03.017.

Taddei, S., & B. Contena. (2013). Privacy, trust and control: Which relationships with online self-disclosure? *Computers in Human Behavior* 29:821–826. doi: 10.1016/j.chb.2012.11.022.

Tokunaga, R. S. (2015). Interpersonal surveillance over social network sites: Applying a theory of negative relational maintenance and the investment model. *Journal of Social and Personal Relationships*, 1–20. doi: 10.1177/0265407514568749.

Tom Tong, S., B. Van Der Heide, L. Langwell, & J. B. Walther. (2008). Too much of a good thing? The relationship between number of friends and interpersonal impressions on Facebook. *Journal of Computer-Mediated Communication* 13:531–549. doi: 10.1111/j.1083-6101.2008.00409.x.

Toma, C. L., & J. T. Hancock. (2011). A new twist on love's labor: Self-presentation in online dating profiles. In K. B. Wright & L. M. Webb (Eds.), *Computer-mediated communication in personal relationships* (pp. 42–55). New York: Peter Lang.

Walther, J. B. (1996), Computer-mediated communication: Impersonal, interpersonal, and hyperpersonal interaction. *Communication Research* 23:3–44. doi: 10.1177/ 009365096023001001.

Walther, J. B., B. Van Der Heide, L. Hamel, & H. Shulman. (2009). Self-generated versus other-generated statements and impressions in computer-mediated communication: A test of warranting theory using Facebook. *Communication Research* 36:229–253.

Walther, J. B., B. Van Der Heide. S. Y. Kim, D. Westerman, & S. T. Tong. (2008). The role of friends' behavior on evaluations of individuals' Facebook profiles: Are we known by the company we keep? *Human Communication Research* 34:28–49.

Williams, A. L., & M. J. Merten. (2008). A review of online social networking profiles by adolescents: Implications for future research and intervention. *Adolescence* 43 (170): 253–274.

Chapter Four

Mobile Social Networking

Giuseppe Lugano

Mobile social networking refers to social networking practices enabled, supported, or mediated by mobile communication technologies including, but not limited to, old-generation 3G mobile phones, new-generation 4G smartphones, or laptops and tablets using mobile links to surf the Web.

The inclusion of 3G CDMA and GSM mobile feature phones may sound surprising in this context, however, the traditional mobile services such as phone calls and short text messages (SMS) are, first of all, about interpersonal communication (Katz & Aakhus, 2002; Ling, 2004), which was by and large the main purpose of mobile telephony throughout the whole 1990s. With the turn of the millennium, new uses of the SMS and other emerging technologies, such as Bluetooth, were experimented with to offer additional interaction modalities such as colocated mobile social networking (Persson & Jung, 2005), group communication (Rantanen, Oulasvirta, Blom, Tiitta, & Mäntylä, 2004), and SMS-based geolocation (Melinger, Bonna, Sharon, & SantRam, 2004). Although none of this type of application reached critical mass, early mobile social networking platforms such as Dodgeball or Nokia Sensor evolved in parallel to the spreading of mobile access to the World Wide Web. Academic research and industrial innovation supported each other in this field in rapid development: This factor made the United States and some Nordic countries, Finland and Sweden in particular, at the forefront of research and innovation on mobile social networking.

Instead of focusing on interpersonal exchange, mobile social networking applications are inherently linked to one-to-many and many-to-many communication models (Rheingold, 2002, 2003; Shirky, 2003). These models broadened the scope of mobile telephony from interpersonal communication towards a wider range of network or community-based activities such as digital sharing, social awareness, collaboration, and collective action. Consequently, both mobile and Internet devices can operate, according to the desired use, to reach a specific audience and function as personal media or mass media. In addition to the "size" of the targeted audience (i.e., single person, small group, large community, everybody), interaction can take place either synchronously or asynchronously, and the message can be conveyed in any form (e.g., text, images, sound, or video clips). Because of their numerous features and options, an almost unlimited number of variations in mobile social networking are possible.

The aim of this chapter is to explore mobile social networking and how it has evolved throughout the last decade not only from a technological and a commercial viewpoint but also from the perspective of its social role, impact, and usefulness.

The appearance of the iPhone in 2007 marked a landmark for mobile social networking applications because it accelerated smartphones' adoption and the use of mobile Internet services. The huge success of the iPhone put strong pressure to all key players of the mobile market to reconsider and adapt their strategy to the new successful paradigms of mobile technology based on touch screens, large displays, and a high degree of versatility and customization enabled by large online repositories of mobile "apps."

Resembling the popular label of "Web 2.0" (O'Reilly, 2005) driven by online social networking sites (boyd & Ellison, 2007), some scholars talked about the rise of a "Mobile 2.0" (Holmquist, 2007) brought about by smartphones and social networks. Being both based on the underlying trend of technological convergence, the Web 2.0 and Mobile 2.0 can be regarded as two sides of the same coin resulting in the integration of offline, online, and mobile social networking modalities (Lugano, 2010). Jenkins (2006) argued that technological convergence entails also other forms of convergence. In the context of human social networking, this means that the digital convergence of computer networks, telecommunication networks, and the media implies convergence and seamless integration of one's social networks into the "hybrid" social space of digital community where offline, online, and mobile spaces intersect.

The transition towards digital communities has relevant implications also for the sociology of community, which already acknowledged the shift from densely knit, bounded groups to more distributed and sparse social networks (Wellman, 2001). This shift is relevant for the design of mobile social networking applications, which indeed typically follow the egocentric perspective of "personal communities" (Wellman, Carrington, & Hall, 1988). Interestingly, the design of early "social" applications of the Internet such as the ones described by Rheingold (1993) in the "Virtual Community" were not about one's individual connections but rather about shared collective values, principles, interests, and individual contributions to achieve common objectives. While a proper treatment of this subject is beyond the scope of this chapter, it is sufficient to underline that this emerging configuration of the social space no longer allows us to clearly separate and distinguish between online and mobile social networking, or even to completely understand their relation to and impact on offline (i.e., face-to-face) social networking. As a matter of fact, popular online social networking sites (ONS) such as Facebook or LinkedIn—originally conceived for a "desktop" use—have evolved and become "cross-media" applications (Lugano, 2010; Humphreys, 2013) to acknowledge the centrality of mobile use as well. Consequently, mobile apps for social network access have been designed for enhancing use on the go and updates are regularly released. Thus, today the distinction and classification between social networking sites, mobile social software applications, and the like is not as useful as it was ten years ago as the offline, online, and mobile social spaces are perceived and experienced as a common and integrated interaction space accessible with any device able to connect to the Internet. Even mobile social networking apps still designed for exclusive use on smartphones such as Instagram and WhatsApp can be run on desktop computers via powerful emulators of popular mobile operating systems such as iOS or Android.

The evolving technological scenario corresponds to an evolving context of research and use of mobile social networking applications. We may identify two main periods, namely a first "exploratory" one until the appearance of iPhone in 2007 and a second period of "growth and maturity" that has followed.

The "exploratory" period is characterized by "smart" uses of the SMS and early smartphone apps for enhancing social communication. These have been grouped and studied under the umbrella term of Mobile Social Software (MoSoSo) applications (Churchill & Halverson, 2005; Counts, Ter Hofte, & Smith, 2006; Eagle & Pentland, 2005; Lugano, 2007; Smith, 2005).

The subsequent period of "growth and maturity" is characterized by the completion of digital convergence described in the scenario of digital communities. From a research viewpoint, studies on mobile social networking seldom refer to MoSoSo but rather employ a variety of different terms. One of the most commonly used is social media, a concept adopted by the media industry and largely employed within business and economics research communities (Hanna, Rohm, & Crittenden, 2011). Among these terms it is also worth mentioning mobile social media, which has been defined as "software, applications, or services accessed through mobile devices that allow users to connect with other people and to share information, news, and content" (Humphreys, 2013, p. 21). This concept closely resembles that of MoSoSo, the term which is employed in this chapter. The choice of adopting new terms and of no longer using related ones with rather similar meanings has already characterized earlier shifts in social computing history, for instance when social software was introduced and groupware and related technologies were considered as something from the past (boyd, 2007; Lugano, 2012).

The remaining sections of this chapter provide a comprehensive overview on mobile social networking applications. This is done by first positioning mobile social networking as a research area. Then, the meaning of a mobile social network is illustrated by adopting a network analytical perspective grounded on the concepts of social actor and social relationship. Next, further details on the developments of mobile social networking are provided by following three key complementary lines of analysis which focus respectively on the technological developments, on the evolution of the mobile market, and on the societal aspects. Finally, the chapter offers an outlook on possible evolution of the area in the near future.

MOBILE SOCIAL NETWORKING AS A RESEARCH AREA

Mobile social networking is an inherently interdisciplinary area across research disciplines and applications. Consequently, our understanding of the theory and practice of mobile social networking draw from a broad amount of approaches and perspectives.

A first reflection emerges from the outcome of a Google Scholar search on the keyword "mobile social network": Before 2000 there are no studies related to the use of mobile applications for social networking while on the move. Instead, the term is used in a report from the US Census Bureau (2003) about residential mobility trends: as a matter of fact, in the report a mobile social network was understood as a social network of highly mobile people. While not linked to ICTs, this report hints that the study of mobile social networks would be naturally associated to the SNA tradition. Fortunati (2001), one of the pioneers of the sociology of mobile communication, relates the term mobile social network to mobile technology to refer to the social network of contacts accessible through phone numbers stored in the mobile phone. Similarly, Crabtree, Nathan, and Reeves (2002) mention mobile social networks within the context of ICTs penetrating everyday life:

> Moreover, voice over telephony (much like email) expresses social network effects. Put crudely, the more your friends and colleagues use them, the more you need them also. Combine these two factors—technologically mobile social networks and personal behaviour—and use moves quickly to reliance. . . . This is the "technology-pull" view of ICT and change. Technology does not push people into new ways of living. Instead, people pull technology into their lives, based on a perception of need or utility, and then begin to integrate it into their day-to-day existence.

Following this initial insight, around 2005 the study of mobile social networks becomes part of the research on social networks and mobile communication. These two traditions are acknowledged by Lugano (2008), who argued that the study of mobile social networks is first of all anchored to the tradition of social network analysis (SNA), which has as object of analysis "a finite set or sets of actors and the relation or relations defined on them" (Scott, 2000; Wasserman & Faust, 1994). This strand of mobile social networking studies received contributions mainly from human and social sciences scholars, who had an opportunity to better understand social structure and social action in communities and social networks thanks to large and rich datasets (Raento, Oulasvirta, & Eagle, 2009).

At the same time, we cannot forget that mobile social networking applications are also about mobile and Internet communication technology: for this reason the "technological" tradition of mobile social networking studies is also relevant and connects to existing research perspectives on groupware, context-aware computing, and pervasive/ubiquitous computing. Unlike these related research areas, "technology-oriented" studies on mobile social networking have found their natural development in the world of start-ups. Indeed, the technological outcome of such efforts has resulted in business opportunities linked to MoSoSo applications (Crowley, 2005; Melinger et al., 2004; Persson & Jung, 2005). This is in line with the history of the Internet and more generally of the ICTs, which features successful enterprises (e.g., Microsoft, Apple, Google, Facebook) driven, at least in their initial phase, by the creative curiosity and innovation of young "geeks."

Another relevant perspective, linked to both the sociological and the technological traditions, concerns studies on the economics of mobile social networking. This includes, for instance, studies on social media marketing (Hettler, 2010), a field that relies much on the social use of mobile technologies, or on "community-driven" open innovation (Piller, Vossen, & Ihl, 2012).

The three interlinked scientific areas and related fields contributing to mobile social networking are summarized in the table 4.1 below proposed by Lugano (2010). This classification will be adopted in this chapter to logically illustrate mobile social networking from its key perspectives. Before passing to the review of these perspectives, the concept of mobile social network is described by adopting a network analytic approach.

A mobile social network is a special type of social network in which a central role is played by mobile social software, a class of mobile applications specifically designed for enhancing social interaction (Lugano, 2007). Being a social network, a mobile social network consists of a set of social actors and dyadic social ties connecting such actors. MoSoSo represents the access point to one's personal community (Wellman et al., 1988), thus implying an egocentric and networked view of the social world.

Specific area	Perspectives
Technology-oriented (natural sciences)	Social computing and mobile social computing, context-aware computing, wearable computing, pervasive computing, ubiquitous computing, complex networks, groupware, social software
Social orientation (human & social sciences)	Social media and mobile social media, communication theories of new media, SNA, emerging forms of social organization, online and mobile social networking, social impact of ICT in everyday life
Economic orientation	Web 2.0 and Mobile 2.0, digital service development, open/community innovation studies

Table 4.1.

Social actors are typically represented as "contacts" stored in mobile address-books or accessible via installed apps. The mobile address-book, present since the early versions of mobile phones, is the prototypical form of MoSoSo as it enables access to a wide range of interaction modalities with the registered contacts. Smartphones and tablets extend this range of possibilities even further via specialized apps or through sophisticated versions of the address-book, which have the capacity to import and aggregate contacts and other types of information from various social networking websites and to conveniently display, search, and filter social feeds that are updated in real time.

The representation of contacts as user profiles changed significantly over time and became increasingly richer in parallel to the advances of mobile technology. In the early times it was extremely simple and static: it consisted of a phone number and a few other text fields (e.g., postal address, birthdate, email address) manually entered when registering the contact. The set of contacts displayed in the address-book was basically the digital equivalent of personal paper phone notebooks. Lonkila (2004) conducted an interesting study on the evolution of one's personal community by comparing entries listed in personal paper phone notebooks over time. Although not sophisticated, the resulting snapshot of the social network allowed deriving meaningful conclusions on lifestyle and social relationships. Reflecting on the nature of mobile communication technology, the author concluded that

> the increasing availability of mobile phones offers new opportunities for obtaining data on personal networks. Compared to PNN [phone notebook networks] data, the mobile phone notebook networks (MPNN) seem to be more valid data in the sense that they cover more accurately both the weak and the

strong ties, the interaction network and the network of significant others. . . .
The MPNN may open up new perspectives on the ways of communicating and
interacting in a "mobile culture." (Lonkila, 2004, p. 60)

Lonkila's intuition was correct, as mobile communication logs have been
increasingly used to gain a better understanding of the structure and dynamics of mobile social networks. Within this area of investigation the MIT
"Reality Mining" study (Eagle & Pentland, 2006; Eagle, Pentland, & Lazer,
2009) is probably the most relevant and well-known, as it has opened up a
whole stream of interdisciplinary research based "social sensing" (Kiukkonen, Blom, Dousse, Gatica-Perez, & Laurila, 2010; Rosi et al., 2011; Rachuri, Efstratiou, Leontidas, Mascolo, & Rentfrow, 2014). This area of research
is often referred to as "computational social science" (Lazer et al., 2009;
Raento et al., 2009; Gilbert, 2010; Cioffi-Revilla, 2013; Mason, Vaughan, &
Wallach, 2014).

Unlike the early exploratory studies (Lugano, 2008), which were mainly
based only on a small amount of participants and mobile communication logs
related to a limit period of time, more recent research in this area may
involve even hundreds of participants to collect rich-data on their mobility
and communication behaviors over several months.

While the concept of representation of the social actor is relatively
straightforward, the notion of social tie that can be derived on the basis of
sensed data is less obvious. Lugano (2006) describes social ties in mobile
social networks in terms of "mobile relationships":

Mobile social software supports interaction among networked mobile users.
The definition considers the crucial property of mobile users, mobility, and the
fact that there is an invisible "social link" which keeps them interconnected . . .
Hence, it is of crucial importance to understand the meaning of "social link"
and associate it with "interaction-styles", which should include a certain control over the resources and information; not only with whom we want to
interact, collaborate or share, but also which information will be shared.

In brief, the social tie can be anything that can be used to connect a social
actor to another one. It can be the relationship of "family," "friend," or "work
colleague," a shared interest, matching objectives (e.g., dating), a participation in the same event, a shared physical space (e.g., a meeting room), or the
fact of being tagged in the same photo. In principle, every possible association that entails information sharing or some form of interaction recorded on
the device can be used and interpreted as a social tie in a mobile social
network. These ties can be either ephemeral—think of Bluetooth interactions
at a concert—or long-lasting ones. It goes without saying that two social
actors can be linked through multiple social ties, for example, because they
are friends, work colleagues, and members of the same interest group. Often

this multiplicity of relationships implies social actors' profiles being connected in several online social networks such as Facebook, LinkedIn, WhatsApp, and Instagram.

To summarize, mobile social networks can be described as representations of social actors interconnected through social ties. These ties can be inferred by applying methods of social network analysis to datasets collected through mobile devices. The understanding of the structure and dynamics of mobile social networks has not only a sociological value, but also direct implications for the design of mobile social networking applications. In other words, the more we understand how individuals interact and what their expectations are, the better we can design technologies to support their sociability needs and orientations.

MOBILE SOCIAL NETWORKING: THREE COMPLEMENTARY PERSPECTIVES

Technological Perspective

Human social networking has been historically firmly grounded on local proximity interactions consisting of face-to-face verbal and nonverbal communication. Throughout the centuries these basic interaction modalities have been regularly enhanced by several technological innovations. Ling (2004) reminds us that the history of mobile communication has its ancestors in the telegraph and in the postal service, which both supported written asynchronous communication, and later in the landline telephone that enabled synchronous verbal communication at distance.

In the last two decades the amount of communication modalities has increased enormously, in particular within the rich communication contexts of Web 2.0 (O'Reilly, 2005). Besides the various types of media formats that can be easily shared online, also text-based interactions assumed new meanings and functions; two popular examples are the "like" feature on Facebook and the Twitter "hashtag."

In the context of mobile social networking, the small amount of characters available in text messages has been used in creative and innovative ways to implement friend-finders (Crowley, 2005), serendipity-based social matching (Eagle & Pentland, 2005) or to indicate locations for flashmobs or mass mobilizations (Rheingold, 2002; Hirsch & Henry, 2005). SMS-based MoSoSo applications, popular in the "exploratory" phase of mobile social networking history, supported only textual and asynchronous mobile social networking. The design typically shifted most of the work to the server side. In the case of Dodgeball, designers developed a query language that was able to interpret the various commands. For instance, "@TheClub" had to be parsed by the server as a description of the current location to search in the database of local places. SMS-based MoSoSo benefited from the GSM infrastructure, which was popular and suitable to implement this type of application. However, the availability of cheap and almost ubiquitous access to the mobile Internet with powerful smartphones, tablets, and the like has made the SMS-based approach obsolete. Nowadays, SMS notifications are still used by more recent mobile social networking applications, but they do not represent the core of the application.

In addition to the SMS-based MoSoSo, which relied on an existing mobile service, another technology commonly adopted to implement a MoSoSo solution was Bluetooth. While SMS-based MoSoSo supported mobile social networking at a distance, Bluetooth-based MoSoSo focused on social proximity interactions. A commercial product was Nokia Sensor, an evolution of the Scent/DigiDress prototypes (Persson & Jung, 2005). The application was designed for light entertainment in bars, restaurants, and the like. It placed emphasis on identity expression by offering the opportunity to create a simple user profile that was made publicly available. Through the scanning of public users' profiles, users could seek and communicate with other nearby users. While interesting as a concept, this type of MoSoSo is almost useless if not used in a densely populated social environment.

Neither SMS-based MoSoSo nor Bluetooth-based MoSoSo ever reached critical mass. This challenge was overcome only quite recently thanks to a variety of factors, such as the spreading of the mobile Internet, the widespread availability of technologies such as WiFi and GPS, as well as the integration of MoSoSo with online platforms such as Facebook and Twitter. A notable example of such integration is provided by the Lumia smartphone series, which embeds social network integration within the design of the device. At the software level, this integration is otherwise achieved either by connecting via the mobile browser or through specialized apps, client applications installed on the device. The MoSoSo evolution towards client-based applications corresponds to the phase of "growth and maturity" of mobile social networking.

It is worthwhile at this point to make a distinction between two categories of client-based mobile social networking applications, namely the ones that are primarily designed for the mobile context such as Foursquare, WhatsApp, and Instagram, and the others like Facebook or Twitter that first developed online and were later optimized for use in mobile contexts. For instance, Instagram allows creating a user profile only through its specialized mobile client, but the functionality to access photos shared online is available independently of the technological platform used. Similarly, WhatsApp has recently announced its desktop version and it may soon also offer voice call functionality. These moves seem oriented to compete with Skype, social networking software that first gained popularity in desktop environments and then also became available as a client application for smartphones.

A common aspect to all categories of client-based mobile social networking applications is that they are cross-media (Lugano, 2010; Humphreys, 2013). The idea of cross-media MoSoSo is to offer access via multiple and different access points to maximize their diffusion. This approach was also experimented with in early types of MoSoSo such as Slam (Counts & Fisher, 2008) with the objective of overcoming the issue of obtaining critical mass. In that case, since smartphones were not yet as widespread as today, the application was designed to be used on either GSM phones or on smartphones. However, only this latter version included the full range of features. Many popular mobile social networking applications today aim at exploiting cross-media opportunities: for instance, updating Facebook or Twitter status can be done by sending a text message. Similarly, a Facebook user can decide on what kind of notifications (e.g., friends' birthdays) to receive on his device via SMS.

Hence, when regarded from a technological viewpoint, mobile social networking applications can be grouped in three main categories: SMS-based, client-based, and cross-media (Lugano, 2010).

The technology-centric approach to MoSoSo presents also a key limitation, namely the difficulty of clearly identifying what constitutes a mobile social networking application. This approach was viable in the early times of MoSoSo, but is no longer adequate today due to the blurring boundaries between offline, online, and mobile social spaces. Rather than focusing on a specific technology, mobile social networking can be more precisely studied in relation to a set of available technologies, devices, and services supporting social networking practices while on the move.

Market Perspective

The market value of mobile social networking applications is strictly linked to the problem of critical mass, which was not overcome until the success of the iPhone. The adoption of mobile social networking applications is linked to the phenomenon of online social networking and it is strongly affected by the availability of smartphones and other related technologies like tablets. It is therefore useful to provide some statistics on the overall growth of these technologies and applications. According to the Pew Research Center's Social Networking Fact Sheet (2014), the growth of social media and social networking witnessed an explosive growth from 2006 to 2010, and since then it has continued to grow, even if at a slower pace.

Global smartphone penetration has also been constantly rising, particularly in the last few years. According to eMarketer (2014a), 1.76 billion people globally were owners of a smartphone by the end of 2014. This statistic represents a rise of 25 percent compared to the previous year. The first country to pass 50 percent of smartphone penetration, already in 2012, was

South Korea, followed in 2013 by Norway, Sweden, and Australia. The United States reached this target during 2014 together with countries such as the United Kingdom, the Netherlands, and Japan. It is foreseen that 2015 will be a year of massive growth, with Canada and several other European countries (such as: Spain, Italy, Germany, France, and Finland) passing 50 percent smartphone penetration. A study by comScore (2014) indicates even higher smartphone penetration rates in the United States (71.6 percent corresponding to 173 million users). Another relevant trend for mobile social networking applications concerns the diffusion of tablets, which has reached around 35 percent penetration in Europe with the United Kingdom leading (eMarketer 2014b). In the United States, data from late 2013 showed that 42 percent of adult Americans own a tablet (Pew Research Center, 2013).

The penetration rates give an estimate of the potential reach that a mobile social networking application can achieve. According to comScore (2014) among the top fifteen smartphone apps, five are mobile social networking applications (Facebook and Facebook Messenger, Instagram, Twitter, and Google+). It is worth noting that apart from Instagram, all other apps are based on websites that were not originally designed just for use in mobile contexts.

As previously mentioned, none of the pioneers of the MoSoSo market such as Dodgeball (Crowley, 2005; Ziv & Mulloth, 2006), TXTmob (Hirsch & Henry, 2005), Socialight (Melinger et al., 2004) or Nokia Sensor (Persson & Jung, 2005) managed to survive and to adapt to the rapid technological development. These MoSoSo applications probably appeared too early and in a highly fragmented market to achieve long-lasting success. Around 2005 there was a kind of "MoSoSo bubble" with far too positive predictions on the growth and maturation of the market. Ziv and Mulloth (2006) presented forecasts indicating a growth of revenues generated by mobile social networking applications from $31.4 to $215 million in the period from 2005 to 2009. In the same study, it was reported that SMS.ac—one of the market leaders back then—claimed having a base of 50 million users and expectations of exponential growth.

Dodgeball, one of the most promising MoSoSo applications, was acquired by Google in 2005 and integrated in Google Latitude, a location-aware feature of Google Maps. Despite the efforts, Google Latitude was discontinued in 2013. On the other hand Dennis Crowley, one of the Dodgeball cofounders, launched Foursquare, a MoSoSo application that enhanced some of the concepts already employed in Dodgeball (such as the location "check-in") thanks to a more mature smartphone technology. Foursquare is still today one of the most popular mobile social networking applications with more than 55 million active users having made over 6 billion location check-ins globally.

In conclusion, even though mobile social networking applications had already appeared in the market around 2004, it was only after 2010 that they acquired a real commercial value based on continuous and active use by millions of users globally. This trend goes hand-in-hand with the increase in smartphone and tablet penetrations. Therefore, early MoSoSo applications like Dodgeball can be considered more as creative and innovative explorations of an emerging niche market than as real and sustainable goldmines. Most likely, the highly fragmented but also incredibly rich landscape of applications was necessary to achieve the mature and sustainable mobile social networking applications that have recently earned much success. New successful applications will certainly emerge thanks to creative and innovative start-ups. However, these will most likely be the targets of acquisitions by the key Internet players, who will use these innovative products as strategic assets to preserve and expand their influence in the overall Internet market.

Societal Perspective

More than ten years have passed since the publication of the first studies on MoSoSo and mobile social networking applications. During this period, science and technology, as well as society, have undergone relevant developments. It is therefore legitimate to ask: What has been the role and impact of MoSoSo in everyday life, and how has the design of mobile social networking applications influenced social practices and behaviors?

A good starting point to answer these questions is the critical analysis of mobile social software by Thom-Santelli (2007). It is noted that although the premise of mobile social networking applications is to offer anybody the opportunity to enrich social interactions within one's social sphere, in reality the design of these applications privileges only a certain type of urban experience based on an idealized category of users. In particular, these applications are best experienced in dense urban environments and encourage interactions, especially serendipitous ones, with similar users based on the homophily hypothesis (McPherson, Smith-Lovin, & Cook, 2001). Furthermore, the aim of such interactions is typically associated with light entertainment and consumption behavior. According to the author, this is a missed opportunity for offering a richer and more inclusive experience of cities and, more broadly, of societies.

Studies on the use of Foursquare, a popular MoSoSo typically used in cities, found that this application was regarded not only as a social networking tool, but also as an urban game, a spatial search engine, and even as a personal memory tool (Frith, 2014). For instance, individual comments and photos on specific locations like restaurants were used to remember one's own past experiences in those restaurants. On the other hand, the gaming aspect of the application seems predominant as mayorships and badges represent an incentive to regularly check in. This incentive seems in many cases to outweigh privacy concerns related to sharing of one's own location and places, even when practices of selective disclosure are put in place (Guha & Birnholtz, 2013). Apart from the social dynamics of competition, this logic of application use has been also exploited for marketing purposes to combine check-ins with special offers and deals in partner shops. Furthermore, it was also found that the design of Foursquare provides little value for social coordination and friend-finding (Frith, 2014), tasks that were considered as central in MoSoSo. Hence, although Foursquare users connect to each other on the basis of the type of social relationship, the application goes beyond this form of social networking and allows experimentation with different types of social links associated to locations and tags.

Similarly, Instagram social networking service is centered on the sharing of photos that, unless set as private, can be viewed by anyone. Also, in this case, the search and browsing of photos via hashtags is a popular practice. According to Yang et al. (2012) hashtags have a dual function in this type of application, namely they serve as bookmarks of content and as a sort of "virtual community" membership. In a way, this virtual community resembles the one described by Rheingold (1993) rather than an egocentric one. Indeed, hashtags reveal a sense of belonging, shared identity, and values; when widely utilized by a large number of users over a short period of time this becomes a global online trend. Twitter has been a pioneer in this form of communication, which scales up from the individual level of social networking to the global level of viral campaigns and mass communication. Probably due to this important function, hashtags have been recently integrated also on Facebook. Even if this application is primarily grounded on the individual user profile, it is also possible to navigate content and contacts through hashtag associations.

Being at the edge between private and public contexts, personal and collective use, privacy has traditionally been a major concern of online and mobile social networking applications. In one of the early studies on MoSoSo, Anderson (2005) provided a description of this issue within the broad context of distance learning:

> This sense of presence can also operate to support presence in physical space, as provided by tools for mobile social networking or in the capacity to help identify those in social proximity who share a common interest in educational or discipline related interest. Of course, this sense of presence must be under the control of the individual learner since there are times when I welcome presence of other "kindred souls", while there are other times when I need the freedom to protect and maintain my privacy and anonymity. (p. 5)

The design of online and mobile social networking applications has been gradually enhanced to best meet all types of needs, practices, and expectations concerning personal privacy management. A side effect of the choice of enforcing personal privacy by not sharing some information (e.g., location) may be the unavailability of some functionality of the application. For this reason, applications increasingly implement the principle of allowing users to establish their preferred trade-off between sharing of personal resources and application functionalities (Beresford, Rice, Skehin, & Sohan, 2011). Instead of following a "black or white" approach of choosing whether to disclose information or not, users can choose to selectively disclose personal resources in a mobile social network: a resource may be shared only in some cases by taking into account measures of social trust, type of relationship, or interaction context (Consolvo et al., 2005; DiCrescenzo & Lipton, 2013; Lugano & Saariluoma, 2007; Sadeh et al., 2009).

Personal privacy management is tightly associated with the digital sharing of personal information and content stored. As observed by Lugano (2010), the more general challenge concerns users' control over outgoing and incoming information flows. This broader context connects, from a design perspective, the issue of personal privacy with the problem of social information overload due to lack of proper mechanisms and features to adequately display relevant content. This issue obviously cannot be addressed only by means of an optimally designed technology; it also requires adequate human strategies and an understanding of the possible implications. Concerning the technological side, the offering of search and filtering features, combined with relevance algorithms, already provides some degree of support. In a few years these features may become obsolete as personal virtual assistants like Apple Siri or Microsoft Cortana may become relevant actors in future mobile social networking applications, and more. Personal virtual assistants are currently employed in tasks such as translating text to speech in mobile contexts (Williams et al., 2012; Vieri & Vieri, 2013). However, these advanced virtual agents are very versatile and can potentially be employed to support any type of user decision, as recently shown in the movie *Her*, which presents a potential scenario in which personal virtual assistants are part of our everyday lives. Intelligent software agents may represent only the tip of an iceberg that is about to emerge: as we will see in the next section, the future outlook of mobile social networking is likely to experience a new form of convergence, that with robotic services and applications.

MOBILE SOCIAL NETWORKING:
TOMORROW AND BEYOND

Information and communications technologies have supported existing practices of human social networking and at the same time opened up new opportunities for social interaction. As we have discussed, technological advances in the last two decades have resulted in the convergence of computer and telecommunication networks with the media. A notable consequence of this trend is the blurring boundaries between online and mobile social spaces. For this reason, mobile social networking applications cannot be easily distinguished from other types of applications for social communication available on smartphones, laptops, and tablets. As a matter of fact, almost all applications on these devices offer "social" functions of communication, sharing digital content, georeferencing, tagging, and the like. To say it differently, rather than discussing the impact of mobile social networking applications, one could focus more generally on the function of mobile devices in everyday life.

It is worth underlining that technological advances are continuous and new mobile technologies with rich social functions will appear. Among them, we can include all sorts of wearable technologies and in particular eyewear technology such as Google Glass. Among others, this type of technology will represent another source of personal information to share in real time with one's social network while on the move. It may be possible, for instance, to make accessible to personal contacts one's own view of reality by means of continuous video streams. As it already happens today with shared photos and videos, comments, ratings, and "likes" may be associated with such video stream. Other possible applications of Google Glass, which may have several types of social networking implications, are represented by activity recognition (Ishimaru et al., 2014) and identification of other persons by means of pattern recognition (Wang, Bao, Choudhury, & Nelakuditi, 2013).

Another emerging area of great relevance for social networking is represented by what Esposito, Fortunati, and Lugano (2014) define as "socially believable robots and ICT interfaces," intelligent machines that are able to establish rich and emotional interactions with humans. This concept embeds and extends the whole range of social robots to capture their most recent developments:

> On the one hand, because of space and security constraints, there is a tendency
> to deconstruct the "classical" robot into intelligent agents, automated person-
> al assistants, future smart environments, ambient assistive living technologies,
> computational intelligent games/storytelling devices, embodied conversational
> avatars, and automatic health-care and education services. On the other hand,
> the re-structuring of robotic agents as drones, humanoids, swarms, cleaning,

manufacturing, emergency and space exploration robots is motivated by un-
pleasant, tedious or dangerous tasks, as well as tasks requiring a certain
amount of strength and precision abilities." (Esposito et al., 2014, p. 626)

The technological trend towards an increasingly interconnected world
implies that we will soon not only speak and investigate on social networks
made of humans, but also of networks of socially believable robots and ICT
interfaces. This is not completely a new trend, since related phenomena such
as socialbots are well-known and documented (Mavridis et al., 2009; Hwang,
Pearce, & Nanis, 2012; Boshmaf, Muslukhov, Beznosov, & Ripeanu, 2013).
Existing trends will be amplified by the shift from industrial robots to domestic robots, which is already ongoing. Bicchi and Tamburrini (forthcoming)
describe the visionary scenario of "societ[ies] of robots operating within the
physical environments of everyday human life, developing rich robot-robot
social exchanges, and yet refraining from any physical contact with human
beings." This scenario therefore envisages noninteracting human social networks and robotic social networks. If these two types of networks will be
allowed to interact—at least in some contexts or situations—new forms of
mobile social networking will emerge and imply new technological solutions, commercial opportunities, and societal impacts.

It would be a mistake to consider these scenarios just as science fiction.
Bright minds like Stephen Hawking and Elon Musk have recently signed an
open letter stating research priorities for robust and beneficial artificial intelligence (Russell, Dewey, & Tegmark, 2015). These concerns against the
progress of artificial intelligence directly affect social networking practices,
as we may envisage an extension of current personal virtual assistants to
make decisions or even communicate with others on behalf of their owners.
Several challenges of mobile social networking applications are still open
and under investigation. By taking into account the above-mentioned trends,
it would be a wise strategy to consider how well any suitable solutions to
such challenges would work when applied to future human-robotic social
networking applications.

REFERENCES

Anderson, T. (2005). Distance learning–Social software's killer ap? In *Proceedings of the 17th Biennial Conference on the Open & Distance Learning Association of Australia* (ODLAA).
Beresford, A. R., A. Rice, N. Skehin, & R. Sohan. (2011). MockDroid: Trading privacy for application functionality on smartphones. In *Proceedings of the 12th Workshop on Mobile Computing Systems and Applications* (pp. 49–54). San Diego, CA.
Bicchi, A. & G. Tamburrini. (forthcoming). Social robotics and societies of robots. *The Information Society* 31 (3).
Boshmaf, Y., I. Muslukhov, K. Beznosov, & M. Ripeanu. (2013). Design and analysis of a social botnet. *Computer Networks* 57 (2): 556–578.

boyd, d. (2007). The significance of social software. In T.N. Burg & J. Schmidt (Eds.), *Blog-Talks reloaded: Social software—Research & Cases* (pp. 15–30). Norderstedt: Books on Demand.

boyd, d., & N. B. Ellison. (2007). Social network sites: Definition, history and scholarship. *Journal of Computer-Mediated Communication* 13 (1).

Churchill, E. F., & C. A. Halverson. (2005). Guest editors' introduction: Social networks and social networking. *IEEE Internet Computing* 9 (5): 14–19.

Cioffi-Revilla, C. (2013). *Introduction to computational social science: Principles and applications.* New York: Springer.

comScore. (2014). comScore reports June 2014 U.S. Smartphone subscriber market share. Retrieved from http://www.comscore.com/Insights/Market-Rankings/comScore-Reports-June-2014-US-Smartphone-Subscriber-Market-Share.

Counts, S., & K. E. Fisher. (2008, January). Mobile social networking: An information grounds perspective. In *Hawaii International Conference on System Sciences, Proceedings of the 41st Annual* (pp. 153–153). Waikoloa, HI: IEEE.

Counts, S., H. Ter Hofte, & I. Smith. (2006). Mobile social software: Realizing potential, managing risks. In *Proceedings of the CHI 2006 Workshop on Mobile Social Software* (pp.1–5), Montreal, Canada.

Consolvo, S., I. E. Smith, T. Matthews, A. LaMarca, J. Tabert, & P. Powledge. (2005, April). Location disclosure to social relations: Why, when, & what people want to share. In *Proceedings of the SIGCHI Conference on Human Factors in Computing Systems* (pp. 81–90). New York: ACM.

Crabtree, J., M. Nathan, & R. Reeves. (2002). *Reality IT—Technology & everyday life.* London: Work Foundation.

Crowley, D. (2005). An ubiquitous approach to mobile applications. In *Proceedings of the 32nd International Conference on Computer Graphics and Interactive Techniques* (ACM SIGGRAPH 2005), Los Angeles, USA.

DiCrescenzo, G., & R. J. Lipton. (2013). Social network privacy by means of evolving access control. US Patent No. 8,370,895, filed August 2, 2010, and issued February 5, 2013.

Eagle, N., & A. Pentland. (2005). Social serendipity: Mobilizing social software. *IEEE Pervasive Computing* 4 (2).

———. (2006). Reality mining: Sensing complex social systems. *Personal and Ubiquitous Computing* 10 (4): 255–268.

Eagle, N., A. S. Pentland, & D. Lazer. (2009). Inferring friendship network structure by using mobile phone data. *Proceedings of the National Academy of Sciences of the United States of America* 106 (36): 15274–15278.

eMarketer. (2014a). Worldwide smartphone usage to row 25% in 2014. Retrieved from http://www.emarketer.com/Article/Worldwide-Smartphone-Usage-Grow-25-2014/1010920.

———. (2014b). The UK leads the EU-5 in Tablet Adoption. Retrieved from http://www.emarketer.com/Article/UK-Leads-EU-5-Tablet-Adoption/1010810.

Esposito, A., L. Fortunati, & G. Lugano. (2014). Modeling emotion, behavior and context in socially believable robots and ICT interfaces. *Cognitive Computation* 6 (4): 623–627.

Fortunati, L. (2001). The mobile phone: An identity on the move. *Personal and Ubiquitous Computing* 5 (2): 85–98.

Frith, J. (2014). Communicating through location: The understood meaning of the Foursquare check-in. *Journal of Computer-Mediated Communication* 19 (4): 890–905.

Gilbert, G. N. (2010). *Computational social science.* London: Sage.

Guha, S., & J. Birnholtz. (2013, August). Can you see me now? Location, visibility and the management of impressions on Foursquare. In *Proceedings of the 15th International Conference on Human-Computer Interaction with Mobile Devices and Services* (pp. 183–192). New York: ACM.

Hanna, R., A. Rohm, & V. L. Crittenden. (2011). We're all connected: The power of the social media ecosystem. *Business Horizons* 54 (3): 265–273.

Hettler, U. (2010). *Social media marketing.* Oldenbourg: Verlag.

Hirsch, T., & J. Henry. (2005). TXTmob: Text messaging for protest swarms. In *Extended Abstracts Proceedings of the 2005 Conference on Human Factors in Computing Systems* (pp. 1455–1458). Portland, OR: CHI.

Holmquist, L. E. (2007). Mobile 2.0. *Interactions* 14 (2): 46–47.

Humphreys, L. (2013). Mobile social media: Future challenges and opportunities. *Mobile Media & Communication* 1 (1): 20–25.

Hwang, T., I. Pearce, & M. Nanis. (2012). Socialbots: Voices from the fronts. *Interactions* 19 (2): 38–45.

Ishimaru, S., K. Kunze, K. Kise, J. Weppner, A. Dengel, P. Lukowicz, & A. Bulling. (2014, March). In the blink of an eye: Combining head motion and eye blink frequency for activity recognition with Google Glass. In *Proceedings of the 5th Augmented Human International Conference* (p. 15). New York: ACM.

Jenkins, H. (2006). *Convergence culture: Where old and new media collide*. New York: New York University Press.

Katz, J. E., & M. Aakhus. (2002). *Perpetual contact: Mobile communication, private talk, public performance*. Cambridge, UK: Cambridge University Press.

Kiukkonen, N., J. Blom, O. Dousse, D. Gatica-Perez, & J. Laurila. (2010). Towards rich mobile phone datasets: Lausanne data collection campaign. In *Proceedings of the 7th International Conference on Pervasive Services*. Berlin: ACM.

Lazer, D., A. S. Pentland, L. Adamic, S. Aral, A. L. Barabasi, D. Brewer, & M. Van Alstyne. (2009). Life in the network: The coming age of computational social science. *Science* 323 (5915): 721.

Ling, R. (2004). *The mobile connection: The cell phone's impact on society*. Burlington, MA: Morgan Kaufmann.

Lonkila, M. (2004). Phone notebooks as data on personal networks. *Connections* 26 (1): 53–61.

Lugano, G. (2006, June). Understanding mobile relationships. In *Human Centred Technology Workshop* (HCT 2006; Pori, Finland).

Lugano, G. (2007). Mobile social software: Definition, scope and applications. In P. Cunningham & M. Cunningham (Eds.), *Expanding the knowledge economy—issues, applications, case studies*. (Vol.2) (pp. 1434–1441). Amsterdam: IOS Press.

———. (2008). Mobile social networking in theory and practice. *FirstMonday* 13 (11).

———. (2010). *Digital community design: Exploring the role of mobile social software in the process of digital convergence*. Jyväskylä, Finland: University of Jyväskylä.

———. (2012). Social computing: A classification of existing paradigms. *Privacy, Security, Risk and Trust (PASSAT), International Conference on Social Computing (SocialCom)*, 377–382. doi: 10.1109/SocialCom-PASSAT.2012.54.

Lugano, G., & P. Saariluoma. (2007). To Share or not to share: Supporting the user decision in Mobile Social Software applications. In *User Modeling* (pp. 440–444). Berlin: Springer Berlin Heidelberg.

Mason, W., J. W. Vaughan, & H. Wallach. (2014). Computational social science and social computing. *Machine Learning* 95 (3): 257–260.

Mavridis, N., C. Datta, S. Emami, A. Tanoto, C. BenAbdelkader, & T. Rabie. (2009, March). FaceBots: Robots utilizing and publishing social information in Facebook. In *Proceedings of 2009 4th ACM/IEEE International Conference on Human-Robot Interaction (HRI)*, (pp. 273–274). La Jolla, CA: IEEE.

McPherson, M., L. Smith-Lovin, & J. M. Cook. (2001). Birds of a feather: Homophily in social networks. *Annual Review of Sociology* 27:415–444.

Melinger, D., K. Bonna, M. Sharon, & M. SantRam. (2004). Socialight: A mobile social networking system. In *Proceedings of the 6th International Conference on Ubiquitous Computing*. Nottingham, England.

O'Reilly, T. (2005, September 30). What is Web 2.0: Design patterns and business models for the next generation of software. Retrieved from www.oreillynet.com/pub/a/oreilly/tim/news/2005/09/30/what-is-web-20.html.

Persson, P., & Y. Jung. (2005). Nokia sensor: From research to product. In *Proceedings of the 2005 Conference on Designing for User eXperience (DUX'05)*. San Francisco, CA: ACM.

Pew Research Center. (2013). *Three technology revolutions*. Retrieved from http://www.pewinternet.org/three-technology-revolutions.

Piller, F., A. Vossen, & C. Ihl. (2012). From social media to social product development: The impact of social media on co-creation of innovation. *Unternehmung* 66 (1): 7.

Rachuri, K. K., C. Efstratiou, I. Leontiadis, C. Mascolo, & P. J. Rentfrow. (2014). Smartphone sensing offloading for efficiently supporting social sensing applications. *Pervasive and Mobile Computing* 10:3–21.

Raento, M., A. Oulasvirta, & N. Eagle. (2009). Smartphones: An emerging tool for social scientists. *Sociological Methods Research* 37 (3): 426–454.

Rantanen, M., A. Oulasvirta, J. Blom, S. Tiitta, & M. Mäntylä. (2004). InfoRadar: Group and public messaging in the mobile context. In *Proceedings of the Third Nordic Conference on Human-Computer Interaction* (pp. 131–140). Tampere, Finland.

Rheingold, H. (1993). *The virtual community: Homesteading on the electronic frontier*. Reading, MA: Addison Wesley.

———. (2002). *Smart mobs: The next social revolution*. New York: Basic Books.

———. (2003). Mobile virtual communities. Retrieved from http://www.thefeaturearchives.com/topic/Culture/Mobile_Virtual_Communities.html.

Rosi, A., M. Mamei, F. Zambonelli, S. Dobson, G. Stevenson, & J. Ye. (2011, March). Social sensors and pervasive services: Approaches and perspectives. In *Pervasive Computing and Communications Workshops* (PERCOM Workshops), IEEE International Conference (pp. 525–530). Seattle, WA: IEEE.

Russell, S., D. Dewey, & M. Tegmark. (2015). Research priorities for robust and beneficial artificial intelligence. Retrieved from http://futureoflife.org/static/data/documents/research_priorities.pdf.

Sadeh, N., J. Hong, L. Cranor, I. Fette, P. Kelley, M. Prabaker, & J. Rao. (2009). Understanding and capturing people's privacy policies in a mobile social networking application. *Personal and Ubiquitous Computing* 13 (6): 401–412.

Scott, J. (2000). *Social network analysis: A handbook*. 2nd ed. London: Sage.

Shirky, C. (2003). A group is its own worst enemy. In J. Spolsky (Ed.) *The best software writing I* (pp. 183–209). Berlin: Springer.

Smith, I. (2005). Social-mobile applications. *Computer* 38 (4): 84–85.

Social Networking Fact Sheet. (2014). Retrieved from http://www.pewinternet.org/fact-sheets/social-networking-fact-sheet/.

Vieri, R., & F. Vieri. (2013). Text to speech conversion of text messages from mobile communication devices. US Patent No. 8,345,665, filed December 1, 2009, and issued January 1, 2013.

Wang, H., X. Bao, R. R. Choudhury, & S. Nelakuditi. (2013, February). InSight: Recognizing humans without face recognition. In *Proceedings of the 14th Workshop on Mobile Computing Systems and Applications* (p. 7). Jekyll Island, GA: ACM.

Wasserman, S., & K. Faust. (1994). *Social network analysis: Methods and applications*. Cambridge, UK: Cambridge University Press.

Wellman, B. (2001). Computer networks as social networks. *Science* 293 (5537): 2031–2034.

Wellman, B., P. J. Carrington, & A. Hall. (1988). Networks as personal communities. In B. Wellman & S. D. Berkowitz (Eds.), *Social structures: A network approach* (pp. 130–184). Cambridge, UK: Cambridge University Press.

Williams, J. D., K. Yu, B. Chaïb-Draa., O. Lemon, R. Pieraccini, O. Pietquin, & S. Young. (2012). Introduction to the issue on advances in spoken dialogue systems and mobile interface. *IEEE Journal of Selected Topics in Signal Processing* 6 (8): 889–890.

US Census Bureau. (2003). Ethnographic social network tracing of highly mobile people. Census 2000 Evaluation J.2. Retrieved from https://www.census.gov/pred/www/rpts/J.2.pdf.

Yang, L., T. Sun, M. Zhang, & Q. Mei. (2012, April). We know what@ you# tag: Does the dual role affect hashtag adoption? In *Proceedings of the 21st International Conference on World Wide Web* (pp. 261–270). Lyon, France: ACM.

Chapter Five

Students, the Ivory Tower, and Educational Uses of Social Networking Sites

Anastacia Kurylo and Yifeng Hu

Overwhelmingly, students are not taking full advantage of social networking sites in order to pursue their professional goals. Although naiveté about online professional networking may cause some pause for students, these are the same people for whom the personal use of social networking sites is second nature. This chapter looks at the Ivory Tower stereotypes of academics as a lens through which to understand the technology gap between students' personal and professional uses of social media technologies and the role educators play in narrowing this gap. The main components of the Ivory Tower stereotype are discussed to help elucidate the problems facing academia in fostering student engagement with social networking sites as a professional undertaking. Exemplars of educators and educational institutions where social networking sites or SNSs are incorporated to bridge this divide are explored.

STUDENT USE OF SOCIAL NETWORKING SITES

According to the highlights of the Pew Research Center, in the United States 74 percent of online adults use SNSs (Social Networking Fact Sheet, 2014). For ages 18–29, a traditional age range for the majority of college students, that usage statistic increases to 89 percent (Social Networking Fact Sheet, 2014). Among the most popular SNSs in the world, the three often ranked highest are Twitter, Facebook, and LinkedIn (Milanovic, 2015). Yet, despite how integral SNSs are to the personal and professional relationships of adults, college students in particular are less likely to use SNSs professionally than personally. For example, "LinkedIn announced [in January 2013] that the site has attracted more than 200 million users, but only 43 percent of college students use the site" (Friedman, 2013).

Amongst students who do use SNSs professionally, many may not be adept at doing so. Students tend not to use advanced features on LinkedIn such as the recommendation and endorsement features; they underappreciate and underutilize their current networks to grow their professional networks online, and they may be more likely than graduates to make spelling and grammatical errors that can garner negative reactions from recruiters (Friedman, 2013).

Ultimately, "having [a] LinkedIn profile [or other professional SNS presence] in an age of technology is absolutely crucial for college students" (Friedman, 2013). However, as some human resource and business communication professionals suggest, students wait too long to create LinkedIn pages because they are concerned about having too little work experience to start the process and they over-rely on career fairs and company websites for job opportunities (Hall, 2013). In articles providing advice about how to improve professional social media networking for students, a recurring lament is the juxtaposition of the fluency and frequency of students' personal social networking use with the paucity of their professional social networking endeavors.

While graduates find their way to LinkedIn and other professional networking sites like Doximity, Sermo, and RallyPoint (Bischke, 2014), college students seem to be less able to do so. High school students, though active on social media with 71 percent reporting as Facebook users, are understandably not well equipped to tackle the professional networking required in a Web 2.0 society (Lenhart, 2015). With college admissions counselors invoking the pre-professional training that students will receive at their college to transition high school students to post-college professionals, the relatively low rate of college student engagement with LinkedIn is puzzling. LinkedIn has noticed and taken proactive steps to facilitate high school and college students' engagement including allowing teenagers to have a presence on LinkedIn and having university based LinkedIn pages (Lunden, 2013).

PROFESSIONAL USES OF SNSS

SNSs can be used in productive professional ways that impact engagement with professional, civic, social, and other groups. One study reported that organizational engagement through SNSs can allow users to "draw attention to an issue," "connect with other groups," "impact society at large," "organize activities," "raise money," "recruit new members," "impact local communities," and "find people to take leadership roles" (Rainie, Purcell, & Smith, 2011). Additionally, professionals and businesses use SNSs to advertise, manage their public relations, and engage in marketing campaigns. Small businesses, as well as large corporations, use SNSs to tap into their target audience's psyche, collect market data, and expand their reach in seemingly grassroots ways. For certain professions, experience with SNSs would be incorporated as part of practical training.

Corporations are even finding the value in facilitating SNS use during work hours. According to the Society for Human Resource Management (Managing and leveraging, 2012), social media:

- facilitate open communication
- lead to enhanced information discovery and delivery
- allow employees to discuss ideas, post news, ask questions, and share links
- provide an opportunity to widen business contacts

Companies are finding that SNSs are useful for recruitment, sales, public relations, diversity and inclusion, and building company culture (Falls, 2014; Managing and leveraging, 2012; Westwood, 2015).

The use of SNSs in employee recruitment is even more directly and imminently relevant to college students as a rationale for the incorporation of professional SNS experience into their college experience. After all, "many top search firms and recruiters also depend on LinkedIn to gather information on prospective employees. In fact, in a 2012 Jobvite social recruiting survey, 93 percent of respondents—comprised of more than 1,000 human resources and recruitment professionals—said LinkedIn is a primary recruiting network, and 89 percent have hired from the site" (Friedman, 2013). Considering the importance of SNSs to corporations for recruitment and across a variety of their communications functions as well as for civic, social, and religious engagement, student professional use of SNSs warrants some attention among academics.

Some may argue that the main purpose of secondary and higher education is not to prepare students for corporate life. Some may go so far as to say that the mission of higher education, especially that of many liberal arts learning institutions and programs, is not to produce future labor power and, rather, that it is the job of vocational schools or institutions that offer professional degrees to prepare students for employment. For those who do see value in training students for the professional use of SNSs, the following discussion may be of merit.

THE IVORY TOWER

According to the RationalWiki, the Ivory Tower stereotype "is an expression used to indicate that someone is out of touch with common experience, usually due to spending much of their life in academia . . . . [and is] perceived to be so caught up in their worlds of elitist isolation they lose touch with the everyday world. . . . The term is also used contemptuously [to describe] academics and intellectuals lacking common sense and basic life skills" (Ivory tower, 2015). The Ivory Tower stereotype of academics does not describe a reality. Rather, as with all stereotypes, the ivory tower stereotype is merely a rigid one-dimensional picture of a group (Kurylo, 2012). The stereotype posits that academics are elitists, distant from common experience, isolated, and lack common sense. Nonetheless, it is through this lens that the antipathy some academics might have towards SNSs may be understood. This is not to say the stereotype is true; rather, compartmentalizing the individual components that comprise the stereotype elucidates why an aversion to SNSs might exist for some academics. In particular, four components of the stereotype of the Ivory Tower stand out as relevant and will be discussed below.

Academics as Elitists

As elitists, the stereotype suggests that academics present themselves in such a way as to forestall contact with anyone outside of their perceived stature. One way this is communicated is through language use wherein the language of the researcher is often verbose and philosophically or methodologically inaccessible to the nonacademic, also known as academese ("Beware of 'Academese,'" 2011). The academic does not engage in common discourse, according to the stereotype, as doing so would be beneath the academic's status.

Academese contrasts with how some teachers view student communication styles that do not use "proper" language when writing course papers. For academics, students who use social media language (e.g., abbreviations) represent an outgroup whose members are distinctively different (and lower in social status) from themselves. Therefore, academic elites may refuse to adopt the same language and instead may diverge from it.

According to Communication Accommodation Theory, communicative behaviors represent important dimensions of social identity (Giles & Giles, 2012). One strategy people use to present their identity is divergence, which is to adjust communicative behaviors to accentuate verbal and nonverbal differences with outgroup members who have a different perceived identity. People may also engage in maintenance, which is sustaining one's "default" way of communicating without adjusting for others. Through academese, SNS communication conventions, and social media language choices, divergence and maintenance may be used by academics and students to establish positive intergroup distinctiveness and to differentiate themselves from members of relevant outgroups. This distinction in language choice, unintentionally reinforcing the stereotype of academics as elites, helps to explain why academics may not embrace SNSs as students do.

Academics as Distant from Common Experience

This component of the stereotype suggests that academics are removed from common experience. Social networking is a common part of lived experience with the majority of adults interconnected through SNSs (Social Networking Fact Sheet, 2014). Over time social networking activity has increased substantially from its origins. For example, Facebook continues to show an upward trend (Number of Monthly Active Facebook Users Worldwide, 2015) as does Twitter (Number of Monthly Active Twitter Users Worldwide, 2015) even in their most recent quarters. SNSs can no longer be viewed as a trend in the face of these metrics. While certainly there are instructors and programs incorporating SNSs into their research and curriculum, higher education in particular has not embraced professional SNSs. Rather, on course syllabi technology is often forbidden as part of the class rules in part to deter SNSs use during class.

From the instructor's perspective, it can be a distraction for the whole class if even one student diverts his or her attention to a phone during a lecture. For example, someone speaking about class-relevant material may pause, fidget, or completely forget what they have to say as a result of such a distraction. Moreover, if a student constantly looks at his or her phone while in the classroom, that student may neglect important instructions because it is hard to focus on a speaker while trying to multitask. He or she may miss opportunities to participate in the class discussion as well. From a mindfulness perspective, multitasking with social media in the classroom can have negative consequences on cognitive processing such as missed information, recording inaccurate information, and so forth (Fiske & Taylor, 1984; Langer, 1989; Nisbett & Ross, 1980). Finally, playing with one's phone is often simply considered disrespectful to whoever is talking at that time whether instructors or peers.

This aversion to SNSs by instructors is a practical one largely due to the tendency for the technology to distract students. The image of a student distracted by a cell phone is palpable even beyond academia. An online image search for "distracted student" yields images of students seemingly ignoring their teachers and print materials opting instead to presumably check Facebook and Twitter on their laptops or cell phones. There is certain legitimacy to this picture of SNSs as distractions to academic pursuits inside and outside the classroom (Kelly, 2015). However, the aversion of some faculty to SNSs because of their perceived tendency to distract students may be a missed opportunity given how seamlessly and intuitively SNSs are incorporated into students' everyday lives in integral and commonplace ways (Anderson & Rainie, 2010).

Academics as Isolated

This component of the Ivory Tower stereotype stresses the academic's stereotypical preoccupation with isolation in order to foster intellectual pursuits. Academics often have the summer months, winter breaks, and sabbaticals to work on their academic pursuits in idealized seclusion from their students, teaching, and other work responsibilities. Communication conventions of SNSs such as the option to choose amongst hundreds of emoji, the expectation of quick response times in Facebook messaging, the ability for anyone to request to "friend" or "link in" to you, and Twitter's 140-character limit contrast with this isolationist component of the stereotype.

Of course academics are not always alone in their offices as the stereotype would suggest. However, students and academics perhaps often feel best understood through their fellow student and academic peer relationships (Walker, Golde, Jones, Bueschel, & Hutchings, 2008). Networks in academia can easily, and ideally for some, center around building an intellectual community comprised of academic peers, alumni, mentors, mentees, advisors, faculty, and scholars with the admirable goal of creating a support network, encouraging collaboration, and fostering professional relationships that can be maintained over one's career (Nelson, Pearson, & Kurylo, 2008). These ingroup networking opportunities often involve face-to-face relationship development in the form of departmental events, classes taken together, study groups, research labs, and informally over meals or beverages. Though not isolated entirely, the groups within which one travels as an academic may increasingly begin to settle into a theoretical and methodological comfort zone as noted anecdotally in the preface of Kurylo (2013) in which she discusses an abrupt ending to a conversation when methodological orientations are revealed.

In contrast to a content-focused intellectual community, SNSs, even professional ones, often require unrefined, potentially inane, online social interaction with unknown others. Therefore, academics may avoid broad professional SNSs and opt instead for academic-centered sites like Academia.edu, ResearchGate.net, and Google Scholar. However, even on these more academic research-oriented SNSs, rather than utilizing these for networking and collaboration, academics may inadvertently reinforce traditional professional hierarchies, maintain familiar ties rather than create new ones, and allow the SNS to serve as a supplemental, rather than primary, avenue for collaboration (Jordan, 2014). Through examining the practices and usage of one academic SNS, Jeng, He, and Jiang (2015) found that participants did not engage with social-based features as frequently and actively as they did research-based features. Thus, academics who use academic SNSs may reinforce their current intellectual communities and stereotyped isolation and, themselves, not benefit from the full opportunities of SNSs.

Academics as Lacking Common Sense

This aspect of the Ivory Tower stereotype is related to a long-term orientation, a cultural value that academics may share (Kurylo, 2011). Conducting research and publishing is a protracted process. Academics may spend considerable time reading, studying, and writing. Academics may focus so much on these activities, along with teaching and service work, that they may ignore other aspects of the world around them, appearing to lack common sense through being oblivious. Academics may even intentionally avoid exploring the everyday reality of the topics they study lest they become distracted or even debilitated by trying to help a group they are studying, keeping up with the constant current of new information on a topic in any given moment, or getting overwhelmed by the minutia of detail related to every aspect of their research.

In this sense, that some academics are distanced from the practical everyday details of life, including SNSs, is not surprising when they are mired in the details of their long-term academic pursuits. It may seem like common sense for academics to be involved in social networking as another avenue for intellectual pursuit. However, the long-term orientation of an academic may suggest their time be spent in other ways. Academics may focus on the long-term outcomes of their efforts rather than the short-term activities and events around them. SNSs, then, become one more detail overlooked in the process. Consider, for example, the recent headline on an academic job search site, "Should Academics Use Social Networking Sites in Their Professional Lives?" (Armstrong, 2009). So poignant is the gap between SNS use by academics and SNS use by students that a comparable headline, "Should students use social networking sites in their professional lives?" would be more likely to appear in the satirical newspaper *The Onion* than on a serious job search site for which the answer is obvious.

The four components of the Ivory Tower stereotype discussed here provide a lens through which to understand why SNSs are not of prominent importance, generally speaking, to many academics. Despite this, SNSs have become incorporated into the repertoire of an academic's toolkit in secondary schools and in higher education. This next section will explore how teaching and learning can occur and flourish through online social networks when SNSs are incorporated into the curriculum.

TEACHING AND LEARNING THROUGH
SOCIAL NETWORKING SITES

Education can play a role in the practicality of preparing students for corporate SNS use. This attention is warranted in academia because there is a gap between students' professional and personal use of SNSs that may have consequences for their professional lives. However, academia has not ignored the use of SNSs entirely, particularly in areas that are more pertinent to education. In actuality, many secondary schools and higher education institutions have integrated SNS in teaching and learning.

At the beginning scholars believed that SNSs were merely extensions of the dot.com bubble and were therefore not worthy of integrating into the traditional higher education arena (e.g., Anderson, 2007). Selwyn (2007) suggested that Facebook is better used in an informal way for school-related activities rather than to enhance students' "front-stage" engagement with their formal studies. Another study found that Facebook was used mainly for social reasons, and was occasionally informally used for learning purposes (Madge, Meek, Wellens, & Hooley, 2009).The viewpoint of SNSs as tangential to learning has enjoyed less and less popularity over time.

However, according to Hu (2010), skepticism about whether SNSs can ever be effectively used for learning and instruction still exists, mainly due to potential disadvantages associated with using SNSs in classes, such as the difficulties with engagement, an emphasis on superficial issues, and the lack of coherence (e.g., Boon & Sinclair, 2009; Peters & Slotta, 2010). In addition, there is concern about the appropriateness of such usage in an educational environment including student anonymity, data protection and privacy, lack of control over tools in the public domain, reliability of the service, support from external companies (see Minocha, 2009a, 2009b, 2009c), and instructors' invasion in a supposedly student-based territory such as Facebook (e.g., Mazer, Murphy, & Simonds, 2007). Nevertheless, scholars increasingly argue that SNSs contain versatile features that may be conducive to effective learning, such as reflective elements, mechanisms for peer feedback, and fitting well within the social context of higher education and learning (e.g., Mason, 2006; Minocha, 2009a, 2009b, 2009c; Muñoz & Towner, 2009). The following section discusses how various disciplines have incorporated SNSs into teaching and learning.

THE APPLICATION OF SNSS
IN EDUCATION ACROSS DISCIPLINES

The interactive and collaborative nature of social media is conducive to teaching and learning a variety of subjects. In the following section, we will briefly survey a range of disciplines to give readers a sense of how SNSs are widely applied in education. The areas we will review are: (a) design, (b) literacy and writing, (c) language and culture, (d) journalism and communication, and (e) medical education.

SNSs are being incorporated into design work at various educational levels. Lapolla (2014) evaluated a project that utilizes the social media website, Pinterest.com, in a collaborative learning experience between American fashion design college students and young urban professionals as customers. Similarly, Won, Evans, Carey, and Schnittka (2015) reported that middle school students used social media for design-based learning during an after-school program and benefited from the project.

Social media can also be integrated in literacy and writing classes. Using a blog as a medium for collaboration, students from two universities in Taiwan worked together on a writing project, which demonstrated the educational value of the interactive blogging activities for supplementing formal writing training (Chen, Shih, & Liu, 2015). Page and Reynolds (2015) also reported collaborative and mediated social writing practices through wiki contexts. Thibaut (2015) studied the benefits of using an SNS with learning purposes among primary school teachers and students. It expanded teaching and learning repertoires, engaged students in digital multimodal literacy practices, and promoted self-directed learning and peer-teaching practices.

Social media can be beneficial for learning foreign languages and cultures as well. Melo-Pfeifer (2015) reported a case study where a pedagogical blog was used for the teaching and learning of Portuguese as a foreign language in order to develop plurilingual and intercultural competences. In another study by Terantino (2011), university students used Facebook for a writing project in a beginning-level Spanish course. The students felt more connected to the class and were more engaged in classroom-based activities. They also regarded Facebook as a more open environment for practicing a foreign language and producing more student-centered language learning. In an English as a Foreign Language (EFL) speaking class, YouTube and Facebook were used as platforms to enhance students' public speaking skills, build their confidence in speaking English, and allow them to develop their own learning goals and strategies (Sun & Yang, 2015). Similarly, Chuang and Yang (2010) reported how video podcasts and YouTube were used to deliver instructional materials to language learners who are already often familiar with these platforms.

Journalism schools worldwide are gradually integrating social media into the curriculum. For example, Facebook groups have been incorporated into such staple courses as media writing, promotional writing, and news and magazine editing (Maben, Edwards, & Malone, 2012). Journalism students from a university in Spain used multimedia blogs to gain knowledge about the journalistic work outside the university environment, which contributed positively to students' community integration, and enhanced negotiated decision-making skills and appreciation for others' work (López & González, 2014). Bor (2014) suggested that in order for SNSs to be truly beneficial tools for teaching and learning journalism, the design of the curriculum should include emphasis on ethics, technical skills, and the potential for career development, as well as differentiation between personal and professional social media use.

In addition, social media are adopted by instructors in communication, marketing, advertising, and public relations. For example, Hu (2010) evaluated students' perceptions after using private Facebook groups for a communication class. Both quantitative and qualitative data showed that, overall, students had a positive attitude towards supplementing the class with Facebook. Lester (2012) reported about an applied advertising education project that incorporates a wide range of SNSs such as YouTube, Flickr, MySpace, Facebook, Twitter, Linkedin, Ning, Tagged, and Google+. Infusing social media into a marketing communication strategy enabled students to visually display their creative potential to a real-world business client.

Compared with the pervasive use of social media as learning tools in arts, humanities, and social sciences, incorporating SNSs into medical education has met more obstacles. Early on, there was some skepticism among medical institutions whose faculty members were not necessarily as social media savvy as their students. Schools were also concerned about ensuring professionalism within this communication context (see Johnson, Blackburn, Taite, & Laseur, 2012). In addition, through four case studies, Gray, Annabell, and Kennedy (2010) found that medical students only moderately supported their development of medical knowledge and skills via Facebook. Success levels varied based on technological affordances and group dynamics. They concluded that using Facebook for teaching and learning was as much of a challenge for many medical students as it might be for most educators.

However, a more recent systematic review synthesizing social media use in medical education indicated that in general, using SNSs was associated with students' improved knowledge, attitudes, and skills, and the most commonly reported benefits were promoting learner engagement, feedback, collaboration and professional development (Cheston, Flickinger, & Chisolm, 2013). For example, George and Dellasega (2011) evaluated the integration of Twitter, YouTube, Flickr, blogging, and Skype in two elective courses for Year 4 medical students. Students rated both courses highly, finding the social media resources helpful. By incorporating SNSs into a low-stakes clinical learning environment, Johnson et al. (2012) found that Yammer, an enterprise SNS, provided privacy and ease of access, and allowed posting of all forms of assignments as well as a passionate exchange of ideas that enhanced student engagement. Davis, Ho, and Last (2015) discussed how YouTube videos covering medical topics were incorporated in classroom lectures, and how Facebook and Google were used by medical trainees for online group collaboration.

Regardless of discipline, social media can be powerful tools for teaching and learning in and out of the classroom in primary, secondary, and higher education worldwide. For example, Erjavec (2013) looked at how Slovenian primary school students use Facebook for informal learning. This study found that students used Facebook primarily for exchanging practical information, learning about technology, evaluation of their own and other people's work, emotional support, organizing group work, and communicating with teachers. Asterhan and Rosenberg (2015) conducted empirical research on Israeli secondary school teacher-student contact through Facebook. Through a teacher survey and in-depth teacher interviews, they found that teacher-student Facebook contact comes in different forms and serves three main purposes: Academic-instructional, psycho-pedagogical, and social-relational. Stephansen and Couldry (2014) presented a case study of how Twitter was used to help build a community of practice that enabled mutual learning among teachers and students at a UK college.

CONCLUSION

The use of SNSs in education yields a variety of positive outcomes for students. Lester (2012) suggested that engaging students with social media with which they identified enhanced learning. Their familiarity and expertise with social media increased the likelihood of producing desired learning outcomes. In addition, use of social media in an academic curriculum may expand the interrelational dimensions of students' learning, which may in turn increase students' engagement and the depth and breadth of their learning (Megele, 2015). After using Facebook groups in four sections of a communication class, Hu (2010) found that the social benefits of Facebook use were positively correlated to its educational benefits, implying that due to its unique social functions, Facebook can create a community that may be beneficial to classroom learning. Similarly, using Twitter as an informal learning space, McPherson, Budge, and Lemon (2015) demonstrated that using social media is beneficial for building networks of academics.

Despite the ample evidence that SNSs can be beneficial in learning a variety of subjects, there are still some lingering reservations and concerns. In addition to a reluctance from some teachers and professors as mentioned earlier in the chapter, resistance seems to come from students themselves as well. For example, in a study on the use of Facebook for out-of-class communication between students and instructors, Nkhoma et al. (2015) found that how students perceived the quality of the content of the online social network when it came to their learning had a negative rather than a positive influence on their perceived performance. The authors suggested that this might be due to the distraction of using Facebook for the purposes of learning rather than for socializing or other non-study-related purposes. Other studies found similar challenges of using social media for teaching and learning. Duarte (2015) stated that even though students perceived blogging as a useful learning tool, the capacity of blogging to build and sustain a sense of community was not as strong as expected. Both studies suggested that even though the majority of students thought SNSs were helpful for sharing discipline-related knowledge and information, they were reluctant to participate in a regular and active way unless the instructor built students' participation scores into the grading system. This is consistent with earlier literature that stresses that the use of SNSs for learning rather than socializing demands great attention and desire (e.g., Paul, Baker, & Cochran, 2012) as well as an appropriate curriculum design (e.g., Lumby, Anderson, & Hugman, 2014).

There are certainly some academics who grouse when their institutions introduce changes related to technology-based learning or online teaching tools and who may be naysayers about any technological embrace; however, most academics are not entirely opposed to students using SNSs. Many school teachers and college professors themselves use SNSs personally and professionally and are merely concerned with when and where students use technology and what their purposes are for doing so. While some students may text and post classroom-related information when they use technology during class time most, arguably, do not. In this way students have blurred the boundaries of personal and professional uses of SNSs in ways that can be detrimental to their education.

While it may be unrealistic to change the perceptions of students and instructors towards the main purposes of SNSs, one remedy is that educators play a strong role in encouraging students to participate in SNSs in professional ways (Won et al., 2015). For example, Johnson et al. (2012) found that learning was enhanced when the course director was able to encourage professionalism and facilitate social presence. Megele (2015) also reported how students enhanced their appreciation for e-professionalism and personal learning networks through working via SNSs.

The array of uses of SNSs for teaching and learning, in addition to pre-professional training, discussed here suggest that SNSs have value for students and education that warrants their incorporation into curriculum when appropriate. Although SNSs may be perceived as counter to the stereotype of the Ivory Tower, they are useful tools for academics that can even help to combat the Ivory Tower stereotype when they are incorporated by academics into the curriculum for the educational benefit of students.

REFERENCES

Anderson, J., & Rainie, L. (2010, July 9). Millennials will make online sharing in networks a lifelong habit. Retrieved from http://www.pewinternet.org/2010/07/09/millennials-will-make-online-sharing-in-networks-a-lifelong-habit/.

Anderson, P. (2007, February). What is Web 2.0? Ideas, technologies and implications for education. Retrieved fromhttp://jisc.ac.uk/media/documents/techwatch/tsw0701.pdf.

Armstrong, C. (2009, October). Should academics use social networking sites in their professional lives? Retrieved fromhttp://www.jobs.ac.uk/careers-advice/jobseeking-tips/1341/should-academics-use-social-networking-sites-in-their-professional-lives.

Asterhan, C. S. C., & H. Rosenberg. (2015). The promise, reality and dilemmas of secondary school teacher-student interactions in Facebook: The teacher perspective. *Computers & Education* 85:134–148. doi: 10.1016/j.compedu.2015.02.003.

Beware of "Academese" and write like you speak. (2011, January 2). Retrieved fromhttp://gradpost.ucsb.edu/tools/2011/1/2/beware-of-academese-and-write-like-you-speak.html.

Bischke, J. (2014, June 28). The rise of the "Social Professional" networks. Retrieved from http://techcrunch.com/2014/06/28/the-rise-of-the-social-professional-networks/.

Boon, S., & Sinclair, C. (2009). A world I don't inhabit: Disquiet and identity in Second Life and Facebook. *Educational Media International* 46 (2): 99–110. doi: 10.1080/09523980902933565.

Bor, S. E. (2014). Teaching social media journalism: Challenges and opportunities for future curriculum design. *Journalism & Mass Communication Educator* 69 (3): 243–255. doi: 10.1177/1077695814531767.

Chen, W., Y. D. Shih, & G. Liu. (2015). Task design and its induced learning effects in a cross-institutional blog-mediated telecollaboration. *Computer Assisted Language Learning* 28 (4): 285–305. doi: 10.1080/09588221.2013.818557.

Cheston, C. C., T. E. Flickinger, & M. S. Chisolm. (2013). Social media use in medical education: A systematic review. *Academic Medicine* 88 (6): 893–901. doi: 10.1097/ACM.0b013e31828ffc23.

Chuang, M.-T., & T.-P. Yang. (2010). Using video podcast to support language learning through YouTube: Strategies and challenges. *E-Proceedings of the International Online Language Conference (IOLC)*, 54–59.

Davis, W. M., K. Ho, & J. Last. (2015). Advancing social media in medical education. *CMAJ: Canadian Medical Association Journal* 187 (8): 549 550. doi: 10.1503/cmaj.150248.

Duarte, P. (2015). The use of a group blog to actively support learning activities. *Active Learning in Higher Education* 16 (2): 103–117. doi: 10.1177/1469787415574051.

Erjavec, K. (2013). Informal learning through Facebook among Slovenian pupils. *Comunicar* 21 (41): 117–126. doi: 10.3916/C41–2013–11.

Falls, R. (2014, January 14). The benefits of social media networking at work. Retrieved from http://hrcloud.com/the-benefits-of-social-media-networking-at-work/.

Fiske, S. T., & S. E. Taylor. (1984). *Social cognition.* Reading, MA: Addison Wesley.

Friedman, J. (2013, January 18). Job networking through social media: The advantages of LinkedIn for college students. Retrieved from http://www.huffingtonpost.com/jordan-friedman/college-students-linkedin_b_2506542.html .

George, D. R., & C. Dellasega. (2011). Social media in medical education: two innovative pilot studies. *Medical Education* 45 (11): 1158–9. doi: 10.1111/j.1365-2923.2011.04124.x.

Giles, H., & J. Giles. (2013). Ingroups and outgroups. In A. Kurylo (Ed.), *Inter/cultural communication: Representation and construction of culture* (pp. 141–162). Thousand Oaks, CA: Sage.

Gray, K., L. Annabell, & G. Kennedy. (2010). Medical students' use of Facebook to support learning: Insights from four case studies. *Medical Teacher* 32 (120): 971–976. doi: 10.3109/0142159X.2010.497826.

Hall, B. S. (2013, April 23). Why aren't college students using LinkedIn to find jobs? Retrieved fromhttp://readwrite.com/2013/04/23/why-arent-college-students-using-linkedin-to-find-jobs.

Hu, Y. (2010). Creating a learning community: Social and educational benefits of using Facebook in a mixed-major college classroom. *Electronic Journal of Communication* 20 (1&2).

Ivory tower. (2015, May 9). Retrieved fromhttp://rationalwiki.org/wiki/Ivory_tower.

Jeng, W., D. He, & J. Jiang. (2015). User participation in an academic social networking service: A survey of open group users on Mendeley. *Journal of the Association for Information Science & Technology* 66 (5): 890–904. doi: 10.1002/asi.23225.

Johnson, M. T., M. Blackburn, S. Taite, & D. L. Laseur. (2012). Social media as a support for reflective practice among first-year medical students. *Medical Science Educator* 22 (4): 307.

Jordan, K. (2014, November 3). Academics and their online networks: Exploring the role of academic social networking sites. *First Monday* 19 (11). Retrieved from http://firstmonday.org/article/view/4937/4159.

Kelly, R. (2015, July 7). Study: Smartphones detrimental to learning for first-time users. Retrieved from http://campustechnology.com/articles/2015/07/07/study-smartphones-detrimental-to-learning-for-first-time-users.aspx.

Kurylo, A. (2011, November 20). The case of the ivory tower: Accuracy and stereotypes. Retrieved from http://thecommunicatedstereotype.com/the-case-of-the-ivory-tower-accuracy-and-stereotypes/.

———. (2012). What are *they* like? Non-expert definitions of stereotypes and their implications for stereotype maintenance. *Qualitative Research in Psychology* 9:337–350. doi: 10.1080/14780887.2010.500517.

———. (Ed.) (2013). *Inter/cultural communication: Representation and construction of culture*. Thousand Oaks, CA: Sage.

Langer, E. J. (1989). *Mindfulness*. Reading, MA: Perseus Books.

Lapolla, K. (2014). The Pinterest project: Using social media in an undergraduate second year fashion design course at a United States University. *Art, Design & Communication in Higher Education* 13 (2): 175–187. doi: 10.1386/adch.13.2.175_1.

Lenhart, A. (2015, April 9). Teens, social media & technology overview 2015. Retrieved fromhttp://www.pewinternet.org/2015/04/09/teens-social-media-technology-2015/.

Lester, D. H. (2012). Social media: Changing advertising education. *Online Journal of Communication & Media Technologies* 2 (1): 116–125.

López, N., & P. González, P. (2014). Audioblogs and tvblogs, tools for collaborative learning in journalism. *Comunicar* 21 (42): 45–53. doi: 10.3916/C42-2014-04.

Lumby, C., N. Anderson, & S. Hugman. (2014). Apres Le Deluge: Social media in learning and teaching. *The Journal of International Communication* 20 (2): 119–132. doi: 10.1080/13216597.2014.926283.

Lunden, I. (2013, August 18). LinkedIn growing up: Opens up to high school students over 13, launches dedicated pages for universities worldwide. Retrieved from http://techcrunch.com/2013/08/19/linkedin-growing-up-opens-up-to-high-school-students-over-13-adds-university-pages/.

Maben, S., J. Edwards, & D. Malone. (2012). Online engagement through Facebook groups. *Southwestern Mass Communication Journal* 27 (3): 1–27.

Madge, C., J. Meek, J. Wellens, & T. Hooley. (2009). Facebook, social integration and informal learning at university: "It is more for socialising and talking to friends about work than for actually doing work." *Learning, Media, & Technology* 34 (2): 141–155.

Managing and leveraging workplace use of social media. (2012, December 5). Retrieved fromhttp://www.shrm.org/templatestools/toolkits/pages/managingsocialmedia.aspx.

Mason, R. (2006). Learning technologies for adult continuing education. *Studies in Continuing Education* 28 (2): 121–133. doi: 10.1080/01580370600751039.

Mazer, J. P., R. E. Murphy, & C. J. Simonds. (2007). I'll see you on "Facebook": The effects of computer-mediated teacher self-disclosure on student motivation, affective learning, and classroom climate. *Communication Education* 56 (1): 1–17. doi: 10.1080/03634520601009710.

McPherson, M., K. Budge, & N. Lemon. (2015). New practices in doing academic development: Twitter as an informal learning space. *International Journal for Academic Development* 20 (2): 126–136. doi: 10.1080/1360144X.2015.1029485.

Megele, C. (2015). eABLE: Embedding social media in academic curriculum as a learning and assessment strategy to enhance students learning and e-professionalism. *Innovations in Education & Teaching International* 52 (4): 414–425. doi: 10.1080/14703297.2014.890951.

Melo-Pfeifer, S. (2015). Blogs and the development of plurilingual and intercultural competence: Report of a co-actional approach in Portuguese foreign language classroom. *Computer Assisted Language Learning* 28 (3): 220–240. doi: 10.1080/09588221.2013.818556.

Milanovic, R. (2015). The world's 21 most important social media sites and apps in 2015. (2015, April 13). Retrieved fromhttp://www.socialmediatoday.com/social-networks/2015-04-13/worlds-21-most-important-social-media-sites-and-apps-2015.

Minocha, S. (2009a). A case study-based investigation of students' experiences with social software tools. *New Review of Hypermedia and Multimedia* 15 (3): 245–265. doi: 10.1080/13614560903494320.

———. (2009b). A study of the effective use of social software by further and higher education in the UK to support student learning and engagement. Retrieved fromhttp://www.jisc.ac.uk/media/documents/projects/effective-use-of-social-software-in-education-finalreport.pdf.

———. (2009c). An empirically-grounded study on the effective use of social software in education. *Education and Training* 51 (5/6): 381–394. doi: 10.1108/00400910910987192.

Muñoz, C. L., & T. L. Towner. (2009). Opening Facebook: How to use Facebook in the college classroom. Paper presented at the 2009 Society for Information Technology and Teacher Education Conference, Charleston, SC.

Nelson, P. E., J. C. Pearson, & A. Kurylo, A. (2008). Developing an intellectual community. In S. Morreale & P. Anerson (Eds.), *Getting the most from your graduate education in communication: A student's handbook* (pp. 71–82). Washington, DC: National Communication Association.

Nisbett, R., & L. Ross. (1980). *Human inference: Strategies and shortcomings of social judgment.* Englewood Cliffs, NJ: Prentice-Hall.

Nkhoma, M., H. P. Cong, B. Au, T. Lam, J. Richardson, R. Smith, & J. El-Den. (2015). Facebook as a tool for learning purposes: Analysis of the determinants leading to improved students' learning. *Active Learning in Higher Education* 16 (2): 87–101. doi: 10.1177/1469787415574180.

Number of monthly active Facebook users. (2015). Retrieved fromhttp://www.statista.com/statistics/264810/number-of-monthly-active-facebook-users-worldwide/.

Number of monthly active Twitter users. (2015). Retrieved fromhttp://www.statista.com/statistics/282087/number-of-monthly-active-twitter-users/.

Page, K. L., & N. Reynolds. (2015). Learning from a wiki way of learning. *Studies in Higher Education* 40 (6): 988–1013. doi: 10.1080/03075079.2013.865158.

Paul, J. A., H. M. Baker, & J. D. Cochran. (2012). Effect of online social networking on student academic performance. *Computers in Human Behavior* 28 (6): 2117–27. doi:10.1016/j.chb.2012.06.016.

Peters, V. L., & J. D. Slotta. (2010). Scaffolding knowledge communities in the classroom: New opportunities in the Web 2.0 era. In M. J. Jacobson & P. Reimann (Eds.), *Designs for learning environments of the future* (pp. 205–232). New York: Springer-Verlag.

Rainie, L., K. Purcell, & A. Smith. (2011, January 18). The social side of the internet. Retrieved fromhttp://www.pewinternet.org/2011/01/18/the-social-side-of-the-internet/.

Selwyn, N. (2007, November 15). "Screw Blackboard . . . do it on Facebook!" An investigation of students' educational use of Facebook. *Poke 1.0—A Facebook social research symposium.* London: University of London.

Social networking fact sheet. (2014, January). Retrieved fromhttp://www.pewinternet.org/fact-sheets/social-networking-fact-sheet/.

Stephansen, H. C., & N. Couldry. (2014). Understanding micro-processes of community building and mutual learning on Twitter: a "small data" approach. *Information, Communication & Society* 17 (10): 1212–1227. doi: 10.1080/1369118X.2014.902984.

Sun, Y., & F. Yang. (2015). I help, therefore, I learn: Service learning on Web 2.0 in an EFL speaking class. *Computer Assisted Language Learning* 28 (3): 202–219. doi: 10.1080/09588221.2013.818555.

Terantino, J. M. (2011). Student perceptions of language learning with Facebook: An exploratory study of writing-based activities. *E-Proceedings of the International Online Language Conference (IOLC)* 2:230–249.

Thibaut, P. (2015). Social network sites with learning purposes: Exploring new spaces for literacy and learning in the primary classroom. *Australian Journal of Language and Literacy* 38 (2): 83–94.

Walker, G. E., C. M. Golde, L. Jones, A. C. Bueschel, & P. Hutchings. (2008). *The formation of scholars: Rethinking doctoral education for the twenty-first century.* San Francisco, CA: Jossey-Bass.

Westwood, R. (2015, March 5). Do you "Like" social media in the workplace? Retrieved fromhttp://www.forbes.com/sites/ryanwestwood/2015/03/05/hit-like-if-you-agree-with-social-media-in-the-workplace/.

Won, S. G. L., M. A. Evans, C. Carey, & C. G. Schnittka. (2015). Youth appropriation of social media for collaborative and facilitated design-based learning. *Computers in Human Behavior* 50:385–391. doi: 10.1016/j.chb.2015.04.017.

Chapter Six

The Illusion of Control

*A Historiographical Examination
of Social Media, Bookmarking,
and Perceived Control
in the Digital Sphere*

Pamela E. Walck and Hans K. Meyer

When information was limited to printed pages that were bound in large volumes, readers would place a marker into their book to indicate a place to which they wanted to return some day. Sometimes, lacking other options, they would simply turn down the corner of a page. Bookmarking was beneficial to individual readers, but it could not reach any kind of mass audience. It looked random. Unorganized. Indiscriminate. And, in fact, it was. The lack of organization often meant years later the book's owner could scarcely recall why he or she had marked that page in the first place.

The advent of computer technology meant that for the first time, this human habit of marking pages in the physical sphere merged with the digital world. This chapter will examine how this seemingly self-directed act of *bookmarking*, organizing, and sharing information to be recalled at a later date by the individual or to be consumed by others in the digital sphere has evolved. This study will look at how content was first strictly limited by gatekeepers at news organizations pumping stories through telephone lines. It will also focus on how highly sophisticated algorithms today simulate control but ultimately help determine what appears in modern day newsfeeds and what we, in turn, bookmark. And it will demonstrate how most online users lack control over the information they mark, organize, and share and how the new organizers on the Web, companies built through sharing, such as Facebook, Pinterest, and Twitter, benefit from bookmarking.

While not all social media websites are the same, too often content users employing bookmarks online with the intention of sharing with others have little agenda-setting control over who receives the information they bookmarked or *tagged*. The result is a social media disconnect between intended and actual audiences. The goals and purposes of bookmarking social media have adapted to accommodate more educated audiences as well as advances in new technologies.

BACKGROUND

With printed materials, bookmarking is a physical act. It requires someone to actually place an item, such as a piece of paper, between pages. More formally, professionals in information sciences, such as librarians, have long used categories and organizational techniques to classify information. In the digital world, bookmarking may require less effort, such as a click of a button, but has greater implications. Techtarget.com (Whatis.techtarget.com, 2006) defined digital or social bookmarking as a taxonomy system that is defined by users, which is commonly called *folksonomy*, where individual bookmarks are dubbed tags. But unlike bookmarks, which are stored in folders on individual computers, Techtarget.com (Whatis.techtarget.com, 2006) noted that tagged Internet pages are stored on the Web as a whole and can be accessed from any computer, anywhere. Solis (2011) defined social bookmarks as "sites and communities dedicated to allowing users to share, organize, and search relevant content from around the Web in one place" (p. 162). This tool is unique in that individuals utilizing it can decide if the bookmark should remain private and exclusive for their own use, or if it is something they want to make public and share with others (Dodd & Campbell, 2011).

Swant, Li, and Wang (2011) noted the distinct differences between tags and taxonomies. The researchers defined tags as "personal keywords" that impose "a soft organization on data," compared to taxonomies, which "are restricted by rigid definitions and relationships" (p. 218). Because tags are heavily influenced by colloquialisms and pop culture trends, Swant et al. (2011) said folksonomy quite literally means "folk + taxonomy" (p. 218). In other words, modern bookmarks may seem regulated by the soft organization style of personally organized tags but end up as community-negotiated rigid structures.

The lack of top-down organization can cause challenges, both in searching for particular tags and understanding the user's reasons for tagging items online. Nam and Kannan (2014) said "collections of individually generated tags are called 'social tags' and often spring up online through grassroots efforts" (p. 21). The popularity of tagging and bookmarking items online requires everyone working in mass communication—particularly journalists—to comprehend the significance of tagging online content, both for the promotion of their own work and for that of their news organizations (George-Palilonis, 2013). A historical examination of the phenomenon of bookmarking information online demonstrates how information sharing online has morphed over time; how folksonomy has developed online; how challenging a grassroots taxonomy can be for to end-users and mass communicators alike; how the role of agenda-setting in an algorithmic digital sphere has morphed; and what other areas are ripe for future research.

A REGULATED TAXONOMY

To understand how online behaviors influence the spread of information, it is critical to understand the history of the Internet and the circumstances surrounding its formation (King, 2010). Rogerson and Thomas (1998) noted that when the U.S. Department of Defense funded the creation of a computerized networking program in 1969, its founders, J. C. R. Licklider and Bob Taylor envisioned a borderless network where communities would exist, sometimes geographically connected, but more times not. The Internet's founding fathers envisioned digital communities that could work in small clusters or as individuals, where the thread of common interests would be a stronger pull than the role of geography. Rogerson and Thomas (1998) said, "the Internet, as a behavior space, combines a hierarchical structure of actors within specific spheres (i.e., territories, issues) with an absence of such structures outside those spheres" (p. 430). In other words, the Internet has become a place governed by human behavior and algorithms, where a level playing field allows a head of state to have as much access to the masses as an opinion leader in a small town. But Rogerson and Thomas noted these level playing fields do little to negate the reality that the transportability of online activities "among the spheres limits actor capabilities to regulate interactions" (p. 430). Ideally, user behavior on the Internet is self-controlled. As such, Rogerson and Thomas (1998) said, "Although it is not a political space in the traditional Westphalian sense . . . its users must still interact with economic, cultural, and other types of entities, most of which are still defined politically" (p. 441). At the same time, a great dichotomy seemed to exist online from the very beginning, this paradox of opinions that encouraged an unfettered flow of information while also seeking to control information from within.

An early example of the power of sharing information online emerged in the early 1980s, when a small computer company in Columbus, Ohio teamed with *The Columbus Dispatch*, a large, city newspaper, to offer paying subscribers the free flow of information through their home computers. It was information they wanted, when and how they wanted it. After four months of planning, the first computer-delivered newspaper in America went live Tuesday, July 1, 1980 (Laakaniemi, 1981). The hierarchical order used to present the information to subscribers followed a pattern long established in American newsrooms. Everything was broken down into categories used in the printed publication, such as the front page, sports, local news, features, and obituaries. The categories were predetermined by CompuServe and the *Dispatch*, rather than the end-users, but functioned as a logical taxonomy for subscribers to assist in finding the information they were most interested in. For computer industry leaders, such as Jeffrey Wilkins, president of CompuServe, Laakaniemi (1981) said the move to a digital newspaper "was not a question of whether a market exists for an electronic edition, but when" (p. 67). It was a matter of timing: would the American public buy a home computer in the 1980s or was it a question for the new millennium? Within a year, eleven major U.S. newspaper markets went online as well.

The success of CompuServe and the *Dispatch* prompted a small newspaper, the *Advertiser-Tribune*, in Tiffin, Ohio, to go online as well (Laakaniemi, 1982). For a fixed price of $6 a month, twenty-five subscribers had unlimited access to the newspaper's news database. "Information the user could obtain ranged from major UPI wire stories to local and national sports stories to farm prices, stock quotations, school closing announcements, daily lottery numbers, movie reviews and other items" (p. 38). Again, the information was categorized into nearly a dozen topics, with a taxonomy that included "area news, wire news, sports, farm corner, business/finance, public service, school news, entertainment, better living, advertising and user information" (p. 38). Critical to the early success of sharing information online was organizing it in a way that allowed end-users to find what they wanted.

This early taxonomy for sharing information gave newspaper users a false sense of control over the content they received. The reality was that subscribers only received what gatekeepers at the newspapers—whether in Tiffin or Columbus or beyond—were giving them. Agendas, either online or in print, were a media effect driven by the content offered by the publication's editors, and writers (McCombs & Shaw, 1972). In establishing a tagging nomenclature to disperse online news content, these earliest digital newspapers gave readers the appearance of autonomy, when in fact it was a highly controlled process of information sharing.

The advent of Web 2.0 opened the door for more online interactions. In this environment the gatekeeping controls and the settings of a particular agenda were not limited to professional news organizations. Soon, individuals, with information they deemed worth sharing, had an audience. Social media played a critical role in this purposeful dissemination of information. A digital bookmark that had once been tagged for personal use, the digital equivalent of a printed volume with a turned-down page corner, acquired the ability to be shared with the masses. Over time, this capacity for individuals to use folksonomy to direct the flow of information online has evolved into a tightly controlled, algorithm-driven digital sphere that only gives users the illusion of control.

Gatekeeping

The conceptualization of gatekeeping originated with Kurt Lewin who used it as a metaphor for the process by which information flowed through various channels or gates. Shoemaker (1991) said mass communication theorists repurposed this concept as "the process by which the billions of messages that are available in the world get cut down and transformed into the hundreds of messages that reach a given person on a given day" (p. 57). Although initially limited to examinations of the legacy press (Bleske, 1991; White, 1950), the role of gatekeeping in the media has since expanded to include broadcast news (Berkowitz, 1990) and a wide range of information platforms and media (Shoemaker & Vos, 2010).

The role of gatekeeper expanded dramatically in the wake of Web 2.0, when websites became interactive and end-users began engaging in media in new ways. Technology allowed opinion leaders everywhere to promote a particular agenda over those already touted by news organizations. These advances also helped Internet users gain a sense of control in terms of the taxonomy they used to organize information online, particularly on social media sites such as Flickr, MySpace, and Facebook. The paradigm shift meant that now consumers could actively curate, organize, present, and share information with others.

Credibility and Community

But with the cacophony of noise prompted by so many users, credibility quickly became an issue online. A source's credibility influences how individuals receive messages (Kang, Bae, Zhang, & Sundar, 2011). Borrowing from social psychology, Kang et al. (2011) noted, "credibility has long been perceived as an attribute of the source, and readers' responses to a message are influenced by this attribution" (p. 721). In their study of online credibility, the researchers found that highly involved online users are more likely to scrutinize the credibility of sources both near and far (p. 729). What's more, Kang et al. found that all it takes is a single source of questionable credibility to have a negative impact on news credibility perceptions as a whole on any given website. Ironically, although Web 2.0 began as a participatory medium, the increasing use of complex algorithms to calculate newsworthiness on news aggregation websites began to replace human gatekeepers. For Kang et al., it raises the tantalizing question of whether mass media technologies can be viewed as sources (p. 720) and left some researchers concluding that the perception of credibility of an online website was in part contingent on the reliability of the original news source. Others have countered that appearances impact believability and that audiences take credibility cues from what a website looks like, rather than how reliable the information on the site might be (Flanagin & Metzger, 2007).

This overall Web 2.0 paradigm shift has prompted closer examinations of what it means to share. Jenkins (2006) observed that although "today's participatory culture 'has its roots in practices that have occurred just below the radar of the media industry throughout the twentieth century, the Web has pushed that hidden layer of cultural activity into the foreground'" (p. 137). This participatory culture has redefined how society views the concept of sharing, while at the same time social scientists spend little time expanding on the theoretical underpinnings of the concept (John, 2012). When someone shares computer files, it is not based on a zero-sum loss or gain. Instead John observed, "This kind of sharing involves letting someone else have something that you have (somewhat akin to sharing a candy bar) though without entailing any kind of material sacrifice on the part of the sharer. Not only is this not a zero-sum game, but it is a form of sharing that leaves us with more than when we started" (p. 170).

For example, when an individual goes to the bookmark list on their personal computer and shares a link to a YouTube video on his or her Facebook page, they are not losing anything. The bookmark remains intact on their personal computer favorites list. It doesn't cost them money to share the link either. Nor does this action require a terrific amount of time and effort to click and post the bookmarked video. Similarly, it doesn't cost the individual's digital sphere friends anything to gain access to the bookmarked link. They simply click and watch. Rather than requiring something of the sharer and his or her receivers, both sides of the equation gain from this social media-generated transaction.

Despite this redefined view of sharing, the parceling of information is not equal on all fronts. Companies are making tremendous amounts of money on the backs of individuals inadvertently offering free labor under the guise of content control by engaging in activities online that companies would otherwise have to pay someone to complete. John (2012) noted "Facebook makes money not by asking its users explicitly to perform tasks for Facebook, but rather by aggregating and selling the data produced by the members' interactions with one another on the site" (p. 177). The reality is that every time someone goes online, bookmarks a page, tags it on a social media site or shares the link with friends, she or he is creating added value for unseen digital entrepreneurs in the form of valuable data.

Beyond monetary gains, Web 2.0 has also introduced the less nefarious social capital that individuals can build by sharing and collaborating during information processing. Fulk and Yuan (2013) observed that knowledge is not static. They noted that knowledge "is constructed, shaped and reconstructed as it is interpreted by the participants as they come into contact with it" (p. 32). As a result, Fulk and Yuan contended that knowledge is a construction process woven into a fabric that is influenced by the "lenses, blinders, constraints, and perspectives" that each individual brings to build their own versions of knowledge (p. 32). As a result, social media networks become deeply involved in interpersonal interaction as knowledge is built.

Further, this process is influenced by which online platforms individuals use to gather their knowledge. For instance, a wiki page that permits various authors to write and link to definitions of various subjects through a group-monitored and generated page is much more interactive than an online blog, where one author writes the piece and shares with whoever stumbles upon it.

Fulk and Yuan (2013) said "social capital developed and sustained in enterprise social networking platforms is connective when it buttresses stronger interpersonal connections" (p. 28). Similarly, it is communal when "connective communications among interacting individuals are made visible and public to the whole community" (p. 28). They concluded that communities indeed are strengthened by joint efforts of knowledge sharing, even if it is forged in the digital sphere, rather than the physical sphere. The following paragraphs highlight some examples.

One of the key early players in the online economy was Amazon.com, and it has built itself into the world's largest online marketplace thanks in part to the recommendations and reviews of its users. Ante (2009) writes that many people thought Amazon had lost its mind when it first allowed customers to leave reviews in 1995, but thanks to Amazon's success, reviews are a common part of nearly every e-commerce website. "Amazon has played a central role in the change in consumer behavior by being the first successful web retailer to embrace consumers' views. 'What we try to spend our time on is harnessing customer passion,' says Russell Dicker, Amazon.com's senior manager of community" (Ante, 2009). The most reviewed product on Amazon.com, the Eatsmart Precision Plus Digital Bathroom Scale, with 10,748 reviews demonstrates how important the bookmarks and comments customers make are to the company's overall sales. See figure 6.1.

The site didn't stop with customer reviewers either in the grand scheme of using the community's bookmarks to enhance their shopping experience. Amazon unveiled Wish Lists in 1999, discussion areas for specific products in 2005, and discussion hubs that covered a broad range of topics, such as video production, Harry Potter, or yoga. "All told, Amazon rolls out 50 community features on its site every year. 'We spend a lot of time looking at what customers are doing and seeing what they are saying,' says Dicker" (Ante, 2009).

Figure 6.1.   Amazon.com Review

Although Tumblr began in 2007 as a microblogging platform for self-expression, similar to WordPress or Blogger, it has quickly evolved into a site that relies heavily on users "following" other bloggers and sharing their work, Dewey (2015) writes. A Tumblr user—or "creator" as the company is fond of calling them—was the first to ask the audience to help determine the color of a dress, and quickly generated more than 73 million page views (Guys Please Help Me, 2015). The power of user-created memes and the buzz accompanying them helped Tumblr earn the more than billion-dollar sum that Yahoo paid for the company in 2013. Since then it has more than doubled the number of blogs on its network, from 105 million to 226 million (Dewey, 2015).

Tumblr is not the only site turning bookmarks into viral memes and profiting from it. Both Imgur and Reddit rely exclusively on their audience to post content and have turned that content into multimillion-dollar businesses. Imgur, the photo sharing site, and Reddit, the platform to discuss nearly anything, formalized their partnership when Imgur accepted $40 million in venture capital funding led by Andreessen Horowitz and with participation by Reddit (Konrad, 2014). In internal documents, Reddit has set its sale price at nothing less than $240 million in 2012 (Feigerman, 2012).

The social networking site Airbnb.com offers globetrotters hoping for a more personalized experience than staying in a hotel the ability to preview potential properties in cities they intend to visit, examine reviews of hosts left by past houseguests, and view maps that help determine if the host is in a location convenient to where they want to travel. It uses the popularity of user-generated reviews, such as those on Amazon.com, to help inform potential travelers. Airbnb demonstrates how users can vet potential hosts with the help of reviews. In return, hosts can determine whom they want as houseguests based on reviews of past hosts.

Since Fall 2013, the iOS and Android app, Yik Yak, has created a digital community by allowing users to anonymously post items—about whatever is on any particular user's mind—in a thread that is viewed only by other Yik Yak users within a 10-mile radius. In addition to posting yaks, readers can click an arrow icon up to approve a yak thread or an arrow down to disapprove it. Social media capital is acquired through positive clicks. Posts work to create a community among users, many who are typically college students.

Motivations and Gratifications

Before exploring how platforms and bookmarking have evolved, it is helpful to examine the reasons individuals seek out opportunities to bookmark, tag, and create taxonomies for sharing. To do this, one must take an interdisciplinary approach to understand what drives people to share. Swant et al. (2011) distinguished the difference between what they called "social annotations" and "expert annotations." It is noted that those who leave social annotations are often not certain of what specifically motivated them to share personal knowledge nor are they directed by a specific, work-related task (p. 220). Nam and Kannan (2014) contend that the primary motivation for the creation of social tags and bookmarks is more basic: individuals feel compelled to "describe and efficiently categorize the vast amount of content that users encounter online" (p. 21–22). This organization typically falls into two categories: "content organization (categorization and description of the content) and social communication (information sharing and opinion expression regarding the content)" (p. 24).

Parallels exist between the categories for sharing and the motivations people list for using the Internet. The uses and gratifications paradigm suggests that media audience members actively select the media they think is most likely to fulfill or gratify their needs (Katz, Gurevitch, & Haas, 1973). One common need users seek is socialization (Rodgers & Sheldon, 2002), and the Internet has the potential to gratify this need better than any other medium (Dimmick, Chen, & Li, 2004). Ruggiero (2000) even argues that the emergence of computer-mediated communication has bolstered uses and gratifications as a research paradigm because its flexibility uniquely situates it as a vital way of understanding why we use the Internet and what we hope to get out of it.

In terms of what motivates us to bookmark, however, LaRose and Eastin (2004) suggest researchers need to go further than needs fulfillment. Social cognitive theory, which examines how behavior is related to perceptions of future success, better explains our motivations for Web use, and in turn, bookmarking. One of the primary drivers for Web usage is social support. LaRose and Eastin said, "perhaps by finding like-minded individuals on the Internet and expressing ourselves in those venues we enhance our social status" (p. 373). In other words, the reasons we bookmark items and share them copiously is to build our reputation online, either consciously or subconsciously. This contributes to the illusion of control we think we have over our own behavior (Ryan & Deci, 2000).

Despite all the good intentions and motivations we may have in terms of why we socially tag and bookmark items online for the benefit of others, Swant et al. (2011) found several challenges that are a result of this sharing, including motivations, cultural influences, vocabulary problems, specialized knowledge, and semantic losses. For example, individuals who are motivated to bookmark pages socially online do so because they want others to find and benefit from the knowledge, but often in their haste to share, they don't use the most relevant tags (p. 220). An attempt to share with the masses may be so personalized tHat it misses its target entirely. Similarly, cultural influences and differences direct perceptions and cognitions. An analysis of image tags that were created by European, American, and Chinese users online found that Western participants focused on the foreground and the individuals in the images, whereas Eastern participants were more holistic in their approach to viewing the same objects (Swant et al., 2011).

Akin to the issue of culture are vocabulary issues and specialized knowledge. Swant et al. (2011) found "the spontaneous choice of words to describe the same content varies among different people, and the probability of two users using the same term is very little" (p. 220). The biggest flaw of folksonomy was that various word selections for tags and bookmarks often introduce concerns with polysemy, synonymy, and variations that find both generalized and specified words being assigned to the same concept. This phenomenon differs from specialized knowledge, where tags are embedded with personal references, special characters, or favorite numbers that are so unique to the tagger that they are meaningless to general audiences.

Semantic loss, meanwhile, is a more natural occurrence because annotators are not obligated to associate relevant tags to every image or bookmark link they share (Swant et al., 2011). Adding to this understanding of semantic loss, Nan and Kannan (2014) noted that users often use high-level attribute tags to categorize content, but more semantic or contextual descriptions to describe the content. This disconnect has led some researchers to conclude that nearly half of all the online tag applications on the Internet or within social media collections are "irrelevant for a general audience" (Swant et al., 2011, p. 221). At the same time, this tagging nomenclature for bookmarks and favorite links on social media sites offer insights into individual taggers' personal beliefs and biases (Nam & Kannan, 2014). In other words, the folksonomy of tags online, which veers toward personal definitions, may need the professionalism and organization that taxonomy provides. The ultimate provider of the rules for bookmarking may be the companies, such as Facebook, that allow and encourage the practice.

TRENDS IN BOOKMARKING AND TAGGING

Facebook is arguably one of the largest social media platforms on the Internet. As of June 30, 2014, it boasted 1.32 billion monthly users with 1.07 billion mobile users. Break that activity into daily use, and the numbers total 829 million users each day, with 654 million using mobile devices (Company Info, 2014). It has come a long way from the social networking website started by Harvard University psychology major, Mark Zuckerberg in February 2004 (Phillips, 2007). What began as a social networking tool for college students has since become instrumental in mass communication for everyone from private business owners and massive conglomerate companies to individuals and news organizations.

The realities of this disparate world were most evident when one writer examined the physical-world ramifications of hitting the *like* button on shared bookmarks and video links on one's Facebook page for two full days (Honan, 2014). By the end of the 48-hour analysis, Honan discovered that hitting the like button equated to an economic act every time, as new ads appeared on his newsfeed with each click of the thumbs-up icon. While extreme, it demonstrates how social media users operate under the illusion of control. They may think that they control what they share and with whom, but ultimately, unless they tag a friend by name, they lack the power to ensure that the information reaches its target, purely based on the actions of the audience. Each tap of the like button morphs the unseen, uncontrollable algorithm that dictates what appears on others' Facebook newsfeeds. It prompted Honan (2014) to observe "the like and the favorite are the new metrics of success—very literally. Not only are they ego-feeders for the stuff we put online as individuals, but advertisers track their campaigns on Facebook by how often they are liked" (para. 2). While most Facebook users may assume their feeds are populated by random stories, posts, and tags from friends and acquaintances, this is far from the reality. Facebook's algorithms do more to decide what shows up in your feed than you do (Honan, 2014). "It isn't just a parade of sequential updates from your friends and the things you've expressed an interest in. In 2014 the News Feed is a highly curated presentation, delivered to you by a complicated formula based on the actions you take on the site, and across the web" (para. 4).

Many mass communicators, on the other hand, recognize the power these algorithms bring to reporting news and connecting with audiences. *Broadcasting & Cable*, an industry magazine, noted as early as February 2012 that an increasing number of local television stations were implementing intentional strategies on Facebook to capitalize on improving station ratings, as well as revenue. In a regular feature column, one author noted, "sky-high Facebook followings are good for bragging rights, the bigger challenge for stations is turning them into ratings—and revenue," (Station to Station,

2012). For one station manager, growing the fan base was instrumental in overtaking a long-time local rival in actual television ratings, noting it was important to make an emotional connection with viewers (Station to Station, 2012, p. 20).

Another move television stations have taken is seeking input from viewers online, which are then reflected in the daily newscast. For example, when Disney-ABC announced plans to launch a new talk show featuring Katie Couric, the network turned to Facebook and Twitter—shaping the message for each medium (Albiniak, 2012). David Kite, Disney-ABC Domestic Television's vice president of marketing, said, "Facebook is a great place on which to put content and have conversations, while Twitter is a great place to put the word out" (Albiniak, 2012, p. 23). As the program launched, it planned to tap into both social media platforms as a way to integrate the audience with the show.

Twitter: Lots of Tweets, Few Tweeters

Since Twitter's founding in 2006, the social media site has collected 271 million regular monthly users who blast 500 million Tweets into the ether each day (About Twitter, 2014). Twitter reports that more than 78 percent of all its active users are turning to mobile devices to send and receive tweets, and 77 percent of all Twitter accounts originate outside the United States (About Twitter, 2014). Some researchers contend as recently as 2009 that nearly 75 percent of Twitter's online activity originated with 5 percent of its users. In other words, a majority of Twitter users—some 85 percent—are quiet, tweeting less than once a day (eMarketer, 2009). These tweets can range from random comments to bookmarks to stories, videos, or any other information the sender deems worthy to share.

Even though Twitter allows users to reach audiences that far exceed the limitations of face-to-face communication, why individuals or businesses use Twitter is motivated by the same factors uses and gratifications stipulate. Researchers found in a 2009 study that there were distinct differences in how commercial and public broadcast stations used Twitter (Greer & Ferguson, 2011). For example, commercial stations are more likely to tweet breaking news or promotional tweets than public stations. Similarly, Greer and Ferguson (2011) found that public broadcast stations were more likely than commercial stations to tweet announcements promoting programming other than the local newscast. Greer and Ferguson said these findings "suggest that news is central to commercial stations, while branding and programs are central to public stations" (p. 209). The researchers argued that public broadcast stations might benefit from developing a routine that included tweets about news stories in an effort to make a better connection with potential followers (p. 210).

These findings reinforce the role Twitter plays, in terms of permitting individuals to not only send information to followers, but also to serve as a new form of modern-day bookmarking. Instead of going to a social media bookmarking site, users can use Twitter threads as a holding place for favorite websites, videos, or news stories. The creation of *hashtags* embedded as part of one's Twitter folksonomy means that all it takes is a quick search for past tags to return to those links and the conversations the initial posting may have prompted.

This online activity also demonstrates the power of agenda setting. For Twitter users, whether they have ten or 10,000 followers, a 140-character message blasted into the digital sphere not only tells people what is important, but also sets the agenda to consider (Cohen, 1963). Unlike Facebook, Twitter offers its users greater control. The individual drives what appears in a subscriber's newsfeeds, rather than what an unseen algorithm deems worthy of one's time based on other online activities. Hashtags, first made popular on Twitter, allow all users to search a particular phrase or word to see what is trending, including information that does not originate with people they follow. This level of autonomy preserves the agendas each individual sets and shares with followers. But it is not only individuals who are taking advantage of the agenda Twitter allows them to set. Businesses, such as TV stations, may be better able to use social media to set agendas that can reach large audiences and influence them because it meshes well with what media have always done (Greer & Ferguson, 2011). In fact, the more that news media tap into the conversations their audience members are having on social media, the more they can build credibility, engagement, and ultimately the audience they need to satisfy their profit motives.

Mediating Folksonomy

The need for an organization to make sense of the bookmarks individuals make and an exemplar of how intertwined folksonomy and social media can become online is Delicious. Founded in 2003, the company combines bookmarking and social tagging from an initial post by urging and authorizing its users to share online links with each other. Billed as a free service, Delicious sells itself as a place "designed with care to be the best place to save what you love on the web" (About Delicious, 2014). In more technical terms, it is a social media application that "mediates the bookmarking of Web-available sites and pages" that prompts users to offer not only the link to a favored website, but also a title and a description of the site, to accompany tags that help organize the bookmarks for others to explore (Stolley, 2009). By urging subscribers to fill in tags, Delicious—much like Facebook—benefits from the free labor of its volunteer membership. By empowering users to help organize and tag favorite bookmarks, Delicious also extends a modicum of control to its users.

It currently boasts more than a billion links, carefully organized and tagged and served daily from more than 200 countries (About Delicious, 2014). With this sizeable user-base, Delicious has not been immune to examinations of how user posts are converted into capital for brick-and-mortar industries. Nam and Kannan (2014) observed in their study of the implications of social tagging versus bookmarking that the complex web of tags "can reveal the competitive market structure" (p. 25) whereas a dramatic increase in bookmarks for a brand have little financial impact. From a marketing perspective, examinations of the social act of tagging can reflect both the competitive and complementary relationships that exist between various brands (Nam & Kannan, 2014, p. 25).

For marketing firms, this could mean big business as dramatic increases in popular social keywords can serve as early indicators of a brand's future potential cash flow. These findings beg the question: do these trends work in the same fashion among news organizations? In other words, if a news organization experiences a large surge of social tags based on a particular story or news event, will that convert into a sharp increase in the tangible sale of print publications, an increase in online subscriptions, or a surge in broadcast audiences? Again, we see how the masses willingly, and largely unconsciously, labor for free for the benefit of others. Similarly, it also demonstrates that while individuals posting favorite bookmark links may appear to have control over the content on their favorites list, it is only a perception of control as others post similar content and inadvertently fuel Internet sensations.

When this same scenario—social media users unconsciously laboring for the benefit of others—is applied to health scares or natural disasters, the collective effort and resulting spread of information can be beneficial. For example, when the outbreak of the H1N1 virus, commonly dubbed the swine flu, first struck in the United States in April 2009, social media sites such as Delicious became instrumental in helping spread information to the masses (Freberg, Palenchar, & Veil, 2013). One of the major advantages of social media during such a crisis is "the ability not just to post information and hits related to that information but to learn how that information is shared" (p. 178).

At the same time, many of the previously mentioned pitfalls emerged. Freberg et al. (2013) found that on a platform such as Delicious, the bookmarks often took on many different formats, from websites and blog links to other social media platforms. Legacy media and government agencies, such as *The New York Times* or the Centers for Disease Control and Prevention (CDC), became the most popular bookmarks on Delicious even though the tags used by posters to describe these sites varied. Because information spreads quickly online, private individuals using social media now usurp major health organizations that would have previously directed the narrative. In other words, even in natural disasters or epidemics, the masses exhibit greater control than in the past, but they end up sharing the same message as those in power would have shared anyway. For crisis communication practitioners, Freberg et al. (2013) contend that it remains to be seen how they might "address those stakeholders that are creating their own influence and messages online" (p. 183). Further, it is unknown if legacy media might experience similar challenges while covering major news events.

The Role of Gender and Folksonomy

Up until this point, this chapter has focused largely on the collective, rather than on the role gender might play in how individuals approach bookmarking, sharing, and creating folksonomies to organize favorite websites, links, or ideas with others. Although seminal mass communication studies found no difference in the gatekeeping results of men and women in the newsroom (Bleske, 1991), this is not necessarily the case when it comes to social media. Meyer and Hu (2013) found that women said they were more likely to trust citizen journalism than men. In the social media realm, men and women have demonstrated differences in which platforms they gravitate to—as well as what they do, once they are established on social media.

For example, Reddit.com typically attracts a male audience, who populate the site with news stories and public forum postings they think will interest other readers. On the other hand, Pinterest, has received its share of criticism for being a female-driven digital sphere that defies traditional conventions when it comes to sharing information, especially compared to sites such as Delicious or Google Chrome Bookmarks, because it unites strangers with shared interests rather than through personal connections (Tekobbe, 2014, p. 382). The social media site has been defined, Tekobbe noted, as "a URL-saving and management system that arranges internet addresses into a rhizomatic, digital physical topography, one that is co-curated and navigated by its community members" (p. 382). In other words, it is a digital sphere occupied by dreamers rather than creators.

> If the punditry is to be believed then, Pinterest is a feminized online space that is either about marketing or sharing (or weddings)—it certainly is not about creating. It is not a valid use of the affordances of networked technologies, but then, apparently, in general, women cannot fully engage the robust creative possibilities of online technologies the way men can, either because women are social creatures focused entirely on sharing retail content, or because women do not understand the purpose of the internet. (Tekobbe, 2014, p. 384)

It is hard to deny that female users who are largely based in the United States and remain highly desired by marketers because of their income levels and buying power dominate Pinterest (Smith, 2014) and that the male voice and ethos may dominate Reddit. However, it benefits the corporations behind these sites to be all-inclusive and both have made inroads into diversifying their vast fan bases. When their collective buying power is stripped away, the conversation about gender online degrades into a debate about digital literacy and whether what people do online is an appropriate use of online technologies (Tekobbe, 2014).

Although, other demographics, such as race and ethnicity or even educational levels, have traditionally interested researchers, a 2013 study by the Pew Research Center found that the advent of smartphones is quickly closing many of these common digital divides. For example, in its 2013 survey that asked participants whether they had a smartphone or home broadband service, the researchers found that 80 percent of the respondents who self-reported being white, non-Hispanic replied in the affirmative, while 79 percent of the participants who self-reported being Black or non-Hispanic and 75 percent of Hispanic respondents said they had the same service (Rainie, 2013).

Ultimately, it becomes an even more obvious conversation about power, control, and who should have the right to determine whether these activities are worthy contributions to society. Tekobbe (2014) argues that modern society is so bound by its cultural beliefs, particularly when it comes to digital technology, that "we may unconsciously conflate legacy artefacts (sic) with materially dependent design conventions, causing us to misconstrue emergent literacy practices grounded in reciprocal culture or in broadly shared human experience . . . as error" (p. 385). In terms of gender, she concludes that because society often misconstrues emergent literacy practices as something done in error, it is easier to dismiss the digital actions of women—whether bookmarking a favorite website on a Pinterest board or assigning a folksonomy that others see as unusual—as inappropriate, wrong, or a result of not understanding something. Tekobbe contends it is easier to dismiss women on Pinterest than to admit that the digital sphere is dominated by what she describes as a "hegemonic, masculine technological narrative that privileges 'creating' over 'sharing'" (p. 385).

DISCUSSION

This chapter has attempted to demonstrate how a clear pattern of control has evolved with advancements in technology through an examination of bookmarking practices and the motivations behind them. Although the earliest adapters of bookmarking technology may have felt greater autonomy in terms of how they received information from newspapers—whether in the form of a printed newspaper or through their home computer—it is clear that this was an illusion. Editors and reporters ultimately served as the gatekeepers of information, determining which stories to make available online and which to ignore.

The mass media held firmly to its ability to set an agenda through news coverage until the advent of Web 2.0, when the interactivity and sharing abilities through digital conventions such as hashtags and tagging opened the door to wider control for individuals seeking to share information. This brief period marked a shift in agenda setting as individuals were empowered to share information they found important and with whomever they wanted. But it was short-lived as social media platforms, led by Facebook and Google, began to utilize increasingly stronger algorithms that predetermined what someone was exposed to online, based largely on their own online clicking behaviors.

This period, which remains in its infancy, has been conceptualized as offering the illusion of control to individuals online. While the algorithms don't determine what one posts on Facebook or YouTube, these complex formulas do determine who receives the information. This illusion of control in the digital sphere is only spreading. For example, Twitter recently announced plans to incorporate algorithms for displaying tweets on individual accounts for the first time (McDermott, 2014). As a platform that still caters to legacy media and breaking news, this decision could dramatically change the organic, agenda-setting power of Twitter.

> Twitter's influence in this sense cannot be understated: Conversations on Twitter about Michael Brown's death and the subsequent unrest in Ferguson, Missouri, pushed the story to the national forefront. This was in stark contrast to Facebook . . . where much of the conversation two weeks ago revolved around the ALS Ice Bucket Challenge (McDermott, 2014).

In this later digital sphere event, McDermott contends it was strong Facebook algorithms that pushed videos of people dumping buckets of ice water over their heads in an effort to promote awareness of the progressive neurodegenerative disease commonly known as Lou Gehrig's disease, rather than images and stories that dominated Twitter over the violent race riots that occurred in a small midwestern U.S. town following the police-shooting death of a young African American man in Ferguson, Missouri, in August 2014.

This is not to say that nobody posted videos of Ice Bucket Challenges on Twitter or offered commentary about the Ferguson riots on Facebook. It does help demonstrate, however, how algorithms and computer-driven formulas can control what would appear to be trending stories on social media platforms. The gatekeeper is neither the individual posting nor the legacy media outlet as a bookmarked favorite link, but an unseen force that few take the time to consider. This lack of disclosure and online transparency also prompts larger questions about the agenda behind these unseen, unacknowledged mathematical forces. Who is creating these social media algorithms and what is the agenda? Is it merely done for capital gain? Or is it an intentional effort to tell people what is important and what they should be thinking about? And how can individuals online sidestep these algorithms in an effort to regain the bookmarks they once set online?

CONCLUSION

Social media websites and bookmarking in the post–Web 2.0 era are not created equal. While some social media sites grant enormous control to users in terms of how items are bookmarked, tagged, and shared, others use powerful algorithms to control information shared in the digital sphere. The result is that some social media users maintain a high level of autonomy in terms of agenda-setting control, while others unknowingly settle for merely a perceived control.

This chapter has attempted to highlight current research trends in the largely unexamined area of social bookmarking. It has borrowed from multiple disciplines, including psychology, marketing, and computer engineering. It has also examined the role that gender might play in the functionality and creation of folksonomy on social media platforms, such as Pinterest. Future research should continue to embrace this interdisciplinary approach to examining how individuals in the digital sphere utilize bookmarks, hashtags, and tagging nomenclature to share information online. Examinations of particular interest include those that expand current studies to dive deeper into user motivations for particular folksonomies and online counter-efforts, as well as those that use context-aware tagging models to create a more universal approach to developing nomenclature that will appeal to the masses (Trattner & Helic, 2009).

Additional studies could examine Twitter after it adopts its algorithm, to examine how major world news events are covered. Does Twitter remain the place for breaking news trends, while Facebook becomes more a hotspot for cultural trends? Or does this unseen controlling force of computer-generated algorithms prompt new technologies to step in and replace existing social media platforms? Finally, future studies that examine the role of gender, race, and ethnicity—as well as motivations for posting and user awareness of unseen controls—would lend to a greater understanding of modern-day computer literacy.

REFERENCES

About Delicious. (2014). What is Delicious? Retrieved Sept. 3, 2014 from https://delicious.com/about.

About Twitter. (2014). Twitter Usage. Retrieved Sept. 1, 2014 from https://about.twitter.com/company.

Albiniak, P. (2012, August 20). No stopping until everyone "Likes" Katie: Disney-ABC uses wealth of social media to promote Couric's new talker. Retrieved from http://www.broadcastingcable.com/news/news-articles/no-stopping-till-everyone-likes-katie/113492.

Ante, S. E. (2009, October 19). Amazon: Turning Consumer Opinions into Gold. Retrieved from http://www.bloomberg.com/bw/magazine/content/09_43/b4152047039565.htm.

Berkowitz, D. A. (1990). Refining the gatekeeping metaphor for local television news. In D. A. Berkowitz (Ed.), *Social meanings of news: A text reader* (pp. 81–93). Thousand Oaks, CA: Sage.

Bleske, G. L. (1991). Ms. Gates Takes Over: An Updated Version of a 1949 Case Study. In D. Berkowitz (Ed.), *Social meanings of news: A text reader* (pp. 72–80). Thousand Oaks, CA: Sage.

Christopher, L. C. (2009, February 19). Brave new newspapers: How the future might be better than we think. *The Seybold Report* 9:13–14.

Cohen, B. (1963). *The press and foreign policy.* Princeton: Princeton University Press.

Company Info. (2014). Statistics. Retrieved September 1, 2014 from http://newsroom.fb.com/company-info/.

Dewey, C. (2015, March 11). Move over, Reddit: Tumblr new ground zero of Internet. Retrieved from http://www.washingtonpost.com/news/the-intersect/wp/2015/03/11/move-over-reddit-tumblr-is-the-new-front-page-of-the-internet/.

Dimmick, J., Y. Chen, & Z. Li. (2004). Competition between the Internet and traditional news media: The gratification-opportunities niche dimension. *The Journal of Media Economics* 17 (1): 19–33.

Dodd, M. D., & S. B. Campbell. (2011). *A strategic framework for targeting generation Y via social media: Public relations results and implications.* Paper presented at the International Communication Association Conference, Boston, MA.

eMarketer (2009, August 28). Do you know who's on Twitter? Retrieved from http://www.emarketer.com/Article.aspx?R=1007250.

Feigerman, S. (2012, October 31). Is Reddit worth $240 Million? Retrieved from http://mashable.com/2012/10/31/reddit-valuation/.

Flanagin, A. J., & M. J. Metzger. (2007). The role of site features, user attributes, and information verification behaviors on the perceived credibility of web-based information. *New Media & Society* 9 (2): 319–342.

Freberg, K., M. J. Palenchar, & S. R. Veil. (2013). Managing and sharing H1N1 crisis information using social media bookmarking services. *Public Relations Review* 39:178–184.

Fulk, J., & Y. C. Yuan. (2013). Location, Motivation, and Social Capitalization via Enterprise Social Networking. *Journal of Computer-Mediated Communication* 19:20–37.

George-Palilonis, J. (2013). *The multimedia journalist: Storytelling for today's media landscape.* New York: Oxford University Press.

Greer, C. F., & D. A. Ferguson. (2011). Using Twitter for promotion and branding: A content analysis of local television Twitter sites. *Broadcast Education Association* 55 (2): 198–214.

Guys Please Help Me. (2015). Retrieved from http://swiked.tumblr.com/post/112073818575/guys-please-help-me-is-this-dress-white-and.

Honan, M. (2014, August 11). I liked everything I saw on Facebook for two days. Here's what it did to me. Retrieved from http://www.wired.com/2014/08/i-liked-everything-i-saw-on-facebook-for-two-days-heres-what-it-did-to-me/.

Jenkins, H. (2006). *Convergence culture: Where old and new media collide.* New York: New York University Press.

John, N. A. (2012). Sharing and Web 2.0: The emergency of a keyword. *New Media & Society* 15 (2): 167–182.

Kang, H., K. Bae, S. Zhang, & S. S. Sundar. (2011). Source cues in online news: Is the proximate source more powerful than distal sources? *Journalism & Mass Communication Quarterly* 88 (4): 719–736.

Katz, E., M. Gurevitch, & H. Haas. (1973). On the use of the mass media for important things. *American Sociological Review* 38:164–181.

King, E. (2010). *Free for all: The Internet's transformation of journalism.* Evanston, IL: Northwestern University Press.

Konrad, A. (2014, April 2). Imgur raises $40 million from Andreessen Horowitz after five years going it alone. Retrieved from http://www.forbes.com/sites/alexkonrad/2014/04/03/imgur-raises-40-million-from-andreessen/.

Laakaniemi, R. (1981). The computer connection: America's first computer-delivered newspaper. *Newspaper Research Journal* 2 (4): 61–68.

———. (1982). Electronic newspaper part two: Computer retrieval comes to the small daily. *Newspaper Research Journal* 3:36–40.

LaRose, R., & M. S. Eastin. (2004). A social cognitive theory of Internet uses and gratifications: Toward a new model of media attendance. *Journal of Broadcasting & Electronic Media* 48 (3): 358–377.

McCombs, M. E., & D. L. Shaw. (1972). The agenda-setting function of mass media. *The Public Opinion Quarterly* 36 (2): 176–187.

McDermott, J. (2014, September 5). What a Twitter algorithm could mean for brands, publishers. Retrieved from http://digiday.com/platforms/dont-fear-algorithm-twitters-new-feed-will-mean-brands/.

Meyer, H. K., & H. Hu. (2013, March). Gender stereotypes and citizen journalism: Exploring what effect, if any, gender match has on story credibility for citizen journalism and staff written news. *The Journal of Research on Women and Gender* 6.

Nam, H., & P. K. Kannan. (2014). Informational value of social tagging networks. *Journal of Marketing* 78:21–40.

Phillips, S. (2007, July 24). A brief history of Facebook. Retrieved from http://www.theguardian.com/technology/2007/jul/25/media.newmedia.

Rainie, L. (2013). The state of digital divides. Retrieved from http://www.pewinternet.org/2013/11/05/the-state-of-digital-divides-video-slides/.

Rodgers, S., & Sheldon, K. (2002). An improved way to characterize Internet users. *Journal of Advertising Research,* September/October 2002.

Rogerson, K.S., & G. D. Thomas. (1998). Internet regulation process model: The effect of societies, communities, and governments. *Political Communication* 15:427–444.

Ruggiero, T. (2000). Uses and gratifications theory in the 21st Century. *Mass Communication & Society* 3 (1): 3–37.

Ryan, R. M., & E. L. Deci. (2000). Self-determination theory and the facilitation of intrinsic motivation, social development, and well-being. *American Psychologist* 55 (1): 68.

Shoemaker, P. J. (1991). A new gatekeeping model. In D. A. Berkowitz (Ed.), *Social meanings of news: A text reader* (pp. 57–62). Thousand Oaks, CA: Sage.

Shoemaker, P. J., & T. P. Vos. (2010). Media gatekeeping. In D. W. Stacks & M. B. Salwen (Eds.), *An integrated approach to communication theory and research,* (pp. 75–89). New York: Routledge.

Smith, C. (2014, April 17). This is the behavior on Pinterest that makes the social network so attractive to marketers. Retrieved from http://www.businessinsider.com/demographics-on-pinterest-that-make-the-social-network-attractive-to-marketers-2014-4.

Solis, B. (2011). *ENGAGE! The complete guide for brands and businesses to build, cultivate, and measure success in the new Web.* Hoboken, NJ: John Wiley & Sons Inc.

Station to Station. (2012, February 13). Stations find a "Friend" in social media: Local TV's sharpened Facebook strategy drives ratings and revenue. *Broadcasting & Cable* 20.

Stolley, K. (2009). Integrating social media into existing work environments: The case of Delicious. *Journal of Business and Technical Communication* 23 (3): 350–371.

Swant, N., J. Li, & J. Z. Wang. (2011). Automatic image semantic interpretation using social action and tagging data. *Multimedia Tools and Applications* 51:213–246.

Tekobbe, C. K. (2014). A site for fresh eyes: Pinterest's challenge to "traditional" digital literacies. *Information, Communication & Society* 16 (3): 381–396.

Trattner, C., & D. Helic. (2009). *Extending the basic tagging model: Context-aware tagging.* Paper presented at the IADIS International Conference, Barcelona, Spain.

WhatIs.techtarget.com. (2006, June). Retrieved August 19, 2014 from http://what-is.techtarget.com/definition/social-bookmarking.

White, D. M. (1950). The "Gate Keeper": A case study in the selection of news. In D. Berkowitz (Ed.), *Social meanings of news: A text reader* (pp. 63–71). Thousand Oaks, CA: Sage.

Chapter Seven

Social Networking in Times of Crisis

Hayley Watson, Kush Wadhwa, Lemi Baruh, and Salvatore Scifo

On April 16, 2007 when a single shooter walked into Virginia Tech College in Blacksburg, Virginia, killing thirty-two people and injuring many others, virtual communities responded to the crisis. What emerged from this crisis was not just individuals discussing the unfolding of events online, but an organized group jointly participating in problem solving activities to identify victims, even prior to official news releases. The result was, as argued by Palen, Vieweg, Liu, and Hughes (2009), a form of collective intelligence via online collective action.

The power and abilities of the virtual crowd to respond to a crisis situation has been demonstrated many times and can be traced back as far as 2001 as with the use of blogs to discuss the September 11, 2001 terrorist attacks in the USA (Zoidberg, 2001). As time progresses, according to Palen, Vieweg, Liu, and Hughes (2009), there are countless examples of the use of information communication technologies (ICTs) following a crisis by the public to communicate, collaborate, find information, and help others in an online setting. Some examples include (but are not limited to): the rescue activities and the building of social capital following Hurricane Katrina in 2005 (Procopio & Procopio, 2007), the use of social media for providing localized news during the 2007 California Wildfires (Novak & Vidoloff, 2011), the use of online social networking for organizing volunteers following the 2010 and 2011 earthquakes in Christchurch, New Zealand (Matheson, 2014), citizen journalism for localized news during Hurricane Sandy in 2012 (Knoblich, 2014) and the presence of the crowd in responding to the Boston Marathon attacks in 2013 (Tapia, LaLone, & Kim, 2014).

As illustrated by Watson and Wadhwa (2014), the involvement of the public in communicating during crisis is now a routine activity and is being embraced by various stakeholders taking part in managing and responding to a crisis. Crucial to social organization in communicating in a crisis in this manner is social networking. By the term "social networking" we mean the ways in which groups of people are connected together and how they interact and form relationships. When discussing social networks and their role in times of crisis within this chapter, we are predominantly concerned with the ways in which social networks emerge online, as facilitated by social media, particularly social networking sites (SNS) including Facebook and Twitter. As argued by boyd and Ellison (2007), social network sites are "web-based services that allow individuals to (1) construct a public or semi-public profile within a bounded system, (2) articulate a list of other users with whom they share a connection, and (3) view and traverse their list of connections and those made by others within the system" (p. 211).

Social network sites differ in their function, makeup, and size, with some established with a particular purpose and goal in mind, examples include: the fostering of business relationships (e.g., LinkedIn, XING), the sharing of photographs (Flickr, Instagram), the forming of specialized communities (Academia.edu), and others, like Facebook, Twitter, MySpace, have no specifically expressed function other than facilitating social connectivity, and in some cases providing an advertising space. There are also social network sites that are used by citizens in specific geographic regions, for instance; the use of Sina Weibo in China and IntaFeen in the Middle East and North Africa. Key to accessing these sites and associated applications are those devices—including computers, mobile phones, tablets, and, more recently, smart watches—that facilitate interaction in a virtual setting. Whilst these technologies play an important role in facilitating interaction and networking activities, it is important to avoid a technological determinist perspective, for the public must, themselves, choose to participate in networking activities (Watson, 2011).

Against this backdrop, we aim to explore how SNSs are being used by the public and crisis response organizations in times of crisis. By doing so, we seek to demonstrate the various functions and benefits that these tools provide as well as how they complement crisis management. In doing so, we will examine some of the inherent challenges of social networking in times of crisis and identify a number of open issues to be considered for further research. Prior to considering how social networking is becoming increasingly important in crisis response activities, it is first necessary to clarify what we mean by the term "crisis" and furthermore, why communication is so essential to managing a crisis.

WHAT IS A CRISIS?

At its most basic level, the term "crisis" is defined by the Oxford English Dictionary as "a time of severe difficulty or danger" (Soanes, 2002, p. 193). Within this chapter, when discussing the term "crisis" in relation to ensuring citizens' security, it is commonly attributed and discussed interchangeably with the term "disaster," as seen for instance, in the 2010 *EU Internal Security Strategy in Action: Five Steps Towards a More Secure Europe* memorandum (European Commission, 2010). Although, as often found when defining terms, there is no "agreed upon" definition of the term "disaster," there has been, as outlined by Perry (2007), some consensus. For Perry, a disaster is a social phenomenon; a storm for instance, is not a disaster, it is the scope of the effects of the storm on the social system that causes it to be classified and understood as a disaster. An event might be classified as a disaster according to the number of infrastructure systems damaged, citizens injured or displaced. Importantly, a disaster is also a reflection of the "social structure and reflects the process of social change" (Perry, 2007, p. 12), in that as society evolves so too do the ways in which society is vulnerable to different types of disaster. This approach and understanding is reflected in the *United Nations International Strategy for Disaster Reduction* (UNISDR 2009) which defines a disaster as "a serious disruption of the functioning of a community or a society involving widespread human, material, economic or environmental losses and impacts, which exceeds the ability of the affected community or society to cope using its own resources."

WHY DO WE NEED TO COMMUNICATE DURING A CRISIS?

Central to the management of a crisis is reliable and up-to-date information. The act of communicating is not simply important to responding to a crisis, but when considering the wider management of a crisis. As argued by Vos, Lund, Reich, and Harro-Loit (2011) communication is necessary throughout the different stages of a crisis, where "the goal of communication is to reduce uncertainty about response, resolution, negative consequences, public perception, and blame of the situation" (p. 17). For Leiss (1996) in the preparation and warning phase, communication is often in the form of risk communication, that is, informing others of the risks they potentially face. Alternatively, during the response and recovery phase, crisis communication occurs, referred to by Coombs (2011) as, "the collection, processing, and dissemination of information required to address a crisis situation" (p. 20).

Communication is essential for responders and the public alike, to, among other factors, build their situational awareness, as it helps to build capacity within decision-making. Generally speaking, situational awareness involves "knowing what is going on around you" (Endsley, 2000, p. 5). Although debated, a general definition of situational awareness concerns "the perception of the elements in the environment within a volume of time and space, the comprehension of their meaning and the projection of their status in the near future" (p. 5). Situational awareness then, is crucial for decision-making among stakeholders caught up in responding to and managing a crisis. Consequently, trustworthy and reliable communication is essential for crisis management activities. Why, then, is social networking becoming essential to crisis management?

INNOVATION IN CRISIS COMMUNICATION: THE RISE OF SOCIAL NETWORKING

Social networking in times of crisis is taking place amongst the public and by those involved in responding to crises. The following subsections examine how these different groups are employing SNS to enhance their capabilities.

Social Networking and the Public

The study of the sociology of disaster has provided us with crucial insights into the ways in which society manages and responds to a crisis. For Dynes (2006) an important concept to understanding the ways in which communities deal with a crisis is—capital. As Dynes explains, capital comes in different forms, including: physical (e.g., the tools to build houses, streets to create the environment we reside in on a daily basis), human (e.g., the establishment and running of schools and hospitals to provide society with the required skills) and social (e.g., the social networks and relationships within a community). Consequently, when understanding the role of social networking in times of crisis from the perspective of the public, one way of understanding the growth and importance of the activities associated with social networking is by examining it in relation to social capital. Prior to doing so, it is necessary to note that the presence of physical and human capital in relation to social networking, that is, the hardware and skills to utilize social networking applications and other types of new media, is a prerequisite for any real value to emerge from SNS in the form of social capital. Within a disaster framework, thinking about the emergence of social capital is essential for "seeing social systems as active resources, not passive victims, shifting the focus away from human vulnerability toward an emphasis on human capability. It has the advantage of identifying the creation of social resources in emergency situations, rather than focusing primarily on the destruction of physical capital" (p. 23).

Dynes (2006) draws on the work of James Coleman, by exploring six types of social capital: obligations and expectations, information potential, norms and effective sanctions, authority relations, appropriable social organizations, and intentional organizations. Whilst these different types of social capital are crucial to understanding the value of social relationships in responding to a crisis, for the present chapter, our focus will predominantly be placed on how social networking can help to facilitate the emergence of social capital in a crisis in the form of information potential, which involves obtaining information to support actions to be taken. What then are the different functions and roles that social networking can play in collecting and sharing information during a crisis?

During a crisis, SNSs can be extremely effective tools for the public to use in alerting others and sharing information that they themselves possess, or that they have been exposed to from other organizations. For instance, during Hurricane Sandy in the United States in 2012, social media acted as a useful mechanism for members of the public to share, or relay, critical weather-related information with others in their social networks (Papadimitriou et al., 2013). During Sandy, not only is there extensive evidence of the public using SNSs such as Twitter for looking to share news and information, but the ways in which they did so changed over time, from a global reach to a more localized form of news sharing, through the use of more specific hash tags (Knoblich, 2014). In this sense, SNSs can support one-way communication by pushing and disseminating localized crisis-related information. However, they are also useful tools for facilitating two-way communication. For instance, following the eruption of Eyjafjallajö kull in Iceland in 2010, and the stranding of passengers across Europe (and beyond), Watson and Finn (2013) noted the use of social media, particularly Facebook, for facilitating interaction between stranded passengers and those with local information that were able to support information gathering activities (e.g., train routes).

The emergence of information potential through social networking in times of crisis is evident. However, underlying the growth of this form of social capital is the desire and/or willingness to share information with others in your network, and thus social capital in the form of obligation and expectations also plays a role, and needs to be present, for social networking to be effective in times of crisis. If we take the example of the emergence of citizen reporting during the 2007 California Wildfires, we can see that SNSs enabled citizens to participate in the reporting of local information, via acts of citizen journalism. During their study of the wildfires, Novak and Vidoloff (2011) found that citizens used social networking to develop and run a citizen-led response website, RimoftheWorld.net (ROTW) to provide up-to-date information to other community members and responders. As argued by Novak and Vidoloff, in the past, the media, particularly local radio, acted as a go-to mechanism for communities to find information about unfolding events in a crisis; today, the Internet plays a significant role in enabling communities and local networks to work together to provide timely and accurate local information. Localized knowledge is crucial to supporting community efforts in understanding and responding to a potential threat. Furthermore, such a community-led initiative provides people facing a similar situation to connect with one another. Matheson (2014) recently reported how, following the earthquake in Christchurch, New Zealand in 2010, students utilized Facebook to create an event to organize a mass clean-up effort, where a group of over 2,500 responders cleared 65,000 tonnes of silt. The group, the "Student Volunteer Army," was again mobilized following another earthquake in 2011, by which time 13,000 volunteers had come forward to help in the first week, and the by the third week 27,000 volunteers offered their services. As reported by Matheson, "The tools in our pockets—cell phones, Google maps, Facebook, Twitter and everything in between—were the key to our success" (p. 104).

Social networking has also contributed to the further mobilization of human resources through what has become known as crowdsourcing efforts, in responding to an event. Within crisis management, crowdsourcing involves the process whereby a large group can be called upon, or spontaneously brought together in order to obtain information (e.g., images of destruction, or the processing and checking of information). Countless examples can be provided regarding the joint collaboration of many digital volunteers who operate together as a network of persons using their skills to help respond to a pressing need. For instance, following Typhoon Haiyan, the destruction caused by the typhoon was virtually mapped, care of MicroMappers, by way of volunteers, processing and sifting through tweets that requested help (Hildebrandt, 2013). Furthermore, following the missing Malaysia Airlines flight MH17 in March 2014, the crowd was harnessed by Tomnod, a commercial satellite imaging company which provided a series of satellite images of potential search and rescue sites. Individuals were then provided access to these images to help filter them and search for any potential sightings. This one incident alone attracted over two million volunteers (Fishwick, 2014). Social networking can therefore support the capacity of communities working offline to build their resilience and enhance their response efforts to crises.

Social networking does not simply enable the sharing of information and reporting, but can also be a useful tool for the mobilization of individuals in times of political crisis. The power of social media in political crises has been seen within the Middle East and the Occupy movement. During the revolutions in Egypt in 2011, a study of the use of social media by Tufekci and Wilson (2012) found social media to be of use in individuals' abilities to learn of and organize demonstrations, thereby helping to facilitate their inclusion in the emerging networks participating in the protests. Likewise, our own study of the use of social media in the 2013 protests in Istanbul demonstrated that there were different types of users on Twitter, including: 1) "update hubs" who use Twitter for learning about updates and sharing these updates with others; 2) "update seekers" who use Twitter to get information about the protests; 3) "opinion followers" who were oriented towards learning about opinions rather than information via Twitter; and 4) "voice makers" who used Twitter primarily to share their opinions about the protests (Baruh & Watson, 2014). Elsewhere, work by Castells (2012), as well as others, has demonstrated how the Occupy movement recently relied upon social networking to facilitate what he refers to as networked social movements that were largely conducted through the coordination of decision-making online and local assemblies.

Whilst social networking can be a useful tool for building community resilience and the mobilization of action in times of crisis, particularly in making individuals more proactive in the consumption and sharing of information, as will be seen in the "open issues" section, it is not without its challenges. First however, let us consider how social networking is used by response organizations.

SOCIAL NETWORKING BY RESPONSE ORGANIZATIONS

Preparation and Response

Response organizations use social media in the context of crises both for preparing the public for a crisis and as a tool of response during a crisis. As outlined earlier in this chapter these are distinguished between risk and crisis communication (Blaha et al., 2013). In preparation for crises, the use of social media for risk communication can contribute toward "making diagnoses of vulnerabilities in systems and infrastructures"; where during a crisis, social networks can be "used to facilitate and simplify search and rescue actions"; and, finally, social networks may also be used to "enhance control and community connectedness" in the recovery phase of a crisis (Kotsiopoulos, Yannopoulos, in't Veld, & de Vries, 2013, p. 6). Social networks can help citizens be better prepared for crises by receiving updated information that warns about possible severe disruptions or life-threatening situations. Indeed, the importance of effective preparation of the public is "central to building resilience within the community so as to respond to a crisis" (Watson, Wadhwa, Groenendaal, de Vries, & Papadimitriou, 2013, p. 90). However, it is also important to remember that the use of social media in preparation for a possible crisis has to be planned bearing in mind the audiences and penetration levels of new technologies in a particular area, particularly when considering complexities with the digital divide. As Easton (2014) notes, use of social media and ICT technologies for emergency management may have a "marginalizing impact" (p. 276). For example, certain segments of the population, such as the elderly and people with disabilities, may end up not receiving crucial information due to lack of access to ICTs. Likewise, such segments may be further disadvantaged when emergency planning and response rely on data (e.g., GIS, social media) that disproportionately represents the needs of the population with access to ICTs. In case of communication breakdown the use of battery-powered radios can be a more viable communication tool when electrical power or communication networks break down in the affected areas (Ewart & Dekker, 2013).

In the response phase, social media can be of help to support organizations by enhancing their information-gathering and problem-solving capacities, as well as offering "that unique ability in order to engage and listen in real time to the needs of the citizens" (Herman quoted in O'Connell, 2012). The incoming flow of information can help to play a critical role in directing first responses, by dispatching volunteers to the places where they are needed most and coordinating operations more efficiently (Corbin, 2012).

If the public is well prepared, it can improve its own ability to respond before organized help arrives, as well as assisting response organizations in a common effort to analyze large quantities of data. The use of social media in times of crisis has also shown that response organizations have increasing pressure to adapt to new scenarios as the public might engage with a crisis independently whether the organization is using new media technologies in dealing with a crisis or not.

Engagement with the Public

While the review of relevant research discussed in this chapter seems to suggest that response organizations are increasingly using SNSs to engage with the public, it has also to be noted that social media are still used inconsistently, for example, across different countries that are part of the European Union. Nevertheless, many response organizations have started to more effectively use SNSs to increase awareness and preparedness for emergencies. For example, prior to Hurricane Sandy, the Maryland Emergency Management Agency used Pinterest (http://m.pinterest.com/mdmema/hurricane-sandy/) to post striking pictures to attract the attention of the public to the impending storm and provide instructions on how to prepare for it. However, even when using SNSs, as the example above suggests, most response organizations tend to rely on an approach that communicates "to citizens" rather than "with citizens," therefore limiting the interactive possibilities offered by an increasing number of SNS applications such as Twitter and Facebook. In other words, it has been noted that there is "very scant evidence suggesting that agencies utilize citizens who may have expertise (as a result of their own experience) to help improve emergency preparedness" (Baruh et al., 2014, p. 5).

In the response phase, SNSs have proved to be an increasingly important asset in raising situational awareness and organizing action. At times, members of the public have initiated the use of SNSs. Indeed, in the aftermath of the 2010 Haiti earthquake, an updated mapping of the region, fundraising, and a database of missing people were initiated, developed, and maintained by self-organized members of the public rather than responding agencies (Ward & Wasserman, 2010). On the other hand, organizations are increasingly using SNSs to share updates, collect information, and act on incoming information regarding victims in need of help. For instance, during Hurricane Sandy the New York Fire Department (FDNY) not only provided information through its official Twitter feed (https://twitter.com/FDNY) but also responded to individuals tweeting for help, asking for more information, and relaying the information to dispatch units for assistance. Likewise, in the aftermath of a recent earthquake in Turkey (in the eastern region in Van, 2011), AKUT, a national rescue team, used a small team of volunteers to track requests coming from social media, and reportedly rescued an individual who called for help via Twitter.

Challenge: Resistance and Organizational Structure

The use of social media in helping the response to crises has been met with a number of challenges, the first being the will, or not, of a responding organization to engage proactively in the use and management of such tools. Indeed, they might still resist using new media technologies for issues related to their own organizational structure. Whilst organizations such as the Federal Emergency Management Agency (FEMA) or the Red Cross in the United States have been leading the efforts for benefitting from social media, by the end of 2013 the national coordinating authority of a large European country like Italy, the National Civil Protection Service (NCPS), still resists the widespread use of SNSs at the national level. As its head of Volunteering, Training, and Communication stated in an interview, the NCPS would use social media only for preparation and awareness campaigns, keeping a "responsible observation" approach by looking at use of social media in situations of crisis elsewhere. The main reason for this approach is the fear that, if a bidirectional channel is opened for communication, it is "difficult to pretend that communication will go only one-way" and that, therefore, the management of such flows of communication can be something that the current systems used by the NCPS would not be adequately equipped to deal with (Licata, 2013).

Interestingly, Rapisardi (2010) noted that in the Italian context there is still much to do to fully utilize the potential of citizens in emergencies, to make the best use of the public efforts in providing reliable information to deal with emergencies in a more efficient way. Rapisardi has pointed out that factors including low levels of Web literacy and collaboration among NCPS bodies and the lack of investment in experimenting with and implementing such technologies is hindering the potential of citizens to be proactive actors in emergency situations. This case highlights the risks of not harnessing the opportunities offered by the use of social media in a crisis, but also, the issue of information overload which is a major challenge for responding authorities to deal with when flooded by the public's response during or in the aftermath of a disastrous event.

Challenge: Information Overload

While in the past access to the media was limited by the traditional gateway function performed by print and broadcast media producers, there has been an exponential increase in the quantity of information that is posted, tagged, and shared in countries where the public has access to SNS platforms. As a leading expert in this area has stated, "one of the major challenges of humanitarian response is to adapt to this changing environment and extracting out the informative, actionable and credible information out of unstructured and noisy data generated" (Meier, 2014). However, it is also important to point out that the interest of public and private institutions in harnessing the potential of Big Data has also meant that there is a constant development of tools that are able to extract information that can be relevant to responding authorities (Imran, Elbassuoni, Castillo, Diaz, & Meier, 2013). In fact, such tools can help to improve situational awareness, help to provide precious information to first responders, monitor public health, and anticipate population displacement related to crisis (Cassa, Chunara, Mandl, & Brownstein, 2013).

Whilst the use of social media applications can indeed benefit the management of crises, it is important to note that there are a number of open issues that must be considered in order to optimise the use of SNSs as part of crisis management activities.

OPEN ISSUES

As the preceding sections have outlined, the use of SNSs by members of the public and emergency response organizations may offer important benefits in all stages of crisis management. However, the use of SNSs during emergencies also brings about a number of issues, particularly pertaining to dissemination of misinformation and the privacy of individuals. In the remainder of this chapter, we will focus on these two challenges by providing examples from recent case studies and summarize scholarly work regarding their implications.

Misinformation

The pace with which a rumor, defined as an "unverified account or explanation of events circulating from person to person" (Peterson & Gist, 1951, p. 159), can disseminate via SNSs has made misinformation an increasingly relevant ethical concern in emergency communications.

In general, misinformation can be either the result of certain groups or individuals within a society trying to manipulate an event to deceive others or it can stem from the dissemination of inaccurate information about an event without any malicious intent. An illustrative example of the former type of misinformation transpired in the aftermath of the Boston Marathon bombing, when a single, fake, tweet, posted on the hacked *Associated Press* official Twitter account, reported that there were explosions at the White House and that President Obama was injured. Until minutes later, when it was noticed that the *AP* account had been hacked, Dow Jones had already lost 140 points, wiping out close to 140 million US dollars of financial value (Foster, 2013).

The Boston Marathon bombing incident also provides a landmark example of how social media users may have unintentionally contributed to dissemination of misinformation, when sharing information via SNS platforms and social media outlets such as Reddit (mis)identifying Mr. Sunil Tripathi, an innocent man, as the bomber in the aftermath of the April 15, 2013 Boston bombings. Indeed, in a study that focused on how social media was utilized to disseminate information in the aftermath of the Boston bombings, Starbird, Maddock, Orand, Achterman, and Mason (2014) have observed that out of the 10.6 million tweets they collected, 29,416 contained misinformation identifying Mr. Tripathi and only 4,485 tweets correcting the information. During a timespan of six hours, one to three tweets per minute linked Mr. Tripathi to the bombing.

It should be noted that a number of factors might contribute to the spread of rumors. First, rumors are more likely to spread at times of uncertainty when people try to make sense of what is happening (Bordia & DiFonzo, 2004). Second, according to Pezzo and Beckstead (2006), any traumatic event or threat that increases situational anxiety of the public will induce members of the public to spread misinformation as an adaptive behavior, to warn their loved ones against a potential threat just in case the threat is true. Third, where situational anxiety is high, individuals will be more likely to seek socialization and share the rumors as a way of socialization (Pezzo & Beckstead, 2006). Namely, the anxiety that misinformation creates may often be a factor that leads to the further dissemination of misinformation. This may explain findings suggesting that whilst word of mouth continues to be the most common way through which such misinformation spreads, the use of SMSs and SNSs have been shown in various crises, such as the SARS epidemic in 2003, to amplify rumors (Bai, 2012).

Another factor to consider in the dissemination of misinformation concerns the role that the public may play as citizen reporters during emergencies. Thanks to the wide dissemination of mobile devices that can allow the recording of incidents and the ease with which individuals can use SNSs, including but not limited to microblogging sites, to disseminate information, citizen reporting is becoming a key component of emergency communications. As Liebes and Kampf (2010) note, immediacy is among the most important aspects of newsgathering and sharing via SNSs, making reliability of information an afterthought at best. However, a considerable proportion of citizen reporters are not sufficiently versed in ethical codes of reporting that are used in journalism and conventions related to fact-checking (Riaz & Pasha, 2011). Consequently, particularly at times of crises when pressure for the quick delivery of information is more pressing, citizen reporters may frequently resort to what has been named as "publish, then filter" which involves publishing the received information without engaging in fact-checking and then waiting for the crowds to filter false information (Bowman & Willis, 2003). As the aforementioned data from Starbird et al. (2014) research suggests, the logic of "publish, then filter" may lag behind misinformation both in terms of the level of dissemination and the timing.

One potential solution that has been proposed to address the problem of information reliability in citizen journalism, and particularly within the context of reporting during emergencies, is increasing collaboration between citizen journalists and traditional media. Accordingly, citizen reporting can benefit from the institutional aspects of mainstream media through close collaboration (Riaz & Pasha, 2011). For example, an approach increasingly used by citizen journalism websites like OhmyNews.com and NowPublic.com, called the "tier 1.5 approach" aims to get professional and citizen journalists to cooperate in fact-checking and story editing (Martha, 2010). Yet, recent incidents suggest that mainstream journalism may likewise be susceptible to misinformation spread via social media. For example, after the quick dissemination of rumors in social media misidentifying Mr. Tripathi, who was later discovered to be a suicide victim, as the culprit of the Boston Marathon bombings, *New York Post* printed his photo as one of the culprits. Describing this lapse, Hern (2013) argues that the interlinkage between social media and crowdsourcing "led to images stripped of their context being passed around as though they were confirmed."

The dissemination of misinformation during emergencies may have important short-term as well as long-term implications. For example, while the stock market was quick to recover from the rumor about explosions in the White House (summarized above), the dissemination of such misinformation may have long-term effects on financial markets and the economy. Namely, effects of such rumors on financial markets, according to Kimmel (2004), may be regressive and consequently be "stuck" in an upward or a downward trend depending on the nature of the rumor. Likewise, in addition to the psychological pain it may have inflicted on a family that is already experiencing an important trauma as a result of the loss of their son, the misidentification of Mr. Tripathi as a culprit in the Boston Marathon bombings is indicative of a number of important problems that may, generally, threaten social trust and, specifically, impede on emergency response.

Theories like "terror management theory" suggest that when there is a perceived threat to public safety, such as in the wake of the Boston bombings or more recently when the first case of Ebola appeared in United States in 2014, vigilant attention disproportionately focuses on certain segments of the population who are stereotypically linked to a specific form of threat (Shoshani & Slone, 2008). For example, a study by McCauley, Minsky and Viswanath (2013) indicates that during the H1N1 influenza outbreak, stereotypes about Latinos factored into how Latinos were stigmatized by some Americans as virus carriers. Similarly, in the aftermath of the appearance of the Ebola virus in the United States, reports of stigmatization of individuals of African descent are frequent: "West Africans here say they have been ostracized because of the fear generated by the illness. Some people refuse to shake their hands. A cough brings unwanted attention. Some have been asked to leave work and go home 'to sit for a while'" (Brown & Constable, 2014). Furthermore, even single exposure to information that triggers stereotypical attributions may decrease trust and empathy in racial/ethnic others (Watson & Wadhwa, 2014). This implies that even when false information (or misrepresentation) is corrected through the "publish, then filter" logic, it may still have contributed to the perpetuation of stereotypes. Evidence suggests that such stereotypical perceptions about ethnic others may also influence whether individuals will be willing to assist victims in the wake of an emergency (Saucier, McManus, & Smith, 2010). For example, in a study conducted in the aftermath of Hurricane Katrina, individuals who held stronger negative attitudes about African Americans were more likely to place the blame on victims, more likely to underestimate the severity of the crisis, and less likely to think that the victims needed help (McManus & Saucier, 2012).

Privacy and Confidentiality

The example regarding the misidentification of Mr. Tripathi is also illustrative of how dissemination of information via SNSs may also have severe privacy implications, such as when the undue attention placed on Mr. Tripathi led to widespread publicity of his suicide and the trauma his family went through. Likewise, the use of recording devices, social media, and crowdsourcing applications in the wake of a crisis may result in the exposure of personally identifiable information (including name and other forms of identity or geographical information).

Hence, safeguarding the anonymity of individuals constitutes a necessary but not sufficient precaution. Namely, even when personal identity information may be masked, there is still the threat that the collection and analysis of weak identifiers could lead to a person's true identity being exposed (Palen et al., 2010; Yates & Paquette, 2011). Particularly in a political crisis, the identification of individuals through such means is increasingly common. For example, this was seen during revolutions in Iran in 2009 where officials analyzed social media usage in order to identify and target online dissidents (Joseph, 2012). Likewise, the Turkish government's attempt to control dissidents' use of social media, specifically Twitter, during the Gezi Protests began with police custodies of thirty-eight Twitter users for "encouraging the commission of a crime" via social media (Iacucci & Barrow, 2013).

While the examples above may seem like isolated incidents, the revelations made by the NSA subcontractor Edward Snowden and published by *The Guardian* and *The Washington Post* underline the extent of the threat that government access to information stored in networked settings may be vulnerable to state surveillance (The NSA Files, 2013). Indeed, recently, FBI director James Comey has called for a government-mandated method that would provide a backdoor (although he refrained from using the term as such) for FBI to access any encrypted communication (Timm, 2014).

In a crisis context, the fact that government authorities can have access to increasingly more detailed information about users' activities without their knowledge and consent may have important consequences for freedom of association and freedom of speech. That is, without proper safeguards for privacy, the potential permanence and diffusiveness of data about individuals may have a chilling effect on the extent to which dissenting opinions can be shaped and communicated (Baruh, 2007).

Given the privacy implications of SNS usage during emergencies or crises, balancing the informational needs of various stakeholders, including but not limited to response organizations, with the privacy of individuals presents an important challenge that needs to be addressed both at a theoretical and an applied level. Questions remain, for instance, about whether use of privacy protective frameworks such as "privacy by design" and respect of "contextual integrity" to develop rules of conduct can help enhance protections afforded to individuals while not jeopardizing efficiency of emergency response efforts. Privacy by design principle, for example, argues that rather than adding it as a post-hoc solution, privacy protection should be planned in advance while designing systems (Cavoukian, 2012). This may have important implications for the default level of privacy that should be available in platforms that allow sharing audiovisual material from emergency scenes. At the same time, the concept of "contextual integrity" underlines the notion that data flows about individuals are governed by norms and expectations. These norms and expectations vary depending on a number of factors such as the type of information, actors involved, and the setting. The key to safe-guarding individual privacy is the protection of the contextual integrity of information, which collapses when information that is intended to be used in one context is used in another (Nissenbaum, 2010). This principle may be of crucial importance in developing rules of conduct regarding the secondary uses of information that flow from social media during emergencies.

CONCLUSION

As demonstrated, SNSs are increasingly important tools in the communica-tion of information and building of relationships within the management of a crisis. For the public, SNSs offer the potential for building social capital, providing the public with a role in collecting crisis-related information, and subsequently acting upon this information, thereby helping to build their resilience and therefore enhance their capabilities to respond to a crisis. For those preparing for and responding to a crisis, SNSs offer tools and means for engaging with the public, building trusting relationships and enhancing situa-tional awareness. However, such engagement is not without its challenges. Throughout this chapter we have discussed issues relating to the optimization of social networking in times of crisis including challenges relating to the digital divide, organizations' reluctance to engage with SNSs, the complex-ities and (social) consequences of misinformation and the dangers associated with the use of social networking in times of crises relating to privacy and confidentiality. Moving forward, further research is required to understand and implement good practices in managing these (and other) challenges— only then will it be possible to continue to capitalize on the potential benefits of social networking in times of crisis.

ACKNOWLEDGMENT

This chapter is based on research emanating from the European Commis-sion–funded Contribution of Social Media in Crisis management (COSMIC) project, under grant agreement no. 312737. The views in this paper are those of the authors alone and are in no way intended to reflect those of the European Commission.

REFERENCES

Bai, M. (2012). *Exploring the dynamics of rumors on social media in the Chinese context.* (Unpublished Master's thesis) Uppsala University, Sweden.

Baruh, L. (2007). Read at your own risk: Shrinkage of privacy and interactive media. *New Media & Society* 9 (2): 187–211. doi: 10.1177/1461444807072220.

Baruh, L., A. Papadimitriou, Z. Günel, H. M. Bal, Y. Salman, S. Scifo, & B. Çildaş. (2014). Report on citizens' involvement in emergency communication. Retrieved from http://www.cosmic-project.eu/sites/default/files/deliverables/D4.1.pdf.

Baruh, L., & H. Watson. (2014). Using Twitter for what? A segmentation study of Twitter usage during Gezi Protests. In *Proceedings of the European Conference on Social Media* (pp. 33–41). Brighton, UK: Academic Conferences and Publishing International Limited.

Blaha, M., M.-C. Bonnamour, R. Miskuf, D. de Vries, J. Groenendaal, & I. Helsloot. (2013). Report on the role of main stakeholders in crisis situations. Retrieved from http://www.cosmic-project.eu/sites/default/files/deliverables/D1.3.pdf.

Bordia, P., & N. DiFonzo. (2004). Problem solving in social interactions on the Internet: Rumor as social cognition. *Social Psychology Quarterly* 67 (1): 33–49.

Bowman, S., & C. Willis. (2003). *We media: How audiences are shaping the future of news and information.* Retrieved from http://www.hypergene.net/wemedia/download/we_media.pdf.

boyd, d. m., & N. B. Ellison. (2010). Social network sites: Definition, history, and scholarship. *IEEE Engineering Management Review* 38 (3): 16–31. doi: 10.1109/EMR.2010.5559139.

Brown, D. L., & P. Constable. (2014, October 16). West Africans in Washington say they are being stigmatized because of Ebola fear. Retrieved from http://www.washingtonpost.com/local/west-africans-in-washington-say-they-are-being-stigmatized-because-of-ebola-fear/2014/10/16/39442d18–54c6–11e4–892e-602188e70e9c_story.html.

Cassa, C., R. Chunara, K. Mandl, & J. S. Brownstein. (2013). Twitter as a sentinel in emergency situations: Lessons from the Boston Marathon explosions. doi: 10.1371/currents.dis.ad70cd1c8bc585e9470046cde334ee4b.

Castells, M. (2012). *Networks of outrage and hope: Social movements in the Internet age.* Cambridge: Polity.

Cavoukian, A. (2012). Privacy by design: Origins, meaning, and prospects for assuring privacy and trust in the information era. In G. O. M. Yee (Ed.), *Privacy protection measures and technologies in business organizations: Aspects and standards* (pp. 170–208). Hershey, PA: IGI Global.

Coombs, W. T. (2011). Parameters for crisis communication. In W. T. Coombs & S. J. Holladay (Eds.), *The handbook of crisis communication.* Hoboken, NJ: John Wiley & Sons.

Dynes, R. R. (2006). Social capital: Dealing with community emergencies. *Homeland Security Affairs* II (2): 1–26. Retrieved from http://www.hsaj.org/?article=2.2.5.

Easton, R. C. (2014). The digital divide, inclusion and access for disabled people in IT supported emergency response systems: A UK and EU-based analysis. In S. R. Hiltz, M. S. Pfaff, L. Plotnick, & P. C. Shih (Eds.), *Proceedings of the 11th International ISCRAM Conference* (pp. 275–278). University Park, PA. Retrieved from http://iscram2014.ist.psu.edu/sites/default/files/misc/proceedings/p103.pdf.

Endsley, M. R. (2000). Theoretical underpinnings of situation awareness: A critical review. In M. R. Endsley (Ed.), *Situation awareness analysis and measurement* (pp. 3–32). Boca Raton, FL: CRC Press.

European Commission (2010, May 8). The EU internal security strategy in action: Five steps towards a more secure Europe. Brussels. Retrieved from http://eur-lex.europa.eu/LexUriServ/LexUriServ.do?uri=COM:2010:0673:FIN:EN:PDF#page=2.

Ewart, J., & S. Dekker. (2013). Radio, someone still loves you! Talkback radio and community emergence during disasters. *Continuum* 27 (3): 365–81. doi: 10.1080/10304312.2013.772106.

Fishwick, C. (2014). Why did so many people share graphic images of MH17 crash site on social media? Retrieved from http://www.theguardian.com/world/2014/jul/22/graphic-images-dead-bodies-mh17–malaysian-airlines-crash-site-social-media.

Foster, P. (2013). "Bogus" AP Tweet about explosion at the White House wipes billions off US markets. Retrieved from http://www.telegraph.co.uk/finance/markets/10013768/Bogus-AP-tweet-about-explosion-at-the-White-House-wipes-billions-off-US-markets.html.

Hern, A. (2013). When crowdsourcing goes wrong: Reddit, Boston and missing student Sunil Tripathi. Retrieved from http://www.newstatesman.com/world-affairs/2013/04/when-crowdsourcing-goes-wrong-reddit-boston-and-missing-student-sunil-tripathi.

Hildebrandt, A. (2013). Typhoon Haiyan creates testing ground for crisis mappers. Retrieved October 07, 2014, from http://www.cbc.ca/news/world/typhoon-haiyan-creates-testing-ground-for-crisis-mappers-1.2462119.

Iacucci, A. A., & G. Barrow. (2013). *Social media in emergencies*. Retrieved from http://www.internews.org/sites/default/files/resources/101_report_on_social_media_in_emergencies_2013-12.pdf.

Imran, M., S. Elbassuoni, C. Castillo, F. Diaz, & P. Meier. (2013). Practical extraction of disaster-relevant information from social media. *Proceedings of the 22nd International Conference on World Wide Web Companion*, 1021–24. http://dl.acm.org/citation.cfm?id=2487788.2488109.

Joseph, S. (2012). Social media, political change, and human rights. *Boston College International and Comparative Law Review* 35 (1): 145–188.

Kimmel, A. J. (2004). Rumors and the financial marketplace. *Journal of Behavioral Finance* 5 (3): 134–141.

Knoblich, T. (2014). Hurricane Sandy and the adoption of citizen journalism platforms. In E. Thorsen & S. Allan (Eds.), *Citizen journalism: Global perspectives, Volume Two* (pp. 113–125). Oxford: Peter Lang Publishing, Inc.

Kotsiopoulos, I., A. Yannopoulos, M. in't Veld, & D. de Vries. (2013). Final report on the use of emerging technologies in crisis situations. Retrieved from http://www.cosmic-project.eu/sites/default/files/deliverables/D3.1.2.pdf.

Leiss, W. (1996). *In the chamber of risks: Understanding risk controversies*. Montreal: McGill-Queen's University Press.

Licata, P (2013). Catastrofi. Postiglione: "Su uso dei social network serve cautela." Retrieved from http://www.corrierecomunicazioni.it/it-world/23641_catastrofi-postiglione-su-uso-dei-social-network-serve-cautela.htm.

Liebes, T., & Z. Kampf. (2010). Homullus medius: Transforming the logic of reporting at crisis. *Dynamics of Asymmetric Conflict: Pathways toward Terrorism and Genocide* 3(2): 86–98.

Martha, J. (2010). The social evolution of citizen journalism. *Canadian Journal of Media Studies* 6 (1): 95–158.

Matheson, D. (2014). Tools in their pockets: How personal media were used during the Christchurch Earthquakes. In E. Thorsen & S. Allan (Eds.), *Citizen journalism: Global perspectives, Volume Two* (pp. 99–111). Oxford: Peter Lang Publishing.

McCauley, M., S. Minsky, & K. Viswanath. (2013). The H1N1 pandemic: Media frames, stigmatization and coping. *BMC Public Health* 13:1116.

McManus, J. L., & D. A. Saucier. (2012). Helping natural disaster victims depends on characteristics and perceptions of victims. A response to "Who helps natural disaster victims?" *Analyses of Social Issues and Public Policy* 12:272–275.

Meier, P. (2014, September 4). Keynote Speech, Cosmic Workshop: Involving citizens in emergency preparedness and response. Istanbul.

Nissenbaum, H. F. (2010). *Privacy in context: Technology, policy, and the integrity of social life*. Redwood City, CA: Stanford Law Books.

Novak, J. M., & K. G. Vidoloff. (2011). New frames on crisis: Citizen journalism changing the dynamics of crisis communication. *International Journal of Mass Emergencies and Disasters* 29 (3): 181–202.

The NSA files Edward Snowden: The whistleblower behind the NSA surveillance revelations. (2013). Retrieved from http://www.theguardian.com/world/2013/jun/09/edward-snowden-nsa-whistleblower-surveillance.

O'Connell, M. (2012, December 12). Agencies turn to social media to engage public in an emergency—FederalNewsRadio.com. *Federal News Radio*. Retrieved from http://

www.federalnewsradio.com/445/3152420/Agencies-turn-to-social-media-to-engage-public-in-an-emergency.

Palen, L., K. M. Anderson, G. Mark, J. Martin, D. Sicker, M. Palmer, & D. Grunwald. (2010). A vision for technology-mediated support for public participation & assistance in mass emergencies & disasters." In *Proceedings of ACM-BCS Visions of Computer Science , 8:1–8:12,* British Computer Society. Retrieved from http://dl.acm.org/citation.cfm?id=1811182.1811194.

Palen, L., S. Vieweg, S. B. Liu, & A. L. Hughes. (2009). Crisis in a networked world: Features of computer-mediated communication in the April 16, 2007, Virginia Tech Event. *Social Science Computer Review* 27 (4): 467–480. doi: 10.1177/0894439309332302.

Papadimitriou, A., A. Yannopoulos, I. Kotsiopoulos, R. L. Finn, H. Watson, K. Wadhwa, & L. Baruh. (2013). *Case studies of communication media and their use in crisis situations.* Retrieved from http://pt.slideshare.net/socialmediadna/social-media-case-studies-cosmic-project

Perry, R. W. (2007). What is a disaster? In H. Rodriguez, E. L. Quarantelli, & R. R. Dynes (Eds.), *Handbook of disaster research* (pp. 1–15). New York: Springer.

Peterson, W. A., & N. P. Gist. (1951). Rumor and public opinion. *American Journal of Sociology* 57 (2): 159–167.

Pezzo, M. V., & J. W. Beckstead. (2006). A multilevel analysis of rumor transmission: Effects of anxiety and belief in two field experiments. *Basic and Applied Social Psychology* 28:91–100.

Procopio, C. H., & S. T. Procopio. (2007). Do you know what it means to miss New Orleans? Internet communication, geographic community, and social capital in crisis. *Journal of Applied Communication Research* 35 (1): 67–87. doi: 10.1080/00909880601065722.

Rapisardi, E. (2010). *Building civil protection 2.0.* Retrieved October 19, 2014 from http://www.slideshare.net/elenis/building-civil-protection-20-updated.

Riaz, S., & S. A. Pasha. (2011). Role of citizen journalism in strengthening societies. *FWU Journal of Social Sciences* 5 (1): 88–103.

Saucier, D. A., J. K. McManus, & S. J. Smith. (2010). Discrimination against out-group members in helping situations. In S. Stürmer & M. Synder (Eds.), *The psychology of prosocial behavior: Group processes, intergroup relations, and helping* (pp. 103–120). Oxford: Wiley-Blackwell.

Shoshani, A., & M. Slone. (2008). The drama of media coverage of terrorism: Emotional and attitudinal impact on the audience. *Studies in Conflict & Terrorism* 31:627–640.

Soanes, C. (Ed.). (2002). *Paperback Oxford English dictionary.* Oxford: Oxford University Press.

Starbird, K., J. Maddock, M. Orand, P. Achterman, & R. M. Mason. (2014). Rumors, false flags, and digital vigilantes: Misinformation on Twitter after the 2013 Boston Marathon bombing. In *iConference.* Berlin, Germany.

Tapia, A., N. LaLone, & H.-W. Kim. (2014). Run amok: Group crowd participation in identifying the bomb and bomber from the Boston Marathon bombing. In *Proceedings of the 11th International ISCRAM Conference.* Pennsylvania, USA.

Timm, T. (2014, October 17). The government wants tech companies to give them a backdoor to your electronic life. Retrieved from http://www.theguardian.com/commentisfree/2014/oct/17/government-internet-backdoor-surveillance-fbi.

Tufekci, Z., & C. Wilson. (2012). Social media and the decision to participate in political protest: Observations from Tahrir Square. *Journal of Communication* 62 (2): 363–379.

UNISDR. (2009). *UNISDR terminology on disaster risk.* Retrieved from http://www.unisdr.org/we/inform/publications/7817.

Vieweg, S., L. Palen, & S. Liu. (2008). Collective intelligence in disaster: An examination of the phenomenon in the aftermath of the 2007 Virginia Tech Shootings. In F. Friedich & B. Van de Walle (Eds.), *Proceedings of the 5th International ISCRAM Conference* (pp. 44–54). Washington DC, USA.

Vos, M., R. Lund, Z. Reich, & H. Harro-Loit. (2011). *Developing a crisis communication scorecard.* University Library of Jyväskylä.

Ward, S. J. A., & H. Wasserman. (2010). Towards an open ethics: Implications of new media platforms for global ethics discourse. *Journal of Mass Media Ethics* 25 (4): 275–292. doi: 10.1080/08900523.2010.512825.

Watson, H. (2011). Preconditions for citizen journalism: A sociological assessment. *Sociological Research Online* 16 (3). Retrieved from http://www.socresonline.org.uk/16/3/6.html.

Watson, H., & R. L. Finn. (2013). Privacy and ethical implications of the use of social media during a volcanic eruption: Some initial thoughts. In J. G. & T. M. T. Comes, F. Fiedrich, S. Fortier (Eds.), *Proceedings of the 10th International ISCRAM Conference*, Baden-Baden, Germany. Retrieved from http://www.iscramlive.org/ISCRAM2013/files/241.pdf.

Watson, H., & K. Wadhwa. (2014). The evolution of citizen journalism in crises: From reporting to crisis management. In E. Thorsen & S. Allan (Eds.), *Citizen journalism: Global perspectives, Volume Two* (pp. 321–332). New York: Peter Lang Publishing.

Watson, H., K. Wadhwa, J. Groenendaal, D. de Vries, & A. Papadimitriou. (2013). Report on search and rescue actions. Retrieved from http://www.cosmic-project.eu/sites/default/files/deliverables/D1.2.pdf.

Yates, D., & S. Paquette. (2011). Emergency knowledge management and social media technologies: A case study of the 2010 Haitian earthquake. *International Journal of Information Management* 31 (1): 6–13. doi:10.1016/j.ijinfomgt.2010.10.001.

Zoidberg. (2001). Rage like a fist. Retrieved from http://zoidberg.livejournal.com/2001/09/11/.

Chapter Eight

Social Networking Technologies and Social Movements

Zeynep Günel and Lemi Baruh

Use of social networking sites, henceforth referred to as "SNSs," by the masses has become ubiquitous. Proliferation and integration of SNSs such as microblogging sites into daily lives have allowed people to link and interact with each other irrespective of time or space, causing significant changes in collective movements.

Following the definition proposed by Diani (2000) "social movements can be regarded as networks of informal relationships between a multiplicity of individuals and organizations, who share a distinctive collective identity, and mobilize resources on conflictual issues" (p. 387). Similar to Diani, Gerlach (2001) suggested that the actors of social movements are not isolated from each other, but linked, forming an integrated network of exchange and joint action. Castells (2012) argues that the Internet has created the space for networking; a "space of autonomy" for the individual where exchange of information and linking with others is possible. He posits that online networks give rise to new forms of participation based on horizontal, decentralized, flexible networks forming across multiple levels.

Facilitated by SNSs, activists are able to organize, collaborate, and mobilize at greater speeds and lower costs. Online networks connect physically separated actors together and provide a new means for building instantaneous networks; thereby facilitating real-time communication and coordination that allows them to engage in joint action. Increased, diversified and recurrent interactions boosted by SNSs allow the individuals to get engaged in multiple networks concurrently rather than being part of a single network. Consequently, social activist networks become more individualized, permeable, and loosely knit with overlapping social and spatial boundaries that replace hierarchical, impenetrable structures (Wellman, 2001).

This chapter elaborates on the effects of SNSs on social movements. The authors review examples from recent social uprisings, particularly Occupy Wall Street, 15-M in Spain, Gezi Park in Turkey and Arab Spring where we see how diffusion of SNSs incited the development of networks of relations connecting activists to activists, activists to publics both at the local and global level. The rest of the chapter is structured as follows: The first part discusses how SNSs facilitate the formation of networks thus leading to wide dissemination of information and exchange through networks. In addition, it focuses on the role SNSs play in enhancing group solidarity and facilitating mobilization and diffusion of social movements in a transnational context. The second part of the chapter dwells on the new modes of politics experimented with by the activists. In doing so, it summarizes research regarding the opportunities and challenges faced by this mode of politics. It is argued that the principles adopted by activists in organizing new forms of deliberation are very much interrelated with the logic of networks that is brought about, at least partly, by SNSs. In the last section, the challenges that await the social activism space in relation to increasing dependency of activists on SNSs are summarized.

MOBILIZATION THROUGH NETWORKS

In a public sphere dominated by mass media, the citizens are conventionally seen as only passive receivers in alignment with consumer culture. However, arguably, the Internet and especially the recent growth of social media and SNSs have transformed the power relations between media and individuals by potentially providing a communication platform that allows the formerly passive audiences to become active users that engage in what Castells (2009) names as "mass self-communication." Accordingly, mass self-communication is associated with the resources that individuals nowadays have to create and distribute content/information and even use transnational networks to reach a global audience (Castells, 2009).

This transformation in the communication environment and its effects on activism have become strikingly evident in recent social movements. Challenging the monopoly that mainstream media assumed as a domain for information filtering, sense-making, and political deliberation, protesters have been able to create their own coverage of the protests, "self-direct" their messages through social networks and "self-select" the information deciding on which messages to receive (Castells, 2012, p. 7). In other words, activists now have the means to circumvent mass media gatekeepers and act as publishers and disseminators of information. Even as early as 1999, during the protests known as "The Battle in Seattle," the updates provided by activists via Internet constituted an important alternative to the coverage of the protests in mainstream media sources (Almeida & Lichbach, 2003).

As underlined by recent political unrests, especially—but certainly not only—in relatively more authoritarian regimes within which media is repressed, mass media may often underreport and/or engage in a biased reporting of protests. For example, the 2013 World Press Freedom Index (2013) indicates that, as of 2013, Turkey ranks 154th out of 179 countries in terms of press freedom. Many different factors, including political pressure and conglomeratization of media since the 1990s, have arguably contributed to the formation of a media environment within which dissenting voices are increasingly less likely to be heard. (For a summary of debate regarding the transformation of mass media in Turkey, see Çarkoğlu et al., 2014). In many respects, it was within this context that during the Gezi Protests in Turkey in 2013, 84.2 percent of the protesters reported that their protests were partly a reaction to declining freedom of the press in Turkey (Bilgiç & Kafkaslı, 2013). Indeed, highly critical of lack of reporting and bias in media coverage of the protests, protestors widely utilized social networks both to disseminate and to retrieve up-to-date information (Yüksek, 2014). According to a study in which 4,411 Gezi protesters were interviewed, 69 percent of the protesters found about the events first from social media, while only 7 percent heard them first from TV (Tunç, 2014). Likewise, in a study conducted online, Papadimitriou and colleagues have observed that reliance on mass media as a source of information declined significantly during the protests. For example, while close to half of the respondents reported using websites of newspapers for following news during a typical day, only 6 percent reported using them during the Gezi Protests (Papadimitriou et al., 2014). Conversely, the percent of respondents using social media for getting information during the Gezi Protests increased from 35 percent before the protests to 85 percent during the Gezi Protests (Papadimitriou et al., 2014).

SNSs provide the infrastructure enabling the exchange of information across networks with great ease and speed (Juris, 2004). According to Castells (2012), the contemporary movements are marked by the "viral" diffusion of information through networks. Virally circulating self-produced images and videos in SNSs reaching mass-scale crowds may affect people's decisions to join the protest events. One commonly cited example of the potential of viral images/videos in acting as a catalyst for mobilization of the public is the video blog (vlog) by Asma Mafhouz, famously known as the video which started the Egyptian Revolution 2011. In the video, Asma Mafhouz speaks to the camera and passionately urges people join her in Tahrir Square on the 25th of January, to protest against the government. In the video she said:

> I am making this video to give you one simple message. We want to go down
> to Tahrir Square on January 25th . . . We'll go down and demand our right, our
> fundamental human rights. Your presence with us will make a difference, a big
> difference. (El-Baghdadi, 2011)

The vlog was posted to her personal Facebook account on January 18, 2011, and was put on YouTube on the same day and disseminated over social networks. The fact that the video was posted on YouTube made it almost immediately reachable by a large audience and attracted the attention of the public instantaneously (Wall & Zahed, 2011). On the 25th of January, millions were out in the streets in the major cities, mostly in Tahrir Square in Cairo. Mafhouz's call to her people for action, an individual voice amplified via social networks (Wall & Zahed, 2011), was not the only reason behind the massive protests, but it was a particularly influential one.

Notably, viral videos and images showing citizens being abused and tortured by the police may raise emotions like anger, which may motivate the public to mobilize and react. During the Egyptian revolution, protesters recorded videos showing the police applying violence and shared them via live-streaming platforms, YouTube, and Facebook. Take, for example, a video uploaded to YouTube in December 2011, showing Egyptian soldiers beating a female protester with sticks, hitting her countless times, kicking her in the chest, and then dragging her on the street. It became prominent also in international networks and came to be known as the "blue bra girl" (Blue Bra Girl, 2011). As to the videos showing the police violence, "The viral nature of these videos and the volume and speed with which news on the events in Egypt became available to the wider public in the country and in the world was key to the process of mobilization against Mubarak" (Castells, 2012, p. 59).

Similarly, during the Euromaidan in Ukraine, videos and images showing police were circulated in social media and raised anger which resulted in more people going out into the streets. According to a survey conducted among participants of the Euromaidan, the majority of them (70 percent) said that the police beating of the protesters on November 30, 2013 was one of the main reasons for joining the protests (Maidan-2013, n.d.).

INDIVIDUALS AS THE LOCUS
OF COORDINATION AND ACTION

The open structure of activist networks, combined with the ease with which information can be disseminated via SNSs (and more generally online), makes it possible for every individual to induce or be the locus of a network or a movement. In other words, the individual activist now has the capability to start her own network and disseminate her ideas and even mobilize people.

Castells (2001) names this as the "self-directed networking" referring to the "capacity for anyone to find his or her own destination on the Net" (p. 55). A good case in point is an online organization called VoterMarch. The organization was founded in 2000 by four individuals "who wanted to express their opposition to the irregularities and egregious conduct of Election 2000 and the direction in which an illegitimate administration was taking the country" (About VoterMarch, n.d.). It was founded as an Internet-based activist community using a blog, Google groups, and Twitter to organize its activities. To date, the network created by these four individuals organized several nationwide protests calling for election reform where thousands of people participated (About VoterMarch, n.d.).

According to Lance Bennett, this ability of the individual is in "contrast with the 'modernist' tendency to forge social and political order through mutual identifications with leaders, ideologies and memberships in conventional social and political groups" (Bennett, 2005, p. 112). Similarly, Anduiza and colleagues (Anduiza, Cristancho, & Sabucedo, 2014) suggest that social networks create an opportunity for a new type of participant in social movements: individuals who are not co-members of political parties and who are less institutionally embedded. Hence, Anduiza and colleagues (2014) argue, rather than recruitment of formal members by political parties or unions, the main mobilization channels of social movements are increasingly based on "personal contact and online social networks" (p. 750). Likewise, a study conducted by Baruh and colleagues (2014) suggests that during the Gezi Events in Istanbul in 2013, a considerable proportion of the protestors outright rejected an association with established political parties. And more recently, in Euromaidan protests in Ukraine, social networks were one of the main driving forces enabling people to connect and organize. A survey conducted on the protesters of Euromaidan revealed that around 92 percent of the participants did not belong to any political party or civil organization and said that they came there on their own. On the other hand, only 8 percent of them claimed that their attendance was initiated by the calls of a specific political group (Maidan-2013, n.d.). Notably, the survey was carried out on December 7 and 8, which were the first days of the protests. It was only later that a number of political groups became dominant among the protesters as the clashes between the police and the protesters intensified.

According to Bennett and Segerberg (2011), an important implication of this change is that there is a "growing demand for personalized relations with causes and organizations [which] makes digital technologies increasingly central to the organization and conduct of collective action" (p. 771). In suitable circumstances, SNSs can support people in building collective identities and reinforce their expression of collective identity, which may, in turn, lead to mobilization (Postmes & Brunsting, 2002).

15-M movement in Spain illustrates the potential of online social networks with respect to how they can assist activists to organize, mobilize, and evolve into one massive social movement. The organization of 15-M was actively led by an online platform called "Democracia Real Ya!" (Real Democracy Now). The platform was started as a Facebook group, comprising individuals who thought that the current system was incapable of representing the public. It turned into an activist hub containing nearly 400 organizations. On March 2, they made a call to the public to go out and protest proclaiming: "Real Democracy Now! Go out into the streets. We are not goods in the hands of politicians and bankers" (Castells, 2012, p. 112). In the 15-M protests in Spain there was "intensive use of digital media" and there was "no clear leadership and no involvement of main political organizations" but this did not prevent the call from being heard: 55 percent of the protesters heard about the protests via alternative online media and 49 percent found out via SNSs like Facebook and Twitter (Anduiza, Cristancho, & Sabucedo, 2014). On the 15th of May, thousands of people gathered in the streets in many cities and this was the first one of the protests which became known as 15-M.

TRANSNATIONALIZATION:
MOBILIZATION OF THE DISTANT

Enhanced by social networking technologies, activist networks have become more complex and intertwined (Coopman, 2011). SNSs provide the space for physically disconnected people to exchange information and build ties, thereby increasing the potential of social movements to diffuse to more geographically broader areas (Garrett, 2006). Activists from other countries but working for similar causes are able to exchange information, resources, and tactics as well as build a loose yet collective identity. Regarding the transnational aspect of activism, Tarrow (1998) defines it as "rooted in domestic social networks and connected to one another more than episodically through common ways of seeing the world, or through informal or organizational ties" (p. 184).

Activist networks connected at a transnational level may facilitate the "cross-border" diffusion of the movements by facilitating the networks to share opinions, information about challenges faced, and organizational methodologies (Tarrow, 1998). Especially, common challenges may be effective in creating the space for the diffusion of collective actions across the boundaries. The interaction between 15-M in Spain and Indignant Citizens Movement in Greece in 2011 can provide an example for such a growth of transnational connections related to similar challenges. Just before 15-M, in Spain, the unemployment rate was as high as 20 percent and 70 percent of the population anticipated that the economic situation in the country would be the same or worse the following year (Anduiza, Cristancho, & Sabucedo, 2014). Spanish people took to the streets and, unsurprisingly, one of the main reasons behind the protests was the reaction against the current economic state of the country and the perceived incompetence of the government in coping with the economic crisis (Anduiza, Cristancho, & Sabucedo, 2014).

Similar to Spain, Greece also faced economic problems such as high unemployment which were arguably aggravated further by austerity measures. One of the leading slogans used by the Spaniards in Puerta del Sol was "Shh . . . the Greeks are sleeping" referring to the economic problems Greeks have and their not being on the streets, protesting, at the time (Bennett & Segerberg, 2012). The slogan went viral, diffused through online networks. Greek protesters organized on Facebook networks such as a Facebook page called the "Indignants at Syntagma" (Himanen, 2012). They agreed to go out protesting, and nearly 30,000 people met outside the Greek Parliament on May 25, 2011. As a reply to the call made by Spanish protesters, they hung a banner at the Parliament's front wall, saying "We've awakened! What time is it? Time for them to leave!" (Estamos despiertos, 2011). Activists in Puerto del Sol and Syntagma Square also established live connections and made Skype video calls. Social networking sites were so intensely used in the organization of the protests that the movement was called "May of Facebook" also referring to its connection with 15-M, in addition to its more formal name, "Indignant Citizens Movement" (Himanen, 2012).

However, not all activists are able to harness the benefits of SNSs. First, in many countries, Internet penetration continues to be considerably low, while in others restrictions on Internet use continue to expand. In Cuba, for example, as of 2012 the Internet penetration was as low as 25 percent and only 3.8 percent of households have Internet at home (The little data book, 2014). As such, opportunities for access to international activist networks continue to be limited for Cuban activists. Even so, since 2006, there is a growing group of dissident bloggers whose writing on various topics such as human rights and sexual politics allowed the international community to become more aware of the political problems of daily life in Cuba (Biddle, 2013).

SNSS AND THE ORGANIZATIONAL
STRUCTURE OF ACTIVIST NETWORKS

In addition to influencing how social activists mobilize and how they disseminate/share information, SNSs also have the potential to influence the organizational logic of social activist networks. As Juris argues, the decentralized, horizontal, and self-directed nature of online-networked communi-

cation may indeed have an influence on the organizational structure of activist networks (Juris, 2004). The "networking logic" shaping and carried in
the practices of activists has become inherent to activism space (Juris, 2004).
Specifically, activist networks can emerge to provide information, call for
action, and provide the space for real-time decision-making. As they are
formed by loose initiatives, they may quickly transform, overlap with other
movements, become idle, or even cease to exist as a movement.

Relatedly, network-based politics is based on nonhierarchical horizontal
structures, coordination, and participatory democracy aiming at inclusion of
all members in collective decision-making processes. Many activists from
15-M call it "the new way of doing politics" while some named it "Politics
2.0" emphasizing the linkage between politics and the infusion of online
social networking and other social media platforms into activism.

Creating sustainable and effective decision-making models based on participatory politics was one of the key goals of the Occupy Wall Street Movement during which public spaces were occupied and used as places for gathering. These gatherings were called assemblies. In assemblies, every participant has an equal say, thus they are nonhierarchical. They are based on the
principles of direct democracy, challenging forms of representative democracy and traditional methods of organizing built on top-down, leader-centered
perspectives. David Graeber (2011), one of the leading figures of Occupy
Wall Street Movement, explains the principles adopted in Zuccotti Park as:

> organisers made the audacious decision to operate not only by direct democra-
> cy, without leaders, but by consensus. The first decision ensured that there
> would be no formal leadership structure that could be co-opted or coerced; the
> second, that no majority could bend a minority to its will, but that all crucial
> decisions had to be made by general consent.

Although, there are no leaders or executive committee in assemblies,
people volunteer to moderate discussions and participate in ad-hoc groups
with assigned tasks. In some assemblies, decision-making was based on general and unanimous consent, while other assemblies adopted partial or modified consent which is based on about a 90-percent consensus of the participants. More often than not, within such a decision-making system, the process can become very time consuming with debates lasting for hours, especially in large assemblies. Consequently, in practice, the decentralized, horizontal governance approach may often make it very difficult to achieve even
a modified consensus.

The extent to which this constitutes a problem for loose activist networks
is a question that warrants further debate. On the one hand, the absence of a
demand was seen as one of the main failures of the movement. According to
this view, this failure exposed the movement's weakness as it revealed its

inability to engage in concrete policymaking and, more generally, to unite as a coherent movement (Thomas, 2012). On the other hand, there is also the view that the goal of such movements should not be to propose policy options. For example, activists in the Occupy Wall Street Movement did not formulate and put forth any specific demands. The absence of demands by the movement was interpreted by some as a successful strategy underlining its refusal of the "traditional narrative" of representative democracy. Rushkoff (2013), for instance, sees Occupy Wall Street Movement's resistance as an example of the impact of the network era stimulating the transformation in how people perceive themselves in relation to one another and to institutions. He states, "it is not about winning some debate point and then going home. Rather as the product of the decentralized networked-era culture, it is less about victory than sustainability. It is not about one-pointedness but inclusion" (Rushkoff, 2013, p. 170). Likewise, according to one of the organizers of the Occupy Wall Street Movement, deciding on any clear statement of demands would jeopardize one of the main premises of the Occupy Wall Street Movement as an umbrella for the 99 percent. In this respect, the formalization of an explicit demand would mean the exclusion of some at the expense of others (Bellows, 2012). Hence, in accordance with the participatory model the movement had adopted, if any demand was to be made it had to be developed in consensus, a goal that could hardly be achieved given the heterogeneous structure of the movement. On the other hand, the absence of a demand was also seen as one of the main failures of the movement. According to this view, this failure exposed the movement's weakness as it revealed its inability to unite (Thomas, 2012).

Besides, what may seem like a weakness of a movement like Occupy Wall Street may also be one of the reasons why they are able to allow their members to engage in "maximal coordination and communication" (Juris, 2005, p. 197) at times when there was a need to organize immediate collective action. More generally, as discussed above, loose networks such as the Occupy Wall Street Movement may very quickly change their forms, transform their methods, and even cease to exist in short amounts of time. For example, nearly a year after the Occupy Wall Street Movement, when Hurricane Sandy struck the western coast of the United States, participants of the Occupy Wall Street Movement quickly came together to form Occupy Sandy in order to help the local community recover. Reportedly, in contrast to government authorities which were slow to act, Occupy Sandy was able to mobilize and provide help very quickly, and in many cases, (reportedly) was first to arrive to the disaster (Fauer, 2012). In other words, the OWS movement, partly thanks to its flexible organizational structure, was able to quickly transform itself to into a relief effort.

CONCLUSION

This chapter has discussed the ways in which SNSs affect the process of collective action in social movements. First, it focused on how SNSs may potentially facilitate quicker mobilization. This is partly related to the ways in which SNSs provide the space for activists to have access to more extensive information, discuss with each other, generate, and mass distribute their messages through networks. Accordingly, the costs associated with accessing and disseminating information have reduced notably, equipping activists and the public alike with the ability to challenge the monopoly that mainstream media have on gatekeeping and sense-making functions.

Second, the analysis focused on how SNSs can potentially transform the role that individuals play in initiation of activist networks. Namely, the openness of contemporary activist networks, which is partly enabled by the ease with which information can be created and shared in social networks, "may be shifting the burden of mobilization from organizations to individuals" (Bennett & Segerberg, 2011, p. 772).

Third, the role that SNSs may play in connecting related but independent activist networks on a transnational scale was underlined. Using examples from the 15-M movement in Spain and the protestors in Greece, the chapter discussed how social media was utilized to build rapport between the movements.

Finally, the logic of networking, innate to SNSs, is interrelated with the principles that activists adopt in their practices. The decentralized, nonhierarchical, expanding structure of online networks resonates with conceptions and practices of inclusive, heterogeneous, leaderless, flexible and horizontal forms of organization. The chapter provided an overview of the potential advantages that this form of organizational logic and the ensuing "patterns of social and political interaction" (Juris, 2012, p. 266) may present in terms of challenging the assumptions regarding representative democracy and prioritizing a more participatory form of politics. At the same time, the study summarizes debates regarding whether this organizational logic may implicate the decision-making capability and consequently the long-term sustainability of activist networks.

While the authors' focus has been mostly on the use of SNSs by social activists, it should be noted that use of SNSs works in conjunction with increased utilization of other information and communication technologies, such as smartphones, that enable on-the-spot recording of events and help the communication between activists to be more continuous. In addition, using smartphones and other portable technologies, individuals can engage in sousveillance (first-perspective recording) against police misconduct. Such recordings shared widely in SNSs can be important in creating public awareness. For example, the footage by Ramsey Orta, who witnessed Eric Garner's encounter with police on July 17, 2014, was important in providing an understanding as to how Garner died during the arrest (Speri, 2014). The video became infamous and contributed to the widescale backlash that led to nationwide protests (Kelsey, 2014). Also to be noted is that different SNS platforms may complement each other in terms of fulfilling different functions (Segerberg & Bennett, 2011). For example, while microblogging may often be more useful for activation of networks by notifying others, SNSs, like Facebook, may be more suitable for building spaces of convergence where networks can be sustained through building collective identity among individuals.

While SNSs provide numerous advantages to activists, they also pose various risks. For example, they make their users more susceptible to state monitoring. States are developing new techniques to increase surveillance of online communications and limit the flow of information online. Every year, more countries are "passing new laws to criminalize certain types of political, religious, or social speech" (Kelly, 2013). As also discussed elsewhere in this volume by Watson and colleagues (chapter 7) there is a considerable increase in the number of activists who are arrested and punished for things they have posted on social networks which are seen as against the dominant ideology or critical of the ruling government.

Nonetheless, activists are increasingly mindful of the growing risk of surveillance and seem to be taking some precautions. Activists find ways to circumvent censorship and surveillance by using alternative online tools. Namely, there is a growing tendency to use more "closed" social networking services as alternatives to Twitter and Facebook. For example, Vibe was extensively used during Occupy Wall Street instead of Twitter, for coordinating and sharing information. Vibe doesn't require users to log in and allows its users to determine how far and how long they want their messages to be visible which creates a more secure area for people to communicate through short-range. Likewise, during Turkey's attempt to block social networking sites Facebook and Twitter in March 2014, activists found ways to get around the censorship almost instantly. They used methods like Tor (The Onion Router) and VPN (Virtual Private Network) to hide their IP location. Hotspot Shield, a VPN app, was downloaded 1.1 million times by Turkish people in the first 72 hours and the traffic in Twitter actually went up by 138 percent just after it was banned (Wagstaff, 2014).

Acknowledgment   This chapter is based on research emanating from the European Commission–funded Contribution of Social Media in Crisis management (COSMIC) project, under grant agreement no. 312737. The views in this paper are those of the authors alone and are in no way intended to reflect those of the European Commission.

REFERENCES

About VoterMarch. (n.d.). Retrieved from http://votermarch.blogspot.com/p/about-voter-march.html.

Almeida, P. D., & M. I. Lichbach. (2003). To the Internet, from the Internet: Comparative media coverage of transnational protests. *Mobilization* 8 (3): 249–272.

Anduiza, E., C. Cristancho, & J. M. Sabucedo. (2014). Mobilization through online social networks: The political protest of the indignados in Spain. *Information, Communication & Society* 17 (6): 750–764. doi: 10.1080/1369118X.2013.808360.

Baruh, L., A. Papadimitriou, Z. Günel, H. M. Bal, Y. Salman, S. Schifo, & B. Çildaş. (2014). Deliverable 4.1: Report on citizens' involvement in emergency communication. Retrieved from http://www.cosmic-project.eu/sites/default/files/deliverables/D4.1.pdf.

Bellows, A. (2012). Mind the gap: Connecting the movement to the moderates in India and the United States. *Kennedy School Review* 12:53–57. Retrieved from http://isites.harvard.edu/fs/docs/icb.topic967331.files/Bellows.pdf.

Bennett, W. L. (2005). New media, new movements? The role of the Internet in shaping the "anti-globalization" movement. In W. van de Donk, B. Loader, P. Nixon, & D. Rucht (Eds.), *Cyberprotest: New media, citizens, and social movements* (pp. 109–128). London: Routledge.

Bennett, W. L., & A. Segerberg. (2011). Digital media and the personalization of collective action. *Information, Communication & Society* 14 (6): 770–799. doi: 10.1080/1369118X.2011.579141.

———. (2012). The logic of connective action. *Information, Communication & Society* 15 (5): 739–768. doi: 10.1080/1369118X.2012.670661.

Biddle, R. E. (2013). Rationing the digital: The policy and politics of Internet use in Cuba today. Retrieved from http://blogs.law.harvard.edu/internetmonitor/files/2013/07/IM_RationingtheDigital.pdf.

Bilgiç, E. E., & Z. Kafkaslı. (2013) Gencim, özgürlükçüyüm, ne istiyorum: #direngeziparkı anketi sonuç raporu. Retrieved from http://www.bilgiyay.com/Content/files/DIRENGE-ZI.pdf.

Blue Bra Girl atrocity: Egyptian military police more than brutal. (2011, December18). Retrieved from http://rt.com/news/egyptian-military-cruelty-beating-079/.

Çarkoğlu, A., L. Baruh, and K. Yıldırım. (2014). "Press-party parallelism and polarization of news media during an election campaign: The case of the 2011 Turkish elections." *The International Journal of Press/Politics* 19 (3) (April 27): 295–317. doi: 10.1177/1940161214528994.

Castells, M. (2001). *The Internet galaxy: Reflections on the Internet, business, and society.* Oxford, UK: Oxford University Press.

———. (2009). *Communication power.* New York: Oxford University Press.

———. (2012). *Networks of outrage and hope: Social movemnets in the Internet age.* Cambridge, UK: Polity.

Coopman, T. M. (2011). Networks of dissent: Emergent forms in media based collective action. *Critical Studies in Media Communication* 28 (2): 153–172. doi: 10.1080/15295036.2010.514934.

Diani, M. (2000). Social movement networks virtual and real. *Information, Communication & Society* 3 (3): 386–401. doi: 10.1080/13691180051033333.

El-Baghdadi, I. (2011, February 1). *Meet Asmaa Mahfouz and the vlog that helped spark the revolution.* Retrieved from https://www.youtube.com/watch?v=SgjIgMdsEuk.

Estamos despiertos!—We are awake! (2014, May 26) *Streets of Athens.* Retrieved from http://stamatisgr.wordpress.com/2011/05/26/estamos-despiertos-we-are-awake/.

Fauer, A. (2012, November 9). Occupy Sandy: A movement moves to relief. Retrieved from http://www.nytimes.com/2012/11/11/nyregion/where-fema-fell-short-occupy-sandy-was-there.html?_r=0.

Garrett, R. K. (2006). Protest in an information society: A review of literature on social movements and new ICTs. *Information, Communication and Society* 9 (2): 2002–224. doi: 10.1080/13691180600630773.

Gerlach, L. P. (2001). The structure of social movements: Environmental activism and its opponents. In J. Arquilla & D. Ronfeldt (Eds.), *Networks and netwars: The future of terror, crime, and militancy* (pp. 289–310). Santa Monica, CA: Rand.

Graeber, D. (2014, October 20). Occupy Wall Street's anarchist roots. Retrieved from http://www.aljazeera.com/indepth/opinion/2011/11/2011112872835904508.html.

Himanen, P. (2012). Crisis, identity, and the welfare state. In M. Castells, J. Caraça, & G. Cardoso (Eds.), *Aftermath: The cultures in economic crisis* (pp.154–174). Oxford, UK: Oxford University Press.

Juris, J. S. (2004). Networked social movements: Global movements for global justice. In M. Castells (Ed.), *The network society: A cross-cultural perspective* (pp. 341–362). Northampton, UK: Edward Elgar Publishing Limited.

———. (2005). The new digital media and activist networking within anti-corporate globalization movements. *The ANNALS of the American Academy of Political and Social Science* 597 (1): 189–208. doi: 10.1177/0002716204270338.

———. (2012). Reflections on #Occupy Everywhere: Social media, public space, and emerging logics of aggregation. *American Ethnologist* 39 (2): 259–279. doi: 10.1111/j.1548-1425.2012.01362.x.

Kelly, S. (2013). Despite pushback, Internet freedom deteriorates. Retrieved from https://www.freedomhouse.org/sites/default/files/resources/FOTN%202013_OVERVIEW%20ESSAY.pdf.

Kelsey, R. (2014, December 15). Police Protests: Thousands protest against Eric Garner death. Retrieved from http://www.bbc.co.uk/newsbeat/30480125.

The little data book on information and communication technology. (2014). *The World Bank & International Telecommunication Union.* http://data.worldbank.org/sites/default/files/little_date_book_ict_2014.pdf.

Maidan-2013. (n.d.). Ilko Kucheriv Democratic Initiatives Foundation and the Kyiv International Institute of Sociology. Retrieved from http://dif.org.ua/en/events/gvkrlgkaeths.htm.

Papadimitriou, A., A. Yannopoulos, I. Kotsiopoulos, R. Finn, K. Wadhwa, W. Hayley, & L. Baruh, L. (2014). Deliverable 2.2: Case studies of communication media and their use in crisis situations. Retrieved from http://www.cosmic-project.eu/sites/default/files/deliverables/D2.2.pdf.

Postmes, T., & S. Brunsting. (2002). Collective action in the age of the Internet. *Social Science Computer Review* 20 (3): 290–301.

Rushkoff, D. (2013). Permanent revolution: Occupying democracy. *The Sociological Quarterly* 54(2): 164–173.

Segerberg, A., & W. L. Bennett. (2011). Social media and the organization of collective action: Using Twitter to explore the ecologies of two climate change protests. *The Communication Review* 14 (3): 197–215. doi: 10.1080/10714421.2011.597250.

Speri, A. (2014, August 7). A chokehold didn't kill Eric Garner, your disrespect for the NYPD did. Retrieved from https://news.vice.com/article/a-chokehold-didnt-kill-eric-garner-your-disrespect-for-the-nypd-did.

Tarrow, S. (1998). *Power in movement: Social movements and contentious politics.* Cambridge, UK: Cambridge University Press.

Thomas, F. (2012). To the precinct station: How theory met practice and drove it absolutely crazy. *Baffler* 21. Retrieved from http://www.thebaffler.com/salvos/to-the-precinct-station.

Tunç, A. (2014). Can pomegranates replace penguins? Social media and the rise of citizen journalism in Turkey. Retrieved from http://freedomhouse.org/report/struggle-turkeys-internet/can-pomegranates-replace-penguins-social-media-and-rise-citizen#.VEPm-fmsWv9.

Yüksek, D. (2014). Medialogue: Media as a forum for dialogue in conflicts and peacebuilding new media, social movements and EU policies. Lambert Academic Publishing.

Wagstaff, K. (2014, March 24). Turkey Twitter ban: How 1.1 million people are getting around it. Retrieved from http://www.nbcnews.com/tech/social-media/turkey-twitter-ban-how-1-1-million-people-are-getting-n60716.

Wall, M., & S. E. L. Zahed. (2011). "I'll be waiting for you guys": A YouTube call to action in the Egyptian Revolution. *International Journal of Communication* 5:1333–1343.

Wellman, B. (2001). Computer networks as social networks. *Science* 293:2031–2034.

2013 World Press Freedom Index. (2013). *Reporters without borders*. Retrieved from http://en.
    rsf.org/press-freedom-index-2013,1054.html.

Chapter Nine

Networked Activism in China

Zixue Tai

Market liberalization in the past decades has led China into an era of fast economic growth and rapid social transformation. Among its astounding achievements, China overtook Germany to become the largest global exporter in 2010, and surpassed Japan as the world's No. 2 economy in 2012. As part of the national strategy, the telecommunications sector (Harwit, 2008) and the high tech industry (Lüthje, Hürtgen, Pawlicki, & Sproll , 2013) have been prioritized areas of state investment and vibrant expansion in the reform era. The epitome of China's Internet success finds testimonial in the global e-commerce giant Alibaba, which made the world's biggest IPO debut (worth $25 billion) in the New York Stock Exchange on September 19, 2014 (Reuters, 2014). As a result, technological empowerment through variegated Internet-based applications and smartphone-led personal and portable connectivity has created a brand-new networked communicative sphere that engenders innovative mass collaboration and ingenuous collective action.

The era of economic reform has also witnessed an ancillary development throughout Chinese society in the ever-widening disparity in terms of material benefits and wealth distribution mainly along the lines of social classes and the rural/urban divide. The Gini coefficient (also known as the Gini index), which is often used by economists as a measure of income and wealth inequality within a nation, is pinpointed at 0.73 for 2012 (a surge from 0.45 in 1995) in the most recent China Family Panel Studies (CFPS) report released by the Beijing University Social Survey Center (2014). In general, the threshold index of 0.4 is designated by the United Nations as dangerous and conducive to social instability. Alarmingly, the report reveals that the top 1 percent households own over one-third of the wealth in the country, while the bottom 20 percent claim about 1 percent of the national income.

Against this backdrop, a compounding factor is the absence of any well-established institutional or legal recourse in addressing grievances and disputes for the lower echelons of the socio-political structure, as the current legislation mostly sides with the affluent and powerful elites. Not surprisingly, popular contention focusing on social and economic demands has become a pervasive and routinized form of interest articulation and policy negotiation in recent years (Chen, 2012; O'Brien, 2008). Saturated mass dissent in China, at the same time, coincides with the rising tides of digital activism—the use of networked digital technologies to push for social and political change—across the globe (Joyce, 2012), particularly of note in authoritarian regimes in the Middle East as manifested in the Arab Spring movement (Faris & Meier, 2012; Gerbaudo, 2012). Consequently, variegated formations of networked activism have injected new dynamics into grassroots social movements in China (Lee, 2012; Liu, 2013; Yang, 2014).

This chapter offers an overview of the evolving field of networked activism in China through the lens of three conceptual clusters: mass collaboration, grassroots surveillance, and networks of protest. The discussion is grounded in the socio-political terrain of China's social media environment, and sheds light on the intersection of netizens, digital activism, and collective action in China's networked era.

CHANGING SOCIO-POLITICAL LANDSCAPE AND EVOLVING MEDIA ENVIRONMENT IN CHINA

One conundrum China observers have been trying to grapple with in recent decades has been the stunning achievement of two simultaneous developments in the country: the accelerated pace of economic openness and the tightened hold on power by the Chinese party-state (Laliberté & Lanteigne, 2008). While the market has been constantly pushed to new frontiers in the state-orchestrated laissez-faire expansion, the political system continues to be mostly closed, with the Chinese Communist Party (CCP) monopolizing control over state power, allowing limited public participation in political decision-making. The success and durability of the party-state to adapt to and survive new social and political challenges is touted as proof that the regime has accumulated a certain level of "authoritarian resilience" (Nathan, 2003; Pei, 2012). However, evidence has been piling up in recent years that this "resilience" continues to bend into unchartered boundaries amidst growing manifestations of contestation with an expanding base of participants, actors, and organizers (Reny & Hurst, 2013). Although popular contention is in no way out of control as of yet, the current system of stability maintenance operates at a hefty price for the regime and how it may fare in the future remains unknown (Chen, 2013). The widespread diffusion and integration of networked communication technologies in everyday life has been a major contributing factor in causing this change of tides.

It is hardly possible to understand China's new media culture without delving into its conventional media environment. As part of the state-led commercialization efforts, the media industry has transformed the old state-supported model in the pre-reform era to its current market-based self-financing mechanism in which state subsidies have been cut to the media organizations, and advertising and subscription (or television ratings) define day-to-day success of the mainstream media business. It is routine now for media outlets to engage in fierce competition in grabbing audience attention and thereby generating revenue. This media reform, however, has mostly redrawn the boundaries within which the media can simultaneously serve audience interests and fulfill state demands; it has not unleashed the media into an independent voice in Chinese society. Local and state propaganda departments still often issue directives and pull the strings as to what is to be covered in the media. As a result, the Chinese media have evolved into a "state corporatist" system that hinges on the operational logic of "how to profit the media organizations that are apparatus of the party-state and perform critical state functions" (Pan, 2010, p. 197). The conventional media, therefore, tend to shy away from controversial issues and contentious topics. In other words, the information environment from the media establishment is still highly controlled and heavily regulated.

The participatory nature of the online networked landscape generates different outcomes. It is true that China has implemented a multitiered and multifaceted surveillance apparatus in order to monitor and filter out unwanted information in Chinese cyberspace (Tai, 2010). State directives stipulate that all Internet sites engaging in content publishing be licensed by designated state authorities and comply with demands from official censors. This in essence ensures that state-endorsed information saturates major portal sites. This is not to say, however, that the regime has been able to effectively keep proscribed content and contentious activities out of Chinese online space. As a testimonial to the difficulty of exercising network content control, during the Xinjiang turmoil in July 2009 when race riots between Han and Uighur groups killed hundreds and wounded thousands, the authorities had to totally shut down the mobile and computer networks for weeks in order to stop riot organizers from mobilizing followers.

WEB 2.0 AND USER-GENERATED CONTENT

Chinese Internet users are among the most active in the world in contributing to and relying on a variety of user-generated content (UGC) ranging from

Bulletin Board Systems (BBS), Internet Relay Chat (IRC) rooms, text messaging (SMS), instant messaging (IM), to online communities on the Internet (Tai, 2006). The same pattern holds true for blogs and social media content. Universal McCann, a New York–based global media-marketing consultancy firm, has conducted a series of annual cross-national surveys of global social media use starting from 2006, and its findings consistently show that Chinese netizens are much more likely than their counterparts in other countries to consume (i.e., reading blogs and microblogs) and contribute to content (i.e., writing blogs and microblogs) across multiple social media platforms (e.g., Universal McCann, 2010, 2012, 2014). In a similar vein, the latest survey report on social media use by the China Internet Network Information Center (CNNIC) (2014) released in July 2014 shows that, among China's 632 million Internet users, 89.3 percent do instant messaging (e.g., QQ, WeChat), 61.7 percent visit social networking sites (e.g., Renren, QZone), and 43.6 percent use microblogs (e.g., Sina) respectively, on a regular basis. Overall, 33.7 percent of the online population interconnect to all three social networking platforms regularly.

Meanwhile, Chinese social media users display a much higher propensity than their counterparts in other countries to believe that they can effect change through online participation. In comparing data from multiyear surveys of Internet users across different countries, Tai (2006) found that Chinese individuals display the highest level of online political efficacy, defined as "the self-perceived accessibility and availability of online resources and channels to them in understanding politics and participating in the political process via the Internet" (p. 204). Likewise, they also show a higher level of external political efficacy online than netizens in most other countries in believing that, by using the Internet, government officials can better understand the people and better serve the people.

These tendencies among Chinese online users can be best explained by the controlled nature of China's conventional information environment and the closed setup of the Chinese political system. It is worth noting that the cross-national comparisons from the above findings mostly involve Internet users from countries enjoying varying degrees of a democratic polity and an independent press with the exception of China. The state-controlled arrangement of the media establishment in China, not unexpectedly, produces the effect of channeling user interest to more unconventional, user-centered platforms such as blogs, microblogs, online chat rooms, and other social media applications where user-contributed content dominates. When no freewheeling platforms of democratic exchange and citizen participation exist in the offline world within the one-party authoritarian state, it is natural that Chinese netizens look to the emerging Internet for possibilities unfulfilled elsewhere to vent and make their voices heard.

Mounting evidence has accumulated in recent years corroborating these points. As Tong and Lei (2013) demonstrate, microblogging in China has turned into a battleground for hugely influential opinion leaders and individuals attaining the status of social media celebrities to openly state their positions on controversial issues and breaking events, most often in direct opposition to official stance. Through garnering massive support by accruing tremendous bases of followers within a short span of time, these individuals often achieve an amazing level of success in constructing a "counter-hegemony" and in extracting accountability and responses from the authorities. With regard to mobile communication, Liu (2013) observes that networked mobile phones in China are increasingly used by commoners to bypass state-sponsored blockage of information in mass mobilization and protest organization, essentially to create "an inexpensive *counter-public sphere* which invents and circulates discourses opposed to those featured in the mainstream, making the predominant public sphere more inclusive and open to ordinary people" (p. 1015, emphasis added). Similarly, Esarey and Xiao (2011) conclude that "Via blogs, online video clips, email, and text messages, activists can utilize interactive relationships to garner broad support for their causes" (p. 312).

THE RISE AND RISE OF DIGITAL ACTIVISM

China boasts a rich and variegated history of resistance, rebellion, and revolution (Perry, 2001). During the Maoist era, mass movements were orchestrated by the Communist Party to mobilize ordinary citizens into regime-sponsored ideological campaigns and denunciations. Mass dissent on nonpolitical issues, however, was a rarity. It is since the 1990s that popular unrest driven by economic and social demands has surged, marked by soaring numbers of various forms of petitions, protests, demonstrations, and sometimes riots by different constituents and social groups. As a result, the current Chinese polity has transitioned into what Chen (2012) calls a "contentious authoritarianism" wherein "a strong authoritarian regime accommodates widespread and routinized collective protests" (p. 189).

In his illuminating analysis of social protest and collective movements in China today, Chen attributes this surge to three major factors. First, widespread collective protests are a logical product of the "contradictions and ambiguities" created by tensions between the centralized power structure and the extensive nonbinding consultation the regime puts in place in order to allow ordinary people to lodge complaints and submit petitions; feedback from the people, even when it is negative, is considered essential for the Communist party to maintain responsiveness and to hold ruling legitimacy. Second, epochal economic transitions have fundamentally transformed state structure and reconfigured relations between ordinary people and state agents; they have also created divergent, and often contradicting, economic interests among social groups and local entities. Third, protesters have devised "a strategic pattern of protest opportunism" so as to strike a delicate balance between defiance and obedience in maximizing their bargaining power.

Additionally, I want to add two more factors that have significantly shaped this surge: rising popular awareness among the commoners about their rights and options means that more and more individuals are willing to resort to protest in addressing grievances, and the increasing integration of China into the world politically and economically necessitates more subtle handling of collective actions in order to avoid being put in the negative spotlight of the global media.

Activism takes many forms and shapes. Meikle (2010) identifies four dimensions of activism in analyzing Internet activist campaigns: intercreative texts, intercreative tactics, intercreative strategies, and intercreative networks. Intercreative texts involve reworking or reimagining existing media texts or creating new texts to effect social change; intercreative tactics develop new variations on established tactics and subvert existing media formats; intercreative strategies employ the creation of brand-new alternative media spaces for the expression of dissonant perspectives; and intercreative networks focus on mobilizing resources through collaborative deployment of information networks. What makes this line of scholarship interesting as well as challenging is that the dynamics vary substantially with the specific conditions of the national context and they constantly change to adapt to an ever-evolving technological environment.

In their deliberation on social activism in China, Lee and Hsing (2010) propose a spectrum of politics in three strands—namely, the politics of (re)distribution, recognition, and representation—based on the goals and the basis of the formation of the collective social actors. The politics of (re)distribution "entails struggles and claims for material interests or between social groups and state actors that spring from their common or differential class locations" (p. 3). The politics of recognition is concerned with "the discovery and articulation of needs previously denied or ignored, especially the demand for social recognition of certain groups' moral status, political position and identity" (p. 4). The third strand, the politics of representation, is related to the expression of ideas and symbols, or "symbolic contestations."

With specific regard to online activism, Yang (2009) differentiates among four types of popular contention: cultural, social, political, and nationalistic. Cultural activism expresses concern over values, morality, lifestyles, and identities whereas social activism focuses on issues such as corruption, environmental protection, and the rights of disenfranchised groups. Political activism touches upon topics pertaining to how the country is or should be governed, and online nationalism often permeates China's Internet, especially during particular times of dispute with other countries.

NETWORKS OF PROTEST

While discussing the implications of the Internet and other digital media for global activism, Bennett (2003) observes that "digital communication networks may be changing the political game in favor of resource-poor players who, in many cases, are experimenting with political strategies outside of conventional national political channels such as elections and interest processes" (p.144). This is certainly a fitting characterization of the status quo of online activism in China, in which unconventional, innovative strategies in the network era open up new opportunities for traditionally disenfranchised individuals and groups. Communication in distributed networks can help disseminate information and coordinate plans of action with relative ease, speed, scope, and marginal cost that would be nonexistent within the highly controlled conventional media in China.

Garrett (2006) argues that the influence of new Information and Communication Technologies (ICTs) on social movements can be fruitfully examined in their interconnections in relation to three broad areas: mobilizing structures, opportunity structures, and framing processes. With regard to China, ICTs are profoundly revolutionizing all three of these aspects in shaping the emergence, development, and outcome of contentious activities. In terms of mobilizing structures, online communities and networked communication groups create new dynamics, as conventional social structures, under preempted state cooptation, are typically resistant to contentious activities not endorsed by the state; diversified social groups and networks also make it easy to disseminate information and coordinate activities.

Opportunity structures, which refer to "attributes of a social system that facilitate or constrain movement activities" (Garrett, 2006, p. 212), are apparently institutionalized to repress collective actions outside of state-sanctioned domains in China. The online environment, however, makes it possible to bypass regulated venues and empowers new opportunities; moreover, it can also create formal or informal networks of (moral and logistic) support among like-minded individuals, and thus make contention sustainable. As far as framing processes are concerned, netizen-centered communication unconstrained by state censors effectively frames actions to counter the discourse from the mainstream media, and adds legitimacy to protest actions.

The following examples suggest an overall trend that builds on the empowering potential of networked communication in shaping the course of contentious actions. In a landmark event widely touted as the "Chongqing Nail House Incident,"[1] a couple refused to relocate to make space for a government-designated commercial redevelopment, failing to agree to the terms of compensation, and resorted to blogging to garner public attention and mobilize popular support. Images of their standalone house amid a large stretch of demolished empty land became the rallying cry for individual property rights protection in China, while constant updates online continued to throw this story into the spotlight of the local, national, and overseas media for years before a final settlement was reached. More importantly, this became a source of tactical inspiration for individuals caught in similar situations, as seen in dozens of high-profile nail-house incidents in ensuing years.

Environmental protection has been a hotbed of popular protest in China in recent years. Among the most well-known public protest events is the popular rise to abort a government-supported chemical plant in Xiamen in 2007 for processing p-Xylene (PX), a highly hazardous and inflammable substance. More commonly known as the "Xiamen PX Incident,"[2] this has sparked waves of mass protests across multiple cities against official initiatives in building chemical plants in residential districts. In all contentious activities, self-organizing citizens used QQ groups, online forums, and smartphone-enabled personal networks to bypass government censors and official surveillance in staging public protests (mostly called "walk-ins" by organizers). Following similar steps, local citizens in Luoding, Guangdong Province successfully halted a government plan for a waste-incinerator project seen to be polluting in April 2015.[3]

DISTRIBUTED GRASSROOTS SURVEILLANCE

The penetration of multiple platforms of networked information technologies and applications into everyday life has profound implications for today's society. Ubiquitous connectivity has led to the rise of the "total surveillance society" (Parker, 2001) in which pervasive, perpetual, invisible, and distributed surveillance of individuals becomes a deeply ingrained ritual of our social reality. In that regard, dataveillance—"the systematic use of personal data systems in the investigation or monitoring of the actions or communications of one or more persons" (Clarke, 1988, p. 499)—has become a defining feature of today's surveillance society.

Scholarly deliberation on the current system of social control in the West has been under the heavy influence of Michel Foucault's widely acclaimed classic *Discipline and Punish* (1979) in which he discusses how panopticism (i.e., the principle that the few see the many) has become an effective system of "soul" control in modern society. Compared with the conventional state-centric scheme of social control in the industrial age, many (e.g., Gandy, 1993; Haggerty & Ericson, 2000) have pointed out, the hallmark of surveillance in the network era is the massive participation of, and indeed, oftentimes domination by, commercial interests and nonstate actors in the expropriation of dispersed private data that can be aggregated in different ways to serve specific monitoring functions. This kind of distributed yet ready-to-be-assembled monitoring system is characterized as "surveillant assemblage" by Haggerty and Ericson (2000) and "panoptic sort" by Gandy (1993).

On the other hand, as Mathiesen (1997) has noted, a striking parallel to the panoptical process is "synopticism"—namely, "the development of a unique and enormously extensive system enabling *the many to see and contemplate the few*, so that the tendency for the few to see and supervise the many is contextualized in a highly significant counterpart" (p. 219; emphasis in original). In particular, Mathiesen singles out the role of the mass media, especially television, in laying the synoptical structure of the "viewer society" we live in. This perspective of the media, however, is challenged by Doyle (2011) for being "a narrow one," because the mass media may assume the dual identity of both participating as tools of surveillance and serving as sites of resistance to surveillance at different times at the levels of both production and audience perception. This is in line with the prominent account from critical studies scholars that the media, as a contested space, offer both constraints and potential slots for oppositional voices (e.g., Curran, 2002). Especially in the backdrop of China's authoritarian media environment, structural constraints can and often suffocate dissenting tunes.

The networked culture, however, creates different dynamics. As Pickard (2008) notes, the liberatory nature of Internet-mediated communication fosters participatory and bottoms-up democratic actions from traditionally marginal and disenfranchised groups, and it promises to be a viable locus for democratic, and even radical, collective actions. On one hand, as Gandy (1993) observes, widespread application of information technologies in routine life has institutionalized the practice of panoptic sort—the surveillance apparatus by government and private sectors in *collecting, processing, and sharing* diverse sets of information about individual citizens and consumers. On the other hand, we are also witnessing the rise of the countervailing practice of what I call *synoptic sort* in which dispersed, private individuals observe, record, and share an assortment of information about the select few through voluntary mass collaboration and coordination. Similarly, Koskela (2009) discusses a particular type of amateur surveillance practice—"hijacking surveillance"—in which "people use various items of surveillance equipment for producing visual material for their own purposes with different motivations" (p. 162).

In the following episodes, amateur surveillant gaze through synoptic sort zeroes in on a special group of privileged elites sitting right at the center of China's power structures—government officials and the superrich. On October 16, 2010, a fatal traffic accident on the campus of Hebei University quickly escalated into an online furor and denunciation. The driver was twenty-three-year-old Li Qiming, whose speeding sedan ran over two female students, killing one and injuring the other. Instead of stopping to help the victims, Li tried to flee the scene, and he was immediately confronted by campus security guards and eyewitness students when he was reported to shout at the crowd: "Sue me if you will. My father is Li Gang." It turned out that Li Gang was the deputy police chief of the administrative precinct where Hebei University resides. In no time, smartphone-captured vignettes appeared on Renren.com and QQ.com, two of the most popular social networking websites in China.[4] "My Father is Li Gang" soon rose to be the No. 1 infamous catchphrase in China online—so much so that it became one of the "Top Ten" most-used online phrases for 2010 (despite its short circulation, from late October to December). Enraged individuals demanded punishment, and swelling public outrage forced swift action from the police, leading to Li Qiming's arrest in the following week and his sentence of a six-year prison term in January 2011.

Another sensation featured a video with sexually explicit content involving Lei Zhengfu, the party boss of Chongqing's Beibei District, which went viral after it was posted on Sina Weibo (China's primary microblogging site) in November 2012.[5] In less than a week, Lei was sacked from his post and later sentenced to thirteen years in prison for bribe-taking. Likewise, in a recent scandal that follows the template of a growing number of whistle-blowing revelations online targeting public officials, Yang Pei, the Tobacco Bureau Chief of Weinan City in Shaanxi Province, was accused of having an extramarital affair with a subordinate in an online post in March 2015, alongside snapshots from a surveillance video showing him and a woman walking into the same hotel room next to each other, posted only minutes apart.[6] The same post, which went viral on Chinese social media, also claimed that the official spends over 100K yuan (approximately US$16,230) taxpayer money on hotel rooms annually for his sex encounters. Yang was soon suspended from his post pending an official investigation into these charges.

TECHNOLOGY-EMPOWERED MASS COLLABORATION

The distributed, often anonymous, participatory and freewheeling nature of the Internet works to open windows of opportunity for mass collaboration and collective action. To a great extent, the development of Chinese networked space into a multifaceted, user-empowering platform of public communication has followed the overall trajectory of participatory culture as noted in other parts of the world (Jenkins, 2006; Marshall, 2004)—albeit not without its unique twists and turns. So we have an expanding base of platforms that seamlessly intermingles three core areas of online communication: mass participation, social networking, and creative individuality. As a result,

Web 2.0 turns what used to be mass, passive online surfers into active content contributors, and new forms of applications—such as blogs, microblogs, wikis, social networking sites, RSS feeds, hashtags—allow like-minded users to debate issues, share ideas, and engage in collective actions. This brand-new type of mass-collaborative, user-centered, cooperative content creation and distribution environment has profound implications for the economic, social, and political aspects of our online culture.

One particular form of online, distributed mass collaboration that has caught quite some attention among academics and practitioners alike lately is crowdsourcing. Jeff Howe (2006), who coined the term, acknowledges his intellectual debt to James Surowiecki (2004) in observing that dispersed individuals can outperform highly organized teams at solving singular and complex problems. Crowdsourcing as Howe envisions it is primarily a distributed business model of aggregating the wisdom of the crowd in readily available disparate networks for problem-solving in corporate-driven commercial settings. There has been scant deliberation on the practice of crowdsourcing in nonbusiness-centered environments.

An explosive Web phenomenon in Chinese cyberspace in recent years that bears a lot of resemblance to crowdsourcing is the human flesh search (HFS) engine, or *renrou sousuo* in Chinese. Herold (2011) defines HFS as an online effort to "track down offline individuals by employing as many computer users as possible" (p. 129). In another definition, Wang and colleagues (2010) characterize HFS as "searches that are conducted with help from human users (as opposed to on a purely automated platform, such as Google), often targeted at finding the identity of a human being" (p. 45). Both definitions, noticeably, simply offer broad strokes and lack specificity. This is for a good reason, because, as Wang et al. (2010) note, any existing overly specific definitional effort to understand HFS actually misses more than it clarifies due to the complexity of related activities.

In his sweeping overview of the diversified landscape of HFS, Herold (2011) links it to problem-solving in three areas: satisfying personal interest and addressing personal grievances; inciting (and then mitigating) mob anger as well as seeking populist revenge; and protesting against government officials. In their empirical analysis of a comprehensive set of online HFS episodes from 2001 to 2010, Wang et al. (2010) identified two defining characteristics that interconnect all cases:

> First, most HFS episodes involve strong offline elements, in the form of either information acquisition through offline channels or other types of offline activism. Second, almost all HFS events rely on voluntary crowd-sourcing: a team of Web users join each other to share information, conduct investigations, and perform other actions concerning people or events of common interest. (p. 46)

As a matter of fact, HFS has become such a unique hallmark of China's Web space that it has repeatedly hit headlines of the international media establishment. For example, a *Times* (London) online article calls HFS endeavors "digital witch hunts,"[7] and a *New York Times* story equates HFS to "a form of online vigilante justice in which Internet users hunt down and punish people who have attracted their wrath" (Downey, 2010). The practice of HFS in cyber China as a particular type of massive user-generated online detective collaboration has garnered such global attention that it is the "38th of the 64 things" which will shape the future of our lifetime, according to Ben Hammersley (2012), digital guru and editor-at-large of *Wired* magazine.

The human flesh search (HFS) engine as a special type of crowdsourcing has evolved into a powerful platform of mass collaboration in cyber China. Through numerous cases in the past years, it has fully demonstrated its potential in producing a slew of anticipated and unanticipated consequences under various circumstances. HFS quintessentially stands for what the commoners are willing to confront—degrading moral standards, polarizing events, corrupt officials, outrageous transgressions, and so on—that lie at the fault lines of today's China. At the same time, it can also bring about extreme public humiliation, mass harassment, and mob intimidation to private individuals. On the other hand, grassroots surveillance enabled by new media platforms has led to the rise of a brand-new type of mass collaboration in which dispersed, private individuals collect, process, and share diverse sets of targeted information toward a voluntarily defined goal. Public officials are often at the frontlines of mass scrutiny.

This episode speaks volumes about the power of mass collaboration once a targeted individual becomes the focus of public gaze. In August 2012, a smirking individual was featured prominently in a photograph taken by a passerby in a scene of a fatal highway accident involving thirty-six fatalities; the photo went viral once it was published on a personal blog accompanied with inflaming comments bemoaning the heartlessness of a public official in the face of such a gruesome occasion. Circulation of the story about this so-called "Smiling Brother" on social media amplified public rage, and this person was soon identified to be Yang Dacai, head of the provincial Bureau of Work Safety. Mass scrutiny for incriminating evidence soon focused on his wristwatch in the photo, which was claimed to be an Omega allegedly priced at 38,000 euros. Within hours, coordinated searches online led to fifteen luxurious Swiss watches he wore on different occasions, totaling more than tens of thousands of US dollars at market value. Yang was then nicknamed the "Watch Brother" and was openly questioned for how he could afford such extravagant items with his meager income as a government official.[8] Yang was soon relieved of his official duties, followed by government investigations into bribe-taking and other corruption charges. He was sentenced to fourteen years in prison in September 2013.

CONCLUSION

Bennett and Segerberg (2012) contend that "the logic of connective action" provides the organizational structure for mass mobilization for an emerging genre of contemporary contentious actions worldwide. Contrary to the (conventional and familiar) logic of collective action which typically thrives on formal group identity, membership, and ideology, the (new and less familiar) logic of connective action starts with the "self-motivated sharing of already internalized or personalized ideas, plans, images, and resources with networks of others" (p. 753). While connective action is preconditioned on the prevalence of highly personalized and digitally mediated social networks, its linchpin is the constitutive role of sharing of personally engaging content. This logic, as has been argued in this chapter, finds fertile ground among China's interconnected individuals.

One major facilitating factor that has helped to turn social media into organizing agents of contentious action is the tightly controlled and closely monitored nature of the ecologies of conventional organizations and groups. Because established channels of communication are natural targets of state surveillance apparatus, and because memberships of formal organizations are easily identifiable, these structural elements often inhibit rather than empower resource mobilization in planning contentious activities. On the other hand, the distributed, largely anonymous, and participatory nature of the networked environment makes mass mobilization possible without a clearly identifiable organizational structure. To use the words of Shirky (2008), this power of "organizing without organizations" is particularly enabling for contentiously minded Chinese online users, as it allows mass mobilization without recognizable leaders. This disrupts the three-decade-old practice by the Chinese regime of punishing selective leaders and prominent organizers in mass protests.

Dramatic changes in the socioeconomic landscape as well as rising inequalities in the wake of economic liberalization have turned Chinese society into a hotbed of popular contention, as "key social groups have developed distinctive forms of mobilization and contestation with the state, centered around distinguishable sets of grievances, which elicit at least somewhat predictable responses from the state and lead to particular outcomes" (Reny & Hurst, 2013, pp. 217–218). Meanwhile, the state-controlled conventional media continue to side with government authorities and typically stay away from covering controversial topics and contentious activities, thus eliminating any possibility of functioning either as a trustworthy source of information or as a feasible platform of mobilization. As a result, disgruntled Chinese netizens take to the socially networked online space to disseminate information and coordinate collective action. The pervasive social media have opened up all sorts of new possibilities for grassroots contestation and mass collaboration. These emerging dynamics will likely induce wrenching socio-political changes in the country in the years to come, and remain intriguing areas of scholarly inquiry down the road.

REFERENCES

Beijing University Social Survey Center. (2014). *China Family Panel Studies* 2014. Beijing: Beijing University Press.
Bennett, W. L. (2003). Communicating global activism: Strengths and vulnerabilities of networked politics. *Information, Communication & Society* 6 (2): 143–168. doi: 10.1080/1369118032000093860a.
Bennett, W. L., & A. Segerberg. (2012). The logic of connective action: Digital media and the personalization of contentious politics. *Information, Communication & Society* 15 (5): 739–768. doi: 10.1080/1369118X.2012.670661.
Chen, X. (2012). *Social protest and contentious authoritarianism in China*. New York: Cambridge University Press.
———. (2013). The rising cost of stability. *Journal of Democracy* 24 (1): 57–64. http://dx.doi.org/10.1353/jod.2013.0003.
China Internet Network Information Center (CNNIC). (2014). *China social media user behavior survey report.* Retrieved from http://www.cnnic.net.cn/hlwfzyj/hlwxzbg/201408/P020140822379356612744.pdf.
Clarke, R. A. (1988). Information technology and dataveillance. *Communications of the ACM* 31(5): 498–512. doi: 10.1145/42411.42413.
Curran, J. (2002). *Media and power*. New York: Routledge.
Downey, T. (2010, March 3). China's cyberposse. Retrieved from http://www.nytimes.com/2010/03/07/magazine/07Human-t.html?pagewanted=all&_r=0.
Doyle, A. (2011). Revisiting the synopticon: Reconsidering Mathiesen's "The Viewer Society" in the age of Web 2.0. *Theoretical Criminology* 15 (3): 283–299. doi: 10.1177/1362480610396645.
Esarey, A., & Q. Xiao. (2011). Digital communication and political change in China. *International Journal of Communication* 5:298–319.
Faris, D. M., & P. Meier. (2012). Digital activism in authoritarian countries. In A. Delwiche & J. J. Henderson (Eds.), *The participatory cultures handbook* (pp. 197–205). New York: Routledge.
Foucault, M. (1979). *Discipline & punish: The birth of the prison*. New York: Vintage.
Gandy, O. H., Jr. (1993). *The panoptic sort: A political economy of personal information*. Boulder, CO: Westview Press.
Garrett, R. K. (2006). Protest in an information society: A review of literature on social movements and new ICTs. *Information, Communication & Society* 9 (2): 202–224. doi: 10.1080/13691180600630773.Michel Foucault (Author)
Gerbaudo, P. (2012). *Tweets and the streets: Social media and contemporary activism*. New York: Pluto Press.
Haggerty, K. D., & R. V. Ericson. (2000). The surveillant assemblage. *British Journal of Sociology* 51 (4): 605–622. doi: 10.1080/00071310020015280.
Hammersley, B. (2012). *64 things you need to know now for then*. London: Hodder & Stoughton.
Harwit, E. (2008). *China's telecommunications revolution*. New York: Oxford University Press.
Herold, D. K. (2011). Human flesh search engines: Carnivalesque riots as components of a "Chinese democracy." In D. K. Herold & P. Marolt (Eds.), *Online society in China: Creating, celebrating, and instrumentalising the online carnival* (pp. 127–145). New York: Routledge.
Howe, J. (2006, June 2). Crowdsourcing: A definition. Blog entry available at http://www.crowdsourcing.com/cs/2006/06/crowdsourcing_a.html.

Jenkins, H. (2006). *Convergence culture: Where old and new media collide.* New York: New York University Press.

Joyce, M. (Ed.) (2012). *Digital activism decoded: The new mechanics of change.* New York: IDEBATE Press.

Koskela, H. (2009). Hijacking surveillance? The new moral landscapes of amateur photographing. In K. F. Aas, H. O. Gundhus, & H. M. Lomell (Eds.), *Technologies of InSecurity: The surveillance of everyday life* (pp.147–167). New York: Routledge-Cavendish.

Laliberté, A., & M. Lanteigne. (2008). *The Chinese party-state in the 21st century: Adaptation and the reinvention of legitimacy.* London: Routledge.

Lee, C. K., & Y. Hsing. (2010). Social activism in China: Agency and possibility. In Y. Hsing & C. K. Lee (Eds.), *Reclaiming Chinese society: The new social activism* (pp. 1–13). New York: Routledge.

Lee, M. J. (2012). Online activism by smart mobs and political change in southern China. *Issues & Studies* 48 (4): 1–35.

Liu, J. (2013). Mobile communication, popular protests and citizenship in China. *Modern Asian Studies* 47 (3): 995–1018. doi: 10.1017/S0026749X12000340.

Lüthje, B. , S. Hürtgen, P. Pawlicki, & M. Sproll . (2013). *From Silicon Valley to Shenzhen: Global production and work in the IT industry .* New York: Rowman & Littlefield.

Marshall, P. D. (2004). *New media cultures.* London: Arnold.

Mathiesen, T. (1997). The viewer society: Michel Foucault's "Panopticon" revisited. *Theoretical Criminology* 1 (2): 215–234. doi: 10.1177/1362480697001002003.

Meikle, G. (2010). Intercreativity: Mapping out online activism. In J. Hunsinger, L. Klastrup, & M. Allen (Eds.), *International handbook of Internet research* (pp. 363–377). Dordrecht, Heidelberg: Springer.

Nathan, A. J. (2003). Authoritarian resilience. *Journal of Democracy* 14 (1): 6–17. doi: 10.1353/jod.2003.0019.

O'Brien, K. J. (2008). *Popular protest in China .* Harvard University Press.

Pan, Z. (2010). Bounded innovations in the media. In Y. T. Hsing & C. K. Lee (Eds.), *Reclaiming Chinese society: The new social activism* (pp. 184–206). New York: Routledge.

Parker, J. (2001). *Total surveillance: Investigating the Big Brother world of e-spies, eavesdroppers and CCTV.* London: Piatkus.

Pei, M. (2012). Is CCP rule fragile or resilient? *Journal of Democracy* 23 (1): 27–41. doi: 10.1353/jod.2012.0008.

Perry, E. J. (2001). *Challenging the Mandate of Heaven: Social protest and state power in China.* New York: M. E. Sharpe.

Pickard, V. W. (2008). Cooptation and cooperation: Institutional exemplars of democratic Internet technology. *New Media & Society* 10 (4): 625–645. doi: 10.1177/1461444808093734.

Reny, M. E., & W. Hurst. (2013). Social unrest. In C. Ogden (Ed.), *Handbook of China's governance and domestic politics* (pp. 210–220). New York: Routledge.

Reuters. (2014, September 22). Alibaba IPO ranks as world's biggest after additional shares sold. Retrieved from http://www.nytimes.com/reuters/2014/09/22/business/22reuters-alibaba-ipo-value.html?_r=0.

Shirky, C. (2008). *Here comes everybody: The power of organizing without organizations.* New York: Penguin.

Surowiecki, J. (2004). *The wisdom of crowds: Why the many are smarter than the few and how collective wisdom shapes business, economies, societies, and nations.* New York: Doubleday.

Tai, Z. (2006). *The Internet in China: Cyberspace and civil society.* New York: Routledge.

———. (2010). Casting the ubiquitous net of information control: Internet surveillance in China from Golden Shield to Green Dam. *International Journal of Advanced Pervasive and Ubiquitous Computing* 2 (1): 53–70. doi: 10.4018/japuc.2010010104.

Tong, Y., & S. Lei. (2013). War of position and microblogging in China. *Journal of Contemporary China* 22 (80): 292–311. doi: 10.1080/10670564.2012.734084.

Universal McCann (2010). *The socialisation of brands: Social media tracker—wave 5.* Retrieved from http://www.umww.com/global/knowledge/view?id=128.

————. (2012). *The business of social : Social media tracker—wave 6.* Retrieved from http://www.umww.com/global/knowledge/view?Id=226

————. (2014). *Cracking the social code: Social media tracker wave 7.* Retrieved from http://wave.umww.com/.

Wang, F. Y., D. Zeng, J. A. Hendler, Q. Zhang, Z. Feng, Y. Gao, H. Wang, & G. Lai. (2010). A study of the human flesh search engine: Crowd-powered expansion of online knowledge. *Computer* 43 (8): 45–53. doi: 10.1109/MC.2010.216.

Yang, G. (2009). Online activism. *Journal of Democracy* 20 (3): 33–36. doi: 10.1353/jod.0.0094.

————. (2014). Internet activism & the party-state in China. *Daedalus* 143 (2): 110–123. doi: 10.1162/DAED_a_00276.

NOTES

1. See full coverage of this event from Sina's page titled "Focus on the Chongqing Nail House Incident." Retrieved from http://news.sina.com.cn/z/cqzndzh/.

2. See the Baidu wiki page "The Xiamen PX Project Incident" for a narrative of this incident at http://baike.baidu.com/view/3114002.htm, accessed 12/15/2013.

3. See coverage of this event at "Luoding Government Cancelled Waste-Incinerator Project Amidst Protests by Local Residents." Sohu.com, April 8, 2015. Retrieved from http://news.sohu.com/20150408/n410951888.shtml.

4. The narrative of this episode is based on related information from the Baidu wiki page titled "My Father is Li Gang." Retrieved from http://baike.baidu.com/view/4534118.htm, supplemented by information from searches on Sina, Mop, and Tianya.

5. See full coverage of this event from Sina's page titled "The Chongqing Sex Video Incident." Sina News, no date. Retrieved from http://news.sina.com.cn/z/cqbpscandal2012/.

6. See coverage of this event at "Tobacco Bureau Chief in Shaanxi Province Spotted in a Hotel Affair." *Beijing Morning Post*, April 14, 2015. Retrieved from http://www.morningpost.com.cn/2015/0418/523595.shtml.

7. Hannah Fletcher, "Human flesh search engines: Chinese vigilantes that hunt victims on the web." *Times (London) Online*, June 25, 2008. Retrieved from http://technology.timesonline.co.uk/tol/news/tech_and_web/article4213681.ece.

8. "Watch Brother" Yang Dacai of Shaanxi Found to Have 20-plus CD Bank Accounts." *Oriental Morning Post*, October 10, 2012. Retrieved from http://news.sina.com.cn/c/2012-10-10/054025325894.shtml.

Chapter Ten

Social Network Research Methods

Approaches and Key Issues

Tatyana Dumova

Nearly one billion people around the world are social media users (Ruths & Pfeffer, 2014). Among all social media forms, social networks currently occupy a central place in the social media ecosystem. In 2014, half of all American adults were using Facebook and one in five visited popular social media sites such as Twitter, Instagram, Pinterest, or LinkedIn (see Duggan et al., 2015). Scientists' predictions of social media's pending sizable economic effects (see Heidemann, Klier, & Probst, 2012) were realized in just two years, with Facebook's estimated $227 billion economic impact which affected 4.5 million jobs around the world in 2014 (Deloitte, 2015). In light of these developments, research on online social networks has acquired vital importance, and even business magazines such as *Forbes* are joining the conversation.

It is commonly acknowledged that the field of social network research is thriving (Borgatti, Brass, & Halgin, 2014; Carrington, 2015). For researchers studying society and social behavior, social network analysis provides a means "to identify behavior patterns and the groups or social strata that correlate with those patterns" (Degenne & Forsé, 1999, p. 2). In line with classical sociological theory, it seeks to determine links between social entities (people or groups) in order to conceptualize societal structures (social, political, economic) and study behavioral patterns, social interactions, and social change. The growth and development of this burgeoning area of inquiry has put social network analysis "at the forefront of social and behavioral science research" (Galaskiewicz &Wasserman, 1994, p. xii).

Whereas sociologists are primarily interested in the structure of social relations and networks ranging from small groups to an entire society (Degenne & Forsé, 1999), other academic disciplines—communication, social anthropology, psychology, computer science, economics, political science, geography, ecology—find the concept of networks equally useful and embrace the network perspective with rigor and enthusiasm. The proliferation of social media platforms (such as: online social networks, blogs, microblogs, wikis, podcasts, social bookmarking tools, social tagging, folksonomies, collaborative filtering, mashups) based on advances in Web programming (AJAX, DHTML, HTML5, PHP, JavaScript), and the growth of mobile communications have led to an upsurge of social network research. Ruths and Pfeffer (2014) argue in the journal *Science* that social network researchers are currently poised at "a technological inflection point" (p. 1063):

> Powerful computational resources combined with the availability of massive social media data sets have given rise to a growing body of work that uses a combination of machine learning, natural language processing, network analysis, and statistics for the measurement of population structure and human behavior at an unprecedented scale. (p. 1063)

While academic interest in social media networks is growing, methodologically the study of online social networks poses a plethora of challenges. In order to examine the complexity of interactions enabled by social media networks, researchers must understand both the dynamics of technology-mediated environments and the nature of structural relations in a network. This chapter considers the implications of the network perspective for the study of online social networking sites (SNSs). Emphasis is placed on methodological approaches such as levels of analysis and sampling strategies as well as types of data amenable to network research, data mining and reduction, data archiving, and ethical issues such as seeking consent.

BACKGROUND

Drawing from social theory, mathematics (graphs), and empirical social science research methods, the tradition of social network analysis has been gaining ground since the early 1930s. Its origin is traced to the ideas of *social structure* developed by English anthropologist Alfred Reginald Radcliffe-Brown (1881–1955) and *sociometry*, the study of interpersonal relations and psychological wellbeing in groups of people advanced by Austrian American psychotherapist Jacob L. Moreno (1889–1974). Between the 1950s and 1970s, a number of theoretical conceptualizations and analytical techniques for measuring social relations were more formally defined to focus on the structure of social networks, their organization, and connections among social units in society.

In their landmark work evaluating the theoretical and methodological foundations of social network analysis (SNA) and its evolution, Wasserman and Faust (1994) viewed SNA as both a research perspective and a set of methods for applying network theory. Based on the assumption of the importance of structural relations in social systems, SNA encompasses "theories, models, and applications that are expressed in terms of relational concepts or processes" (p. 4). Social networks have been considered the "primary building blocks of the social world" (Marin & Wellman, 2011, p. 11). Advances in the social network research tradition revealed that many important aspects of societal life may be rooted in social networks and networks may have a profound impact on individual behavior (Galaskiewicz &Wasserman, 1994).

Social network researchers working within this perspective apply quantitative, qualitative, and mixed methods approaches. Some scholars see quantitative methods as predominant in SNA (Knoke & Kuklinski, 1982; Wasserman & Faust, 1994) because it is data-intensive and heavily relies on computations. Others argue that social network analysis is "neither quantitative, nor qualitative, nor both" (Carrington, 2015). On a similar note, Carrington (2014) asserts:

> Observing or calculating quantitative aspects of social networks, such as the average number of individuals with whom an individual is directly connected, or qualitative aspects, such as the nature of social ties among individuals, can be useful analytic techniques, but the fundamental quest is to understand the structure of the network, which is neither a quantity nor a quality. (p. 35)

Carrington (2014) goes on to explain that people may mistakenly perceive "mathematical" as "quantitative," neglecting to consider that the world of mathematics extends beyond "quantity," for example, as in graphs that represent structures rather than quantities.

Methodological advancements that occurred in SNA during the last several decades have led Carrington and Scott (2011) to conclude that social network analysis is a paradigm, rather than a theory or a method: It embraces theory, methodology, and a substantive body of empirical research.

METHODOLOGICAL ISSUES

From a social network perspective, "social life is created primarily and most importantly by relations and the patterns formed by these relations" (Marin & Wellman, 2011, p. 11). According to most definitions (Kadushin, 2012; Wellman & Berkowitz, 1988), a *network* is a structure composed of a set of social entities or *nodes* (individuals, families, companies, organizations). SNA centers on network structure, organization, and relations among social entities. Focusing on relations rather than specific attributes of nodes, social network analysis redefines the fundamental units of analysis used in social and behavioral sciences and shifts the emphasis to social interactions. "The unit is now the relation—for example, kinship relations among persons, communication links among officers of an organization, friendship structure within a small group," emphasize Garton, Haythornthwaite, and Wellman (1999, p. 78). One recent analysis explored the relationship between professional journalism and Twitter use in Germany. Neuberger, vom Hofe, and Nuernbergk (2014) surveyed 157 editors-in-chief of Internet news departments and conducted a quantitative content analysis of 963 tweets sent by media figures listed by Twitter Germany's "Top Tweets" and 355,000 retweets linking to journalistic websites sent by readers. This design allowed researchers to evaluate the Twitter phenomenon structurally, as well as compare the dissemination patterns of tweets among newsroom professionals and audiences. Thus, social network analysis provides a framework for studying patterns of relations and the interplay between social media networks, SNS-based communication, and social processes.

Levels of Analysis

Social network theory,[1] which is at the heart of the social network perspective, provides a set of concepts, each of which, as Wasserman and Faust (1994) explain, is associated with a particular level of analysis: actor, dyad, triad, subgroup, group, or network. At the individual level, which is called the *actor* level, network researchers are concerned with the actor's position in a network, for instance, centrality, prestige, or social roles (Wasserman & Faust, 1994). This level of analysis is considered the simplest as it is focused on one individual called *ego* and all other actors surrounding that individual known as *alters* (Knoke & Yang, 2008, p. 13). Students in classrooms, schools, ethnic groups, communities, and even nations are all examples of actors. An illustration of an egocentric network made of one actor and the surrounding nodes would be a researcher's profile page on ResearchGate.net or Academia.edu—professional online social networking sites (see Kurylo & Hu, chapter 5 in this volume).

A pair of actors forms a *dyad*, and when the number of actors grows to three (*triad*), the distribution of relational ties between them can create sixteen possible configurations, that is, sixteen different types of triads (Knoke & Yang, 2008). Dyadic analysis can provide information about actor distance, reachability, structural equivalence, tie strength, multiplexity, and reciprocity of relationships between two actors (Wasserman & Faust, 1994). Examples can be seen in the investigation of friendship networks in schools, or studies of intimate relationships established through matchmaking and online dating social networking sites like Kizmeet, HeartBroker, and eHarmony (see also Kalbfleisch, chapter 3, this volume). The analysis of triads can assess mutuality, balance, transitivity, and other structural properties of networks. Additionally, analysis may reveal more complicated patterns of social interactions or uncover manifestations of hierarchy (Kadushin, 2012).

A group of actors and associated ties, or a subset within a group, represents the next level of analysis. A group-level analysis is concerned with relations between areas of networks that are larger than a dyad or triad but smaller than a whole network (Prell, 2012), like Facebook groups or Google+ communities. At this level scholars can study interactions between network members and reveal connections such as "collaborations, friendships, trade ties, Web links, citations, resource flows, information flows, exchanges of social support" (Marin & Wellman, 2011, p. 12) or other patterns of relationships between actors. The process of change within a group can also be traced over time. Liberman (chapter 2, this volume) has scrutinized some of the issues related to group memberships—homophily and degree centrality—while focusing on lesser known, special-interest social networking site communities including WeRead, Recipefy, Travellerspoint, and others. Much of the research in the field of computer-mediated communication (CMC) has dealt with group-level social interactions.

Moving beyond interpersonal or group interactions, SNA can concentrate on *complete networks*, also referred to as whole networks. As such, whole networks provide "a bird's-eye view of social structure" (Marin & Wellman, p. 19). The network or macro level is considered the most important level of analysis (Knoke & Yang, 2008); it is also the most complex and has the most powerful implications. Researchers working at this level seek to describe structural characteristics and overall networks of relationships facilitated by social networking sites. For example, one such study examined the interconnectedness ("degrees of separation") of Facebook subscribers using the entire network or 721 million active users with a total of 69 billion ties (Backstrom, Boldi, Rosa, Ugander, & Vigna, 2012). Unlike Milgram's findings in his famous 1967 "small world" experiment, the results of this large-scale study showed that people were only four, not six "worlds apart." In another instance, Leavitt (2014) explored how Internet *memes* or unique cultural forms transmitted with million-scale magnitude (viral videos, images, fashion trends, or jokes) spread across massive social media systems such as Twitter. Leavitt, using both a qualitative analysis and computational methods, asserts that memes are vital for understanding the dynamics of Internet culture.

Determining an appropriate level of analysis requires an assessment of the size of the network and its components, and is driven by research objectives and specific research questions. The researcher's ability to study social media networks at various levels or to focus on multiple levels of analysis is the methodological advantage afforded by SNA.

Data Sources

Social network researchers can use a variety of data. It has been emphasized that data gathering for network studies can be performed using both conventional social science methods including survey, content analysis, and experiments as well as methods specific to SNA, such as various mathematical models and *sociograms* or visual representations of network relationships pioneered by Jacob L. Moreno in the early 1930s.[2] Social network data, however, are different from typical empirical data collected through traditional means in their distinct structural-relational emphasis on *ties* or relationships, connections, or linkages among social entities. Thus, network analysis data collection techniques focus on relations between actors rather than individual actors and their attributes or, as Wasserman and Faust (1994) explicitly put it, researchers collecting network data are interested in the "interrelatedness of social units" (p. 16). This means that network data can capture how actors are related, and how they are similar or dissimilar to each other across attributes or across all actors "embedded" in the overall network (Hanneman & Riddle, 2005).

Among common data sources for social network studies are direct observations, interviews, focus groups, diaries, various written records such as discussions on Twitter, blog posts, wikis, and massive amounts of data extracted by automated data collection means[3] (e.g., streaming APIs,[4] REST APIs,[5] Social Network Importer,[6] RapidMiner,[7] NameGenWeb,[8] and other tools utilizing various application programming interfaces). For example, Burke and Kraut (2014) used server logs and longitudinal surveys of 3,649 Facebook subscribers with 26,134 pairs of friends to determine whether technology-mediated communication facilitated relational closeness. Dyadic analysis displayed a positive association between tie strength and the use of direct (exchanging posts, comments, messages) and indirect (reading status updates, viewing photos) SNS-enabled communication channels.

Data mining refers to the process of extracting meaningful information from large-scale databases or raw data sets. Network analysts use data or text mining to simplify and summarize data, detect clusters of interacting objects, uncover hidden relationships that have not been previously identified, and produce predictions. Tweets, blogs, forums, RSS feeds, and status updates on social media sites present valuable data sources to analyze networked relationships and patterns that affect the attitudes, beliefs, and behaviors of social actors. Through the process of data mining and reduction, scientists extract useful models that summarize large data sets (e.g., cross-sectional, longitudinal) that can be applied in further analyses.[9]

A wealth of data for secondary data analysis can be obtained from various content collecting and archiving initiatives around the world[10] including but not limited to such renowned repositories as the Library of Congress, the

British Library, the National Library of the Netherlands, and the Internet Memory Foundation based in Paris and Amsterdam, among others. The National Library of Medicine (NLM) in the United States collects and preserves health- and medicine-related blogs[11] freely available for researchers interested in doctor-patient relations, nurses' and physicians' networks, and issues of public health. The world's largest biomedical library, NLM announced plans to increase the use of diverse data types to keep pace with the change in biomedical data science and support research in modern health care (NIH, 2015).

Social network data produced in abundance during social media exchanges can also be derived from electronic archives, like Alexa,[12] the Internet Movie Database (IMDb),[13] or Usenet archive.[14] In 2010 the Library of Congress acquired by gift an archive of Twitter messages from 2006–2010 and started archiving the daily stream of public tweets. As of January 2013, it accumulated approximately 170 billion tweets totaling 133.2 terabytes of data (Library of Congress, 2013). The collection, yet to be opened to the general public, holds a goldmine of data for network researchers given that the structure and organization of the archive as well as legal issues associated with disclosure of private information contained within the archive are resolved.[15] Before these issues are addressed, however, researchers often have to rely on customized crawling activities to collect tweet data.

Sampling Strategies

The social network perspective emphasizes that a network is composed of a set of objects and relations among them. As noted by Marin and Wellman (2011), decisions on which entities to include in analysis often present a challenge. Given the highly dynamic and interactive nature of social relationships enabled by online platforms, determining the boundaries around nodes is of particular importance. Butts (2008) warns that inappropriate inclusion or exclusion of actors may have implications that extend far beyond those entities themselves and may negatively affect the results of the analyses. This brings to the foreground the question of the confines of the sample, or *boundary specification*, when collecting data on networks, especially those that may have no apparent limits, as with unstructured P2P networks such as Gnutella or Freenet.

Specific to network studies are two main approaches to sampling: *positional* and *reputational* (Scott, 2013). To ensure that a sample is representative of a population of interest, network researchers applying the positional approach start with identifying group membership that is formally defined by a set of criteria like the size of a corporation or affiliation with a political party. In the field of social network analysis, studies of business or political elites are often cited as examples of the positional strategy. Scholars who study social networking and video-sharing websites as platforms for political communication can use this strategy for analyzing the flow of information or identifying leaders. Reputational strategy, the second approach, is effective when the information on the boundary of the target population needs to be obtained from respondents themselves, such as key informants or knowledgeable experts, or when no listing of natural groupings within the population exists (Knoke & Yang, 2008). Studies utilizing positional and reputational approaches typically employ surveys or interviews, although experimental designs may also be used. Both of these approaches, however, have the potential for sampling bias because selected nodes may be lacking relational ties, as in the case of the former approach, or relevant and influential actors may simply be not included in the sample, as in the case of the latter. To alleviate these concerns and minimize selection bias, researchers may utilize theoretically driven and empirically tested criteria or they may use a combination of sampling techniques.

Yet another strategy, "neither positional nor reputational" (Scott, 2013, p. 46) is event driven, that is, the choice of units is dictated by certain activities or events in which people are engaged rather than affiliations or the existence of enumerated subgroups in the population. One such large-scale analysis focused on users' understanding of the processes through which online networks may influence political preferences and voting behavior. The authors of the study (Bond et al., 2012), published in the journal *Nature*, took measurements on the accounts of 61 million Facebook users on November 2, 2010, the day of the congressional election in the United States. Results of a randomized controlled experiment showed that political mobilization messages diffused through Facebook may have had a direct impact on real-world voting behavior.

Conventional sampling techniques, both random and nonrandom, can also be applied to the examination of online networks. In that case, the extent to which study design enables researchers to draw unambiguous conclusions or generalize more widely should be treated with caution, as when using traditional social science methods. A study by the Pew Research Center (2012) analyzed news consumption patterns in the evolving media landscape by comparing print and digital media. The data collected were based on a telephone survey of 3,003 landline and cell phone owners using a combination of stratified and systematic random sampling. The study found that the most dramatic change occurred in the rise of news consumption on SNSs.

Cluster sampling is the method of choice when a population of interest consists of somewhat homogeneous subgroups (or strata); in this scenario, participants can be selected randomly from each cluster, for example, top and middle managers who comprise specific clusters of organizations. These clusters can be derived from organizational charts and their representative samples can be drawn randomly, for example, to assess interaction patterns and activities of organizations performing social media advertising campaigns. A simple random sample would be instrumental in studying Usenet newsgroups—communities of Internet users centered around a particular topic or hobby.

The snowball technique, on the contrary, is a nonrandom sampling procedure in which a small number of network actors are interviewed and asked to nominate additional participants based on their individual connections. The resulting social network would represent relationships that occur naturally in the target population. This method was used in a study of the MySpace network by Caverlee and Webb (2008) who explored the demographic characteristics and social interaction of MySpace users and analyzed over 1.9 million MySpace profiles, employing a combination of relationship-based snowball sampling and random sampling techniques.

However, traditional sampling methods may be limited when it comes to working with today's high-volume streams of big data generated by social media. As the body of academic research focused on social networks continues to grow, the number of large-scale studies utilizing social media data is also increasing. Still, some scientists question whether people who use social media represent society as a whole. As Ruths and Pfeffer (2014) emphasize, the ability to interpret large-scale data analyses when looking for patterns of human behavior facilitated by technology requires that researchers acknowledge the characteristics inherent in social media platforms like Twitter or Pinterest and the way data streams are filtered by these platforms and released to the public. They stress that Twitter's retweet function links every retweeted message to its original post, but not to the user who initiated the retweet. In particular, researchers note, platform design, user base, access constraints, platform-specific algorithms, nonhuman accounts, and spam messages may all affect the reliability of collected data. Therefore, the extent to which network sampling methods are free of bias has to be taken into account both at the stage of study design and when interpreting the results.

Ethical Issues

It should be noted that since 2010 when the Library of Congress started archiving public Twitter traffic, issues of protecting user confidentiality and privacy have come to light. Some of the difficulties result from the sheer magnitude of accumulated data (Zimmer, 2015). Researchers boyd and Crawford (2012) have called attention to important ethical issues in handling big data and attempts to harvest massive amounts of information from online social networks like Facebook and Twitter. "The process of evaluating the research ethics cannot be ignored simply because the data are seemingly public," they argue (p. 672). They continue, "It may be unreasonable to ask researchers to obtain consent from every person who posts a tweet, but it is problematic for researchers to justify their actions as ethical simply because the data are accessible" (p. 672). While other scholars agree that "a case-by-case decision regarding each individual tweet is infeasible" in dealing with big data (Beurskens, 2014, p. 132), anonymization of data is warranted. "It is certainly insufficient to simply eliminate the usernames from the data set, as the identity of a user may be easily derived from other facts mentioned in the tweet (including locations, other users, etc.)," Beurskens affirms (p. 132).

In September 2008, a group of researchers at the Berkman Center for Internet and Society at Harvard University released a dataset of 1,700 Facebook profiles of first-year students at an "anonymous, northwestern American university" (Berkman Center, 2008). The data set known as "Tastes, Ties, and Time" was intended to become the first phase in a Dataverse Network Project, which began in 2006 in conjunction with the Open Data Assistance Program at Harvard. Additional data sets were to be added in the following three years to generate a complete snapshot of students' social networking activities on Facebook during their four years in college to provide researchers with longitudinal data. Two studies were released at the time—an analysis of friendship patterns among students (Lewis et al., 2008) and a study of students' preferred privacy settings on Facebook (Lewis, Kaufman, & Christakis, 2008). Although the data from personal profiles were collected anonymously with all identifying information removed, this release of social network profile data into the public domain raised concerns about the protection of individuals' privacy. Zimmer (2010) offers a critical account of the privacy risks associated with data collection for the project and identifies three groups of ethical deficiencies: amount of personal information collected, improper access to personal information, and unauthorized secondary use of personal information. Zimmer calls for the unobtrusive use of SNS-generated data, proper data anonymization, and adherence to ethical practices in research.[16]

In January 2012, researchers in Facebook's Core Data Science team conducted a large-scale experimental study of user emotions by tweaking the amount of positive and negative content posted to their Facebook news feeds for a week. The study found that people's emotions could be affected by the emotional expressions of other network users, "leading people to experience the same emotions without their awareness" (Kramer, Guillory, & Hancock, 2014, p. 8788). None of the 689,003 randomly selected users whose newsfeed updates were manipulated for research purposes had given consent to participate or were aware of the interventions. The article, published in the *Proceedings of the National Academy of Sciences*, simply stated that this practice "was consistent with Facebook's Data Use Policy" (p. 8788), which all Facebook users accept before creating their accounts. The results implied that emotions might be manipulated on a large scale through social networking "mega" platforms such as Facebook without people's knowledge, causing much debate pertaining to the ethical implications both in the scholarly community and society at large (see Goel, 2014; Taylor, 2014).

Evidently, data collection from social media networks presents serious ethical challenges, and it is the responsibility of researchers to develop strategies to safeguard participants' social and emotional wellbeing, preserve anonymity and confidentiality, and prevent privacy breaches. Future students of online social networks should recognize that informed consent, distinctions between public and private information, and participant anonymity (Ackland, 2013) remain key to understanding the ethics of research associated with social media networks, particularly when on a larger scale. In addition to data storage and data sharing, participant recruitment via social media, age verification, and issues of data protection and ownership will require careful attention. The range of ethical concerns inherent in online social network research activities is perhaps not completely understood, but the main principles for the protection of human subjects in research—respect for persons, beneficence, and justice—remain pertinent.

The Use of Software

Computer software that can aid with the analysis of social networks[17] is abundant (Huisman & van Duijn, 2011; Wasserman & Faust, 1994). For example, UCINET, developed in the 1980s by sociologists Linton C. Freeman, Martin Everett, and Stephen Borgatti at the University of California, Irvine, is a comprehensive computer-assisted tool that is continuously updated. UCINET allows users to execute positional and role analysis and calculate the properties of graphs and nodes, including measures of centrality, hierarchical clustering, variety of data transformations, and multivariate statistics. Originally written in BASIC, the program runs on the Windows platform, both the 32-bit and 64-bit versions; in addition, it can be installed on a Mac or Linux computer with the help of an emulator or a compatibility layer software application. UCINET can be used as a 90-day free download[18] or purchased for $40 (students) or $150 (faculty). Stanford Network Analysis Platform (SNAP) is another popular software package that provides the ability to capture network dynamics. Written in C++, SNAP can manipulate large-scale graphs, calculate the structural properties of large networks, and analyze the attributes of tens of millions of nodes. SNAP is not to be confused with SNAPP, which stands for Social Networks Adapting Pedagogical Practice, designed specifically for studying online learning contexts. Pajek is an application for analyzing massive sets of network data[19] ; it runs on Windows and is free for noncommercial use. NodeXL, another free tool, is an open source add-on for Microsoft Excel that can execute basic social network analysis functions and visualizations (Hansen, Schneiderman, & Smith, 2010). Network visualizations[20] help researchers to understand the evolving patterns of relationships, for example, those that occur in friendship networks or interactions in national blogospheres. The Pew Research Center, for instance, conducted a longitudinal study of tweet data resulting in network visualization maps using NodeXL that helped to produce a taxonomy of Twitter conversations—the six types of Twitter networks (see Smith, Rainie, Himelboim, & Sheiderman, 2014).

CONCLUSION

This chapter aimed to outline the primary methodological approaches and key issues facing researchers who undertake social network studies in the age of social media. The decision of the Library of Congress to archive Twitter traffic has become recognition of the fact that "society turns to social media as a primary method of communication and creative expression" (Library of Congress, 2013). The emergence and enormous popularity of social networking sites such as Facebook and Twitter have altered the traditional modes of communication in society and affected many aspects of modern-day social interactions. Social networking activity, already penetrating areas as diverse as friendship formation, organizational behavior, politics and civic engagement, social movements and mobilization, and scholarly activity and communication has the potential to occupy an even greater role in people's lives.

Both nonprofits such as Pew Research Center (e.g., Lenhart, 2015) and business analytics companies like comScore (2015) agree that the line between the digital and physical worlds is blurring. The convergence of social media platforms accelerates the expansion of social networking services that are now accessible anytime and anywhere via smartphones, laptop computers, tablets, portable media players, and wearables, among others. Technology-mediated environments enabled by online social networks continue to evolve and are becoming more multifaceted, increasingly embracing the functionality and features of other social media forms, with participatory multimedia-sharing websites and microblogs in particular. Not only text but also photo, audio, and video content is generated and shared in real-time fashion with growing numbers of SNS subscribers around the world. At the same time, the use of social networking applications is becoming more ubiquitous and deliberate. It embraces advances in computing such as location-based tools, touch-screen technology, autostereoscopic 3D imaging, gesture control systems, and speech recognition. Technological progress requires researchers to keep pace with the times and continuously update their research arsenals.

Effectively fitting the developments in digital communication technologies and going far beyond the "network" metaphor, social network analysis has emerged as an interdisciplinary field of knowledge and a set of analytical tools for studying social relations and processes mediated by the explosion of online social networks. A symbiotic relationship between theory and method (Wasserman & Faust, 1994) has created a multidimensional space in which scholars hailing from diverse academic backgrounds and research traditions are equally positioned to explore the complex relationship between social networking sites, SNS-enabled behavior, and social interaction.

Social network analysis offers a conceptual and methodological framework for understanding the patterns of social interactions made possible by social networking websites. It maintains a set of unique assumptions, measures, analytical models, and techniques. Initially geared towards quantitative methods, it no longer privileges a particular approach and affords researchers the ability to analyze social media networks at multiple levels, and with a wide variety of tools. However, both quantitative and qualitative approaches to examining SNS-mediated communication come with limitations inherent in each of these traditions. Among the potential issues are selection bias, small sample size (successfully addressed by large-scale studies), small response rate, accuracy and consistency of measurements, subjectivity, and lack of generalizability. Sample selection bias can arise from nonrandomly selected data sets and participants' self-selection.

As noted, research applying the social network perspective can be conducted at different levels of analysis and can be of small or large scale. Large-scale investigations of online social networks have been effective in utilizing a range of computer programs specifically designed for network analysis and handling large amounts of data. Although data collection from massive social networking sites like Facebook or Twitter is not free of technical difficulties, further challenges relate to issues of data ownership, privacy, anonymity, and confidentiality. As research on social media networks is coming of age, solving the ethical challenges of dealing with big data promises to open new research avenues for the future study of the social networking universe.

REFERENCES

Ackland, R. (2013). *Web social science: Concepts, data and tools for social scientists in the digital age.* London: Sage.

Backstrom, L., P. Boldi, M. Rosa, J. Ugander, & S. Vigna. (2012). Four degrees of separation. In *Proceedings of the 4th Annual ACM Web Science Conference* (pp. 33–42). New York: ACM. Retrieved from http://arxiv.org/pdf/1111.4570v3.pdf.

Berkman Center for Internet and Society. (2008, September 25). *Tastes, ties, and time: Facebook data release.* Retrieved from https://cyber.law.harvard.edu/node/94446.

Berkowitz, S. D. (1982). *An introduction to structural analysis: The network approach to social research.* Toronto: Butterworths.

Beurskens, M. (2014). Legal questions of Twitter research. In K. Weller, A. Bruns, J. Burgess, M. Mahrt, & C. Puschmann (Eds.), *Twitter and society* (pp. 123–133). New York: Peter Lang.

Bond, R. M., et al. (2012). A 61-million-person experiment in social influence and political mobilization. *Nature* 489:295–298. doi: 10.1038/nature11421.

Borgatti, S. P., D. J. Brass, & D. S. Halgin. (2014). Social network research: Confusions, criticisms, and controversies. In D. J. Brass, G. Labianca, A. Mehra, D. S. Halgin, & S. P. Borgatti (Eds.), *Contemporary perspectives on organizational social networks* (Research in Sociology of Organizations Series, Vol. 40, pp. 1–32). Bradford, UK: Emerald.

boyd, D., & Crawford, K. (2012). Critical questions for big data: Provocations for a cultural, technological, and scholarly phenomenon. *Information, Communication & Society* 15 (5): 662–679. doi: 10.1080/1369118X.2012.678878.

Burke, M., & R. Kraut. (2014). Growing closer on Facebook: Changes in tie strength through social network site use. In *Proceedings of the SIGCHI Conference on Human Factors in Computing Systems* (pp. 4187–4196). New York: ACM. Retrieved from http://dl.acm.org/.

Burt, R. S. (1982). *Toward a structural theory of action: Network models of social structure, perception and action*. New York: Academic Press.

Butts, C. T. (2008). Social network analysis: A methodological introduction. *Asian Journal of Social Psychology* 11:13–41.

Caverlee, J., & S. Webb. (2008). A large-scale study of MySpace: Observations and implications for online social networks. In *Proceedings of the 2nd International Conference on Weblogs and Social Media* (pp. 36–44). Menlo Park, CA: AAAI Press.

Carrington, P. J. (2014). Social network research. In S. Domínguez & B. Hollstein (Eds.), *Mixed methods social networks research* (pp. 35–64). Cambridge, UK: Cambridge University Press.

Carrington, P. J. (2015, April 29). *Social network analysis*. [Annotated bibliography and research guide]. Retrieved from http://www.oxfordbibliographies.com/view/document/obo-9780199756841/obo-9780199756841-0100.xml.

Carrington, P. J., & J. Scott. (2011). Introduction. In J. Scott & P. J. Carrington (Eds.), *The SAGE handbook of social network analysis* (pp. 1–8). London: Sage.

comScore. (2015). *2015 U.S. digital future in focus*. [Report]. Retrieved from https://www.comscore.com/Insights/Presentations-and-Whitepapers/2015/2015-US-Digital-Future-in-Focus.

Degenne, A., & M. Forsé. (1999). *Introducing social networks* (A. Borges, Trans.). London: Sage.

Deloitte. (2015). *Facebook's global economic impact*. [Report]. London: Deloitte. Retrieved from http://www2.deloitte.com/content/dam/Deloitte/uk/Documents/technology-media-telecommunications/deloitte-uk-global-economic-impact-of-facebook.pdf.

Duggan, M., N. B. Ellison, C. Lampe, A. Lenhart, & M. Madden. (2015, January 9). *Demographics of key social networking platforms*. [Social media update]. Washington, DC: Pew Research Center. Retrieved from http://www.pewinternet.org/2015/01/09/demographics-of-key-social-networking-platforms-2/.

Galaskiewicz, J., & S. Wasserman. (1994). Introduction: Advances in the social and behavioral sciences from social network analysis. In S. Wasserman & J. Galaskiewicz (Eds.), *Advances in social network analysis: Research in the social and behavioral sciences*. Thousand Oaks, CA: Sage.

Garton, L., C. Haythornthwaite, & B. Wellman. (1999). Studying on-line social networks. In S. Jones (Ed.), *Doing Internet research: Critical issues and methods for examining the Net* (pp. 75–105). Thousand Oaks, CA: Sage.

Goel, V. (2014, June 29). Facebook tinkers with users' emotions in news feed experiment, stirring outcry. *The New York Times*. Retrieved from http://www.nytimes.com/2014/06/30/technology/facebook-tinkers-with-users-emotions-in-news-feed-experiment-stirring-outcry.html?_r=1.

Hanneman, R. A., & M. Riddle. (2005). *Introduction to social network methods*. Riverside, CA: University of California Riverside. Retrieved from http://faculty.ucr.edu/~hanneman/nettext/Introduction_to_Social_Network_Methods.pdf.

Hansen, D. L., B. Schneiderman, & M. A. Smith. (2010). *Analyzing social media networks with NodeXL: Insights from a connected world*. Amsterdam, Netherlands: M. Kaufmann.

Heidemann, J., M. Klier, & F. Probst. (2012). Online social networks: A survey of a global phenomenon. *Computer Networks* 56 (18): 3866–3878.

Huisman, M., & M. A. J. van Duijn. (2011). A reader's guide to SNA software. In J. Scott & P. J. Carrington (Eds.), The SAGE handbook of social network analysis (pp. 578–600) . London: Sage.

Kadushin, C. (2012). *Understanding social networks: Theories, concepts, and findings.* New York: Oxford University Press.

Knoke, D., & J. H. Kuklinski. (1982). *Network analysis: Quantitative applications in social sciences.* Newbury Park, CA: Sage.

Knoke, D., & S. Yang. (2008). *Social network analysis* (2nd ed.). Thousand Oaks, CA: Sage.

Kramer, A. D. I., J. E. Guillory, & J. T. Hancock. (2014). Experimental evidence of massive-scale emotional contagion through social networks. *Proceedings of the National Academy of Sciences* 111 (24): 8788–8790. Retrieved from http://www.pnas.org/content/111/24/8788.full.

Krempel, L. (2011). Network visualization. In J. Scott & P. J. Carrington (Eds.), The SAGE handbook of social network analysis (pp. 558–577) . London: Sage.

Leavitt, A. (2014). From #FollowFriday to YOLO: Exploring the cultural salience of Twitter memes. In K. Weller, A. Bruns, J. Burgess, M. Mahrt, & C. Puschmann (Eds.), *Twitter and society* (pp. 137–154). New York: Peter Lang.

Lenhart, A. (2015, April 9). *Teens, social media & technology overview 2015: Smartphones facilitate shifts in communication landscape for teens.* [Pew Research Center's report]. Washington, DC. Retrieved from http://www.pewinternet.org/files/2015/04/PI_TeensandTech_Update2015_0409151.pdf.

Lewis, K., J. Kaufman, & N. A. Christakis. (2008). The taste for privacy: An analysis of college student privacy settings in an online social network. *Journal of Computer-Mediated Communication* 14:79–100.

Lewis, K., J. Kaufman, M. Gonzalez, A. Wimmer, & N. Christakis. (2008). Tastes, ties, and time: A new social network dataset using Facebook.com. *Social Networks* 30 (4): 330–342.

The Library of Congress. (2013, January). *Update on the Twitter archive at the Library of Congress.* [White paper]. Washington, DC. Retrieved from http://www.loc.gov/today/pr/2013/files/twitter_report_2013jan.pdf.

Marin, A., & B. Wellman. (2011). Social network analysis: An introduction. In J. Scott & P. J. Carrington (Eds.), *The SAGE handbook of social network analysis* (pp. 11– 25). London: Sage.

Milgram, S. (1967). The small world problem. *Psychology Today* 2 (1): 60–67.

Moreno, J. L. (1934/1953). *Who shall survive? Foundations of sociometry, group psychotherapy and sociodrama.* New York: Beacon House.

Neuberger, C., H. J. vom Hofe, & C. Nuernbergk. (2014). The use of Twitter by professional journalists. In K. Weller, A. Bruns, J. Burgess, M. Mahrt, & C. Puschmann (Eds.), *Twitter and society* (pp. 345–357). New York: Peter Lang.

NIH approves strategic vision to transform National Library of Medicine. [Press release]. (2015, June 11). Washington, DC: U.S. Department of Health & Human Services. Retrieved from http://www.nih.gov/news/health/jun2015/od-11.htm.

Nooy, W. de, A. Mrvar, & V. Batagelj. (2005). *Exploratory social network analysis with Pajek.* New York: Cambridge University Press.

Pew Research Center. (2012, September 27). *In changing news landscape, even television is vulnerable: Trends in news consumption 1991–2012.* Washington, DC. Retrieved from http://www.people-press.org/files/legacy-pdf/2012%20News%20Consumption%20Report.pdf.

Prell, C. (2012). *Social network analysis: History, theory & methodology.* London: Sage.

Quint, B. (1998, October 19). A "gift of the Web" for the Library of Congress from Alexa Internet. *Information Today.* Retrieved from http://newsbreaks.infotoday.com/nbreader.asp?ArticleID=17893.

Ruths, D., & J. Pfeffer. (2014). Social media for large studies of behavior. *Science* 346 (6213): 1063–1064.

Scott, J. (2013). *Social network analysis* (3rd ed.). London: Sage.

Smith, M. A., L. Rainie, I. Himelboim, & B. Sheiderman. (2014). *Mapping Twitter topic networks: From polarized crowds to community clusters*. [Pew Research Center's report]. Washington, DC. Retrieved from http://www.pewinternet.org/files/2014/02/PIP_Mapping-Twitter-networks_022014.pdf.

Taylor, V. (2014, June 28). Facebook tweaked news feeds to see if users' emotions are contagious. *New York Daily News*. Retrieved from http://www.nydailynews.com/life-style/face-book-tweaked-news-feeds-experiment-users-emotions-article-1.1847759.

Wasserman, S., & K. Faust. (1994). *Social network analysis: Methods and applications*. Cambridge, UK: Cambridge University Press.

Wellman, B., & S. D. Berkowitz. (1988). *Social structures: A network approach*. Cambridge, UK: Cambridge University Press.

Zafarani, R., M. A. Abbasi, & H. Liu. (2014). *Social media mining: An introduction*. New York: Cambridge University Press.

Zimmer, M. (2010). But the data is already public: On the ethics of research in Facebook. *Ethics and Information Technology* 12 (4): 313–325.

———. The Twitter archive at the Library of Congress: Challenges for information practice and information policy. *First Monday* 20 (7). Retrieved from http://firstmonday.org/ojs/index.php/fm/article/view/5619/4653.

Zimmer, M., & N. Proferes. (2014). Privacy on Twitter, Twitter on privacy. In K. Weller, A. Bruns, J. Burgess, M. Mahrt, & C. Puschmann (Eds.), *Twitter and society* (pp. 169–181). New York: Peter Lang.

NOTES

1. For a comprehensive overview of the theoretical foundation of the social network perspective, see Berkowitz (1982) and Burt (1982).

2. See Moreno (1934/1953).

3. As of July 2015, Facebook policies prohibit third-party data gathering using "automated means (such as harvesting bots, robots, spiders, or scrapers)" without obtaining permission from the company.

4. Streaming APIs allow for customizable access to Twitter's stream of data. See "The Streaming APIs Overview" at https://dev.twitter.com/streaming/overview for more details.

5. REST (representational state transfer) APIs offer an array of methods to access Twitter data including queries of popular tweets, recent tweets, and tweets about places, among other features. REST can be used for extracting data from other social networking sites, mashups, and mobile applications. For more details, see https://dev.twitter.com/rest/public.

6. Social Network Importer (socialnetimporter.codeplex.com) enables direct downloads and imports of a variety of social network data such as Facebook Fan pages and Group networks data.

7. RapidMiner (rapidminer.com) is a free and open source data miner.

8. Developed by the Oxford Internet Institute, NameGenWeb is a Facebook application for collecting personal profile data available for download at https://apps.facebook.com/namegen-web. As of July 2015, NameGenWeb is no longer updated.

9. Among examples of data mining techniques are topic detection and tracking, homophily clustering, sentiment analysis, community detection algorithms, Semantic Web mining, and others. See Zafarani, Abbasi, and Liu (2014) for more information.

10. An index of web archiving initiatives is maintained by the International Internet Preservation Consortium (IIPC) (www.netpreserve.org).

11. The National Library of Medicine collection is searchable and can be accessed from http://www.archive-it.org/collections/2722.

12. An archive of web pages accessible through the Wayback Machine was started in 1996 by Alexa Internet (www.alexa.com). In 1998 Alexa donated two terabytes of digital content with a snapshot of the early World Wide Web to the Library of Congress (Quint, 1998).

13. The Internet Movie Database (IMDb) is comprised of over 3.3 million titles and 6.6 million personalities (see http://www.imdb.com/stats). The IMDb website (www.imdb.com)

features message boards, photo galleries, entertainment news, and a subscription-based social networking service (www.imdbpro.com) for professionals in the entertainment industry. As of July 2015, the IMDb community on Twitter had 1.56 million followers.

14. A searchable archive of over 700 million Usenet newsgroup posts can be accessed via Google Groups at https://groups.google.com.

15. For more information regarding legal issues associated with the Twitter archive at the Library of Congress, see Zimmer (2015).

16. See Zimmer and Proferes (2014) for an overview of Twitter privacy issues.

17. Wasserman and Faust (1994) provided one of the first comprehensive reviews of statistical software packages handy for network analysis. A detailed review of computer programs developed specifically to perform SNA can be found in Huisman and van Duijn (2011).

18. UCINET software can be downloaded from https://sites.google.com/site/ucinetsoftware/downloads.

19. See an introduction to Pajek written by de Nooy, Mrvar, and Batagelj (2005).

20. See Krempel (2011) for more information on network visualization techniques.

Index

About the Editors and Contributors

Lemi Baruh (PhD, Annenberg School for Communication, University of Pennsylvania) is associate professor and chair at the Department of Media and Visual Arts, College of Social Sciences and Humanities at Koç University in Istanbul, Turkey. His research interests include new media technologies, political engagement, identity, surveillance, privacy—especially pertaining to attitudes about privacy—and the culture of voyeurism. He is an associate editor of the *International Journal of Interactive Communication Systems and Technologies* and an editorial board member of the *Journal of Communication*. He can be contacted at *lbaruh@ku.edu.tr*.

Tatyana Dumova (PhD, Bowling Green State University) is a professor in the School of Communication at Point Park University in Pittsburgh where she teaches undergraduate and graduate courses in communication theory, research methods, and multimedia. Her research focuses on the social and cultural implications of Internet-based communication technologies and the role of technology in teaching and learning. She has presented and published her research nationally and internationally. Dumova has lead-edited *Blogging in the Global Society: Cultural, Political and Geographical Aspects* and the two-volume *Handbook of Research on Social Interaction Technologies and Collaboration Software: Concepts and Trends*. She can be contacted at *tdumova@pointpark.edu*.

Zeynep Günel (MA, Sabanci University) is a PhD student at the Design, Technology and Society program at Koç University in Istanbul, Turkey. Her research interests involve social movements, new media technologies, and information visualization. She is a graduate assistant at the Social Interaction

& Media Lab (SIMLab) at Koç University. She can be contacted at *zgu-nel13@ku.edu.tr.*

Yifeng Hu (PhD, Pennsylvania State University) is an assistant professor in the Department of Communication Studies at The College of New Jersey. Her research interests include uses and effects of new media and emerging technologies in health communication, instructional technology and pedagogy, and intercultural communication. She has published peer-reviewed articles in journals such as *Communication Research, Journal of Computer-Mediated Communication, Journalism & Mass Communication Educator*, and *Electronic Journal of Communication*. In her classes, students collaborated with healthcare industry professionals on technology-related projects. She has experimented with integrating a variety of information and communication technologies into teaching and conducted research on intercultural/ intergroup communication topics. She has been invited to give in-person and virtual speeches about her teaching innovations on and off campus. She can be contacted at *hu@tcnj.edu.*

Pamela Kalbfleisch (PhD, Michigan State University) is a professor of communication at the University of North Dakota. Kalbfleisch is author of *Mentoring Enactment Theory* and publishes widely in the area of mentoring and personal relationships. She is interested in issues affecting communication in personal relationships. Kalbfleisch is a member of the Women's Network Executive Council for the American Council on Education. She has served in leadership roles including dean of the College of Arts and Sciences at Concordia University Chicago; special assistant to the president for strategic initiatives and director of the School of Communication at the University of North Dakota; and as chair of the Faculty Senate at the University of Wyoming. She is a 2009–2010 Fellow of the American Council on Education Fellows Program. She can be contacted at *pamela.kalbfleisch@gmail.com.*

Anastacia Kurylo (PhD, Rutgers University) is an assistant professor in the Communication Studies Department at St. Joseph's College. Her research focuses on stereotypes communicated in interpersonal, intercultural, and organizational contexts; her additional interests include intercultural new media research as well as pedagogy. Her recent publications include *The Communicated Stereotype: From Celebrity Vilification to Everyday Talk* and *Inter/Cultural Communication: Representation and Construction of Culture*. She is president of the New York State Communication Association, assistant director of the Center for Intercultural New Media Research, chair of the Board of Trustees of The Quad Preparatory School, and former president of the New York Chapter of the Tri-State Diversity Council. She can be contacted at *anastacia@kurylo.com.*

Corey Jay Liberman (PhD, Rutgers University) is an associate professor in the Department of Communication and Media Arts at Marymount Manhattan College. His research spans the interpersonal communication, group communication, and organizational communication areas. He has coauthored a textbook, *Organizational Communication: Strategies for Success*, and edited a case study book titled *Casing Persuasive Communication*. His recent research examines crisis communication, social practices of dissent within organizations, specifically the antecedents, processes, and effects associated with effective employee dissent communication. He can be contacted at *cliberman@mmm.edu.*

Giuseppe Lugano (PhD, University of Jyväskylä) is a science officer at COST (European Cooperation in Science and Technology) in Belgium, the longest-running European framework for cooperation in science and technology. His research interests center on the conceptual design of technologies and services for community and sustainable living. In particular, he focuses on principles and applications of social networking in mobile contexts. He has recently coedited the book *Social Robots from a Human Perspective* and two special issues on social robotics for the journals *The Information Society* and *Cognitive Computation.* He can be contacted at *giuseppe.lugano@cost.eu.*

Guy Merchant (PhD, Sheffield Hallam University) is a professor in the Sheffield Institute of Education at Sheffield Hallam University, United Kingdom. He specializes in research into digital literacy and is particularly interested in the interrelations between young people, new technology, and literacy. He has widely published in international journals and is a founding editor of the *Journal of Early Childhood Literacy*. His groundbreaking work *Web 2.0 for Schools* was coauthored with Julia Davies and he has also coedited a number of collections including *Virtual Literacies* and *New Literacies across the Globe*. He is active in digital literacy education in the United Kingdom and beyond including writing curriculum materials and professional publications. He can be contacted at *G.H.Merchant@shu.ac.uk.*

Hans K. Meyer (PhD, University of Missouri) is an assistant professor at the E.W. Scripps School of Journalism at Ohio University. His research focuses on creating community online and how news organizations have adapted to reaching their audiences online. His work has been published in *Journalism Practice, Newspaper Research Journal,* and *American Behavioral Scientist.* Before joining academia he worked for nearly a decade as a reporter and editor for community newspapers in Utah, Nevada, and California. At the University of Missouri, Meyer was part of the team that founded MyMissourian.com, one of the first citizen journalism websites in the United States. He can be contacted at *meyerh@ohio.edu.*

Salvatore Scifo (PhD, University of Westminster) is an assistant professor at the Department of Public Relations and Publicity (English), Faculty of Communication, at Maltepe University, Istanbul, Turkey. He has recently concluded his post-doctoral research with the European Union's FP7-funded COSMIC project, titled *The Contribution of Social Media in Crisis Management*, at the Mediated Interaction and Experience Lab (Mixlab) at Koç University, Istanbul. He has published on topics such as social media and crises, citizen involvement in emergencies, the reliability of information in new media, as well as community media policy and practices in Europe. Prior to that, he has worked at Marmara University (Istanbul), London Metropolitan University, and the University of Westminster. He is a former member of the Executive Board and current member of the Advisory Board of the European Communication Research and Education Association (ECREA). He can be contacted at *salvatorescifo@maltepe.edu.tr.*

Zixue Tai (PhD, University of Minnesota) is an associate professor in the School of Journalism and Telecommunications at the University of Kentucky. His research interests pertain to a multitude of issues in the new media landscape of China. He is the author of *The Internet in China: Cyberspace and Civil Society*, and is completing a book on "gold farming" in massively multiplayer online games in China. Besides contributions to about a dozen edited volumes, his numerous publications can also be found in journals such as *International Communication Gazette, Journalism & Mass Communication Quarterly, New Media & Society, Journal of Communication, Sociology of Health & Illness*, and *Psychology & Marketing*. He teaches undergraduate and graduate courses in media effects, world media systems, advanced multimedia, video game studies, and social media theory and practice. He can be contacted at *zai2@uky.edu.*

Kush Wadhwa (MBA, New York University) is a senior partner at Trilateral Research & Consulting, United Kingdom, a research and advisory consultancy bringing together strategy, technology, and policy. He participates in research affecting the future direction of security and surveillance technologies (UAVs, biometrics, cybersecurity), use of technologies in crisis, disaster management, and emerging technologies and applications (e.g., predictive analytics, big data technology, cloud computing). He provides advanced research and advisory services with respect to emerging technologies in security, ICT, and data sciences, focusing upon issues of strategic policy development related to privacy and data protection, socioeconomic issues, and technology assessment. He is a frequent speaker at international conferences and is widely published in industry and peer-reviewed journals. He can be contacted at *kush.wadhwa@trilateralresearch.com.*

Pamela E. Walck (PhD, E.W. Scripps School of Journalism at Ohio University) is an assistant professor in the Department of Journalism & Multimedia Arts at Duquesne University. Her research focuses on the use of technology in the newsroom, history of journalism, and the African American press and race relations during World War II. Prior to entering graduate school, she spent more than a decade in the newspaper industry where she held various positions from reporter to editor to staff writing coach. She can be contacted at *pewalck@gmail.com.*

Hayley Watson (PhD, University of Kent) is a senior research analyst at Trilateral Research & Consulting, United Kingdom, a research and advisory consultancy bringing together strategy, technology, and policy. Her area of expertise involves the role of technology including social media in relation to security. She is particularly interested in the use of ICT in crisis management. Watson has published in peer-reviewed journals on citizen journalism in relation to security, social media, and crisis management and has participated in a number of conferences. She is actively involved in the Information Systems for Crisis Response and Management community (ISCRAM) and cochairs the ethical, legal and social issues (ELSI) conference track and working group at ISCRAM. Prior to joining Trilateral, Hayley worked as a lecturer in sociology at Canterbury Christ Church University. She can be contacted at *hayley.watson@trilateralresearch.com.*

Lightning Source UK Ltd.
Milton Keynes UK
UKOW02n1700010316

269417UK00001B/21/P

9 781611 477382